CONTEMPORARY LANGUAGE STUDIES

GENERAL EDITOR: Professor F. M. Willis, University of Bradford

Based on an original plan, this series is a new venture, in publishing for modern language students, and aims to promote the interdisciplinary study of language and of the sociocultural context in which language is used and evolves.

Its predominant concern at present is with French studies, and this governs the selection of themes. At the outset, however, the programme provides for a general text on linguistics designed for students not only of French but of other European languages also.

The books are of an introductory nature and devised, with appropriate adjustments in each case, on the following general plan:

- a section, in English, with chapters of description and analysis
- illustrative texts, in French, at the end of each chapter, and bearing directly on it
- a section, in French and English, of linguistic exercises followed by bibliographical guidance

The series is addressed to all who are concerned with the study of France and its language, and is of special value to two broad categories:

1. Modern language students who are engaged in a new discipline (e.g. economics, politics, business studies) involving new concepts and requiring them to acquire a new technical lexis and a new style of writing or speech.
2. Students of social sciences and business studies taking a modern language course requiring application of the principles or theory already acquired in their primary discipline.

PUBLISHED

Linguistics for Language Learners by Anthony F. Hartley
Contemporary French Society by Linda Hantrais

IN PREPARATION

The Contemporary French Economy by Graeme M. Holmes and Peter D. Fawcett
Contemporary French Politics by Malcolm Slater

Contemporary French Society

Linda Hantrais

First published 1982
Reprinted 1989

Published by
MACMILLAN EDUCATION LTD
Houndmills, Basingstoke, Hampshire RG21 2XS
and London
Companies and representatives
throughout the world

Printed in Hong Kong

ISBN 0-333-28062-8 (hardcover)
ISBN 0-333-28063-6 (paperback)

Contents

List of Tables

List of Figures

Acknowledgements

I should like to thank Professor F. M. Willis for his constructive advice and encouragement and to express gratitude to Dr G. E. Hare for reading and criticising draft chapters and to Monsieur A. Goupi for preparing the line drawings. Thanks are due to Miss S. Lawrence, who, with assistance from Mrs F. Bannister and Mrs C. D. Ketley, typed the manuscript. The Department of Modern Languages at the University of Aston provided material support for the project. I am indebted to my family for their technical assistance and more especially for their patience and forbearance.

LINDA HANTRAIS

General Editor's Foreword

This book is one of a series designed primarily to meet the needs of two types of students – modern linguists and social scientists with an interest in contemporary France. It is assumed that both will be seeking to acquire a deeper understanding of various aspects of French society and at the same time to improve their command of the language used by members of that society.

Accordingly, while the descriptive and analytical sections of the book are in English, each is illustrated by suitable texts in French aimed at providing examples of an appropriate technical vocabulary as well as an appreciation of the various approaches adopted by French authors who write in different language varieties and for different readerships. Based on these texts are the linguistic exercises which have been constructed not only to develop competence in the foreign language, but also to involve students in a critical appraisal of the arguments and the ways in which they are expressed. The selected and annotated bibliographies at the end of each chapter are intended to give useful guidance to authoritative and specialised works and also to up-to-date source material; here the aim is to provide readers with the stimulus and help to undertake further independent study in areas of particular interest to them.

This presentation of interlinked descriptive, analytical and illustrative materials and their linguistic exploitation is the means by which the authors of the books in the series attempt to promote an interdisciplinary study of French and certain facets of French civilisation which form part of the indivisible sociocultural context in which the language is used and developed.

As an introductory work the present volume should be invaluable to modern linguists who are seeking to understand the unfamiliar concepts of a new discipline and to social scientists who, already familiar with the conceptual framework of their discipline, wish to extend its field of reference to another European society. It is hoped, however, that the book will be of interest and help to more general readers wishing to increase their knowledge of French life and institutions.

FRANK M. WILLIS

Introduction

Introductory works on sociology, defined as the scientific study of society, generally include a survey of the major social sub-systems, namely the family, religion, the educational, economic, political and legal systems. They also treat the main social processes: differentiation and stratification, interaction and organisation, order and change. In the present study of French society, which is aimed primarily at students of the social sciences and humanities, the systems approach has been adopted as the framework, and this is indicated in the chapter headings. The subheadings point to the processes to be examined for each topic.

Since other works in the series concentrate on the French political scene and the French economy, it has been possible to limit the discussion here to more specifically 'social' phenomena. The interdependency of the three areas is constantly stressed: for example, an investigation of social differentiation, in the chapter about welfare provision, emphasises redistributive mechanisms and their effects, whereas the sources of income and wealth and its accumulation are dealt with in full in the companion volume on the French economy; some features of the social changes examined here can be attributed to pressures exerted by trade unions, but the roles of trade unions as an economic force, a political pressure group, or an alternative form of political control, are more properly subjects for the companion volumes on the French economy and French politics.

One of the first precepts in any investigation of society is to ensure that phenomena are interpreted according to the specific factors which have produced them. Consequently it is dangerous to make deductions from and about other societies and other periods. While the intention in this study is to describe and analyse a contemporary society during a particular phase in its social evolution, in this case France in the postwar period and more especially the 1970s, it is important to set in perspective the systems being investigated both temporally and spatially. Provided every effort is made to avoid unjustified generalisations or extrapolations, it is both legitimate and necessary to refer to the

1

historical events which have shaped the present situation, and hypotheses about future trends can make a valuable contribution to an assessment of current policy decisions. Nor does such an approach invalidate comparisons with other contemporary societies. Reference to British society in particular will help the reader to gain a deeper insight into the relative importance of the variables and factors presented and the ways in which they may interact. At the same time comparisons will make it possible to isolate the peculiarities of the French scene. France is today facing most of the same problems as other Western industrialised societies, whether they be the questioning of traditional values and authority, the conflict between generations, the demand for public accountability of government action, increasingly high unemployment or concern about the environment, to name but a few. The manifestations and intensity of these problems, as well as the reactions and policies they engender, are however often peculiarly French.

The basic data for this study are derived from two main sources: statistics collected and analysed by government agencies and other research organisations, many of which were set up in the immediate post-war period specifically for this purpose; information about public opinion based on polls and surveys, carried out by state-financed or private bodies, and related reports and studies. These two sources are complementary in that they provide both a presentation of current trends and the attitudinal data with which to understand them. It must be remembered however that they can never be completely exempt from the problems of bias and error associated with all methods of data collection. The nature of the subjects under study is such that documentation about the most recent developments will inevitably soon lose its topicality; and it may sometimes be several years before all the analyses of large-scale surveys are published. The bibliographical references at the end of each chapter to sources of information about contemporary trends will enable the reader to update his studies. Having been guided through an investigation of the current situation he should be equipped with the necessary analytical apparatus to allow him to interpret new developments within a broader perspective. The themes selected in this work relate to perennial problems (as illustrated in the French texts at the end of each chapter, many of which are drawn from press coverage in recent years) and continue to reflect traditional assumptions and cultural patterns which are likely to remain dominant for many more decades.

The first chapter is of an introductory nature, presenting the demographic features of contemporary French society, defined as the components of growth and change in the distribution and composition of the population, and analysing the issues which are commonly associated with demographic trends. This problem-orientated approach is pursued throughout subsequent chapters. At the same time this survey provides a backcloth against which to situate the systems under study and introduces the main variables which may be considered to shape the social life of the individual in France today: age and sex differences, ethnic and geographical origins, and socio-occupational and cultural factors.

Since family origins continue to be such a dominant force in determining the life chances of the individual in society, present-day patterns of marriage and divorce, family building and size, are examined and an attempt is made to evaluate recent changes in the functions of the family and the roles of its members. The appropriateness of documented family models to different socio-economic categories is assessed and inferences are drawn about the interactive nature of the relationship between the family as a fundamental social unit and society at large, a topic which is a constant preoccupation of governments and the media.

Although a separate chapter is not devoted to the church, the role of religious belief and observance in determining attitudes and behaviour is an important recurring theme, in relation not only to the family but also to other social systems. The way in which the functions previously considered the prerogative of the family and the church are being taken over by outside agencies is reflected in the extension of welfare provision to an ever increasing number of areas of the individual's everyday life from, and even before, the cradle to the grave. The chapter about social welfare pursues this theme and looks at the complexities of the organisational framework of the French social security system. The main social services are examined, namely those providing health care, family and old age benefits; and from an analysis of the disparities in the cover afforded, it is possible to demonstrate the doubtful validity of the concept of national solidarity.

Although chronologically a forerunner of most other forms of collective welfare provision, the educational system can be classified as a subdivision, albeit a major one, of the social services. The traditional subjects of debate within this field in France continue to be of topical interest: secularism, and in particular the perennial discussion about state versus church schooling; democratisation, for although the status of education is that of a public service to which all in theory have access as of right, studies of different levels of education amply demonstrate that in practice social origins still determine the benefits derived by each individual. A study of the main leisure activities, situated in relation to different social categories, illustrates how the disadvantages resulting from the accumulation of socio-economic and cultural handicaps are compounded to reproduce in leisure the inequalities found in the other areas of social life.

The final chapter brings together the interlocking themes which appear like leitmotifs throughout the book: changes in patterns of behaviour and attitudes, with special reference to features which can be considered peculiarly French; the cumulative effect of the different variables determining the life chances of the individual in present-day France, and the resulting social inequalities in all areas of social life; the consequent justification for state intervention under the banner of greater social justice and an improved quality of life for every member of society.

Society has been depicted as an enormous and complex jigsaw. In seeking to present and analyse any society, it is not possible to describe fully every facet, and within the narrow confines of this book some pieces must inevitably be left out. So that these omissions should not detract from the general perception of the overall scene, an attempt is made throughout to guide the reader to complementary materials, both in the illustrative texts and bibliographies, enabling him to complete the picture for himself.

The linguistic exercises following each illustrative text have two main functions: they are designed to assist comprehension of the subject matter and to teach the student of the French language how to analyse and present materials in an appropriate style. By formulating definitions of selected terminology, explaining cultural inferences and the implications of particular sentences, syntactic structures or specific grammar points, and by identifying the idiosyncrasies of a particular author, the rhetorical devices and tone he uses, the student will gain a deeper understanding of both the topic and the language describing it. The productive exercises, involving summaries of the arguments presented and transposition of texts into different language varieties, or evoking reactions to information and ideas, will teach the student how to manipulate the language and to argue cogently in French. The exercises for comparison and application at the end of each group of texts include questions requiring a contrastive analysis of the different language varieties encountered. Finally the suggestions for essay and debating topics are designed to ensure that a critical appraisal is made of the English exposition, the French texts and the works referred to in the bibliographies.

1

Demographic Features

In the context of rapid social and technological change, which has been characteristic of Western industrialised nations since the Second World War, it has become imperative for governments to refine procedures for the collection, analysis and evaluation of detailed up-to-date information about the socio-economic phenomena associated with population growth and variations in its distribution and structure. These data provide the basis for monitoring and understanding contemporary trends, for making forecasts about future developments and for formulating effective policies to meet the needs predicted, whether they be for education, professional training, housing, medical care or other social welfare services and communal facilities.

In 1945 the *Institut National d'Etudes Démographiques* was set up to study and report to the government on demographic matters, and in 1946, during the preparatory phase of the first five-year National Economic Plan, the *Institut National de la Statistique et des Etudes Economiques* was formed to co-ordinate statistical data on a national level. This government agency took over responsibility for the quinquennial national population censuses which have been carried out in France since 1801. The abundant data regularly produced by both these organisations about population growth, movement and composition provide a valuable base-line for a description and analysis of contemporary French society, since they include detailed information about all the phenomena associated with the social processes under discussion.

Population size and growth

A comparison of figures recorded in 1975, the year of the last national population census in France, with those for the United Kingdom and the Federal Republic of Germany, as given in Table 1.1, clearly shows why the French media and politicians devote so much time and attention to the population issue; indeed, as Texte 1.1 suggests, it could be called a national obsession.

5

Table 1.1

Population size and density in 1975*

	Number of inhabitants	Surface area (sq.km)	Density (inhabitants per sq.km)
France	52,913,000	547,026	97
German Federal Republic	61,832,000	248,577	249
United Kingdom	55,962,000	244,046	229

*Mid-year estimates from the *United Nations Demographic Yearbook 1975*, XXVI (1976) p.146.

Although France and the United Kingdom have similar figures for total population, the average density of the two countries is very different, for the United Kingdom has less than half the surface area of France; and the German Federal Republic, with a surface area similar to that of the United Kingdom, has an even higher population density. In European terms France is underpopulated: with the exception of Spain and the North Scandinavian countries, France is the least densely populated state in Western Europe. If the population density of France were the same as that of Germany, it would have more than 136 million inhabitants, and this could radically alter the whole political balance of Western Europe. In 1974 the Hudson Institute estimated that, if Federal Germany's birthrate continued at its relatively low level, the economic strength of the two countries could be reversed by the end of the century. Whereas other countries in Western Europe are advocating policies designed to limit their population growth – in Great Britain, for example, the objective is to ensure exact replacement and no more – French governments and the press, as exemplified in Textes 1.1 and 1.2, have publicised many of the same political, economic and ideological arguments used by the developing nations in support of an expanding population.

The French concern about depopulation and underpopulation is nurtured by the belief that demographic stagnation is one of the reasons why France has lost its former world hegemony. As illustrated by Figure 1.1, when the first censuses were carried out in France and the United Kingdom in 1801, the demographic supremacy of France was such that, with 28,250,000 inhabitants on its present territory, its population was almost two and a half times that of the United Kingdom. France was at that time the most populous state in Europe, including Russia, with approximately 16 per cent of its total population. Although the number of inhabitants in France has almost doubled since 1801, it has, as a

Figure 1.1
Population size in European countries 1800-1976

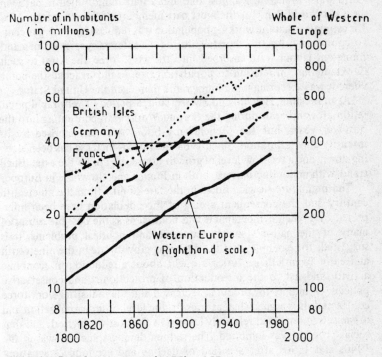

Number of inhabitants (in millions)

Whole of Western Europe

British Isles
Germany
France

Western Europe (Righthand scale)

SOURCE: *Population*, XXXII (1977) p.257.

result of the relatively slow growth rate over the last century and a half, now fallen to fourth position in Europe, excluding the USSR, while the United Kingdom has moved into second place. The most marked difference in growth rates occurred in the second half of the nineteenth century, when other comparable European states were undergoing a period of demographic transition, since their deathrate was declining while the birthrate remained high. In France the decline in the deathrate was slower, due primarily to the poor standards of hygiene in the urban slums and in rural areas and to the prevalence of alcoholism. The practice of birth control, which the French had introduced some eighty years ahead of their neighbours, was already widespread by the second half of the nineteenth century, and the birthrate was falling so steeply that between 1850 and 1914 the number of deaths exceeded the number of births in eleven different years.

The beginning of the twentieth century was characterised in France by a continued decline, which reached its lowest point between the two world wars. France lost almost one and a half million men in battle in the First World War, for the most part members of the work force, and it is estimated that the working population was reduced by 10.5 per cent. To compensate for this shortfall, during the interwar years, women and immigrant labour were absorbed into the work force, the latter to such an extent that, in relation to population size, France reached the point where it was accepting more immigrants than even the United States.

As in Belgium, Holland and Switzerland, a period of very rapid population growth began during the Second World War, continuing into the post-war years, but the French baby boom was characterised by its intensity and its duration. Since 1964 the rate of increase has been slowing down, and a very low level of growth now seems to be the established trend, with minor fluctuations, both in France and elsewhere in Europe.

The premature slowing down in the rate of growth in the nineteenth century and the consequent ageing of the population have been interpreted by French demographers and politicians as the possible causes of many of the nation's social, economic and political problems. It is suggested, for example, that the declining growth rate in the nineteenth and early twentieth centuries brought about a reduction in economic activity and led to the introduction of protectionist and conservative policies, as outlets for products decreased and the industrial work force contracted. It is argued that, as a result, the level of industrialisation and urbanisation remained relatively low up to the post-war period, and that social progress was inhibited. The sudden demographic renewal in the 1940s and 1950s after a period of decline and economic stagnation, while providing a spur for economic expansion, also created many problems: the rapid growth in the number of consumers of goods and services made enormous demands on the nation's resources at a time when it was recovering from two major international upheavals. More recently reports that the birthrate is again slowing down arouse renewed concern about the nation's future, as the problems associated with an ageing population, discussed in Texte 1.2, once more threaten the country's social and economic development.

Contemporary demographic trends and population structure

The main elements which demographers, sociologists and economists examine in their analyses of population trends, and to which reference will be made here, are the general level of fertility and the birthrate, the deathrate, migratory movements and social and occupational mobility. These they explain in terms of the physical and psychosocial characteristics of the population. Fertility and the birthrate are investigated in relation to the number of women of childbearing age and their rate of reproduction, as affected by the age at marriage, its duration, birth control practices and the state of health of the population, which also affects the survival rate of offspring. The desire of couples to have children is seen to be influenced by the general standard of living, the social climate and customs, social origins and group norms, religious belief and practice and regional traditions, as well as by incentives and disincentives provided by governments through legislation. Political circumstances, such as the incidence of wars and conflict, affect both the deathrate and the number of births, as do social and educational conditions, including knowledge about the production and utilisation of food, clothing, shelter and hygiene. Medical advances, improved knowledge about the prevention, diagnosis and cure of disease, economic developments, rising income levels and social reforms controlling living and working conditions are all likely to cause fluctuations in population growth rates and lead to changes in its structure by age and sex. Many of these factors will be discussed more fully in later chapters in reference to particular social systems and processes.

Migratory movements add another dimension to the analysis, as migrants carry with them their own physical and psychosocial characteristics and are themselves influenced to varying degrees by their new environment. Two major types of migratory movements are considered here: those within the country, associated with the rural exodus and the phenomena of urban concentration and industrialisation; those across national borders, determined by the changing social, political and economic circumstances in the countries concerned.

Studies of social and occupational mobility generally include changes in the relative status, power and prestige of social groups and of individuals, both being influenced by the factors associated with population growth and composition. Since family origins and status and the level of educational attainment are the main variables thought to determine individual mobility, this type of social change is dealt with in more detail in the chapters on the family and education, and attention here is focused on the transformation in occupational and socio-economic structure as a result of group mobility.

The birthrate and family size

The 1975 census results brought confirmation of the trends which had been observed in preceding years: the number of marriages had decreased slightly; the number of those remaining celibate continued to decline; and more importantly the number of births was still falling (a trend analysed in Textes 1.1 and 1.3), albeit at a slower rate than in other comparable European countries, for France was still registering fourteen births per 1000 inhabitants, whereas in the United Kingdom there were 11.8 and in the Federal Republic of Germany only 9.5.

It has become standard practice in France for the INED and the *Institut Français de l'Opinion Publique* to carry out regular opinion surveys of the attitudes of the French towards demographic trends, the birthrate and family policy. The results of recent surveys indicate the relative influence of different collective and individual pressures. Answers to questions designed to determine what is considered the most desirable, or 'ideal' family size reveal that in France the preferred number of children fluctuates between two and three. The preference for two rather than three children is however by no means so pronounced in France as in the United Kingdom. Ideal family size does not generally match the actual number of children and tends to fall within a narrower range: few couples express the view that they want no children at all, whereas between 10 and 20 per cent are unable to have children; few couples state that they would like more than five children, whereas families of more than five are by no means exceptional.

According to recent surveys, the decreasing propensity of couples to have a third child, the key factor in demographic growth today, is more and more to be explained by economic problems and the prevailing social climate. When people are questioned about their reasons for preferring a particular family size, they attribute less importance to what might be called the 'collective' arguments or pressures: they give little weight to the imbalance between the working and the dependent population or to the supposed economic incentives of a youthful population. The majority shows more concern about the status of the individual, particularly of the woman, the purchasing power of a household, the desire to ensure educational and professional training for offspring, and the amount of help given to the family. Studies of the effects of a third child on the standard of living of a family show that, in spite of the additional income from family allowances and other benefits, after the first two children a critical point is reached: having more children entails pressures on space, as the need arises for more living accommodation, and on time, making work outside the home less feasible for the mother.

The French government uses the information it is given about population trends, their causes and possible consequences, not only in deciding how best to meet the new demands resulting from the changes observed, but also in determining policies intended to influence these trends and to prevent potentially harmful fluctuations. Texte 1.4 provides an example of the predictions which the government may use as a guideline.

The first attempt by a French government, before the days of regular opinion surveys, to reverse the population decline came in 1920 with the introduction of repressive legislation which punished with fines, imprisonment, and even the death penalty, anyone found guilty of producing propaganda or the means of voluntarily controlling procreation. More positive measures were taken in the interwar years, including financial assistance for unmarried mothers, a bonus for a male child, cheap government housing and a partial system of family allowances (discussed in Chapter 3). The most significant positive and comprehensive legislation was that of 1939: the *Code de la famille* of Edouard Daladier, but it also increased penalties for abortionists (Article 317), and an abortionist was executed in 1943.

Due to the almost impenetrable opposition from the church, the medical profession and politicians, attempts to repeal the 1920 law have only recently met with success. Family planning clinics were legalised in France as late as 1967, and it was only in December 1974 that the contraceptive pill became available under the social security system. Moves to reform the law on abortion roused even more ardent opposition. The issue became such a controversial matter that members of parliament were given a free vote in November 1974 when the bill was before the National Assembly. Even when the vote had finally been carried, making abortion legal in certain circumstances for a trial period of five years, the finance necessary for its enforcement was not immediately forthcoming, and there are still important regional and social discrepancies in access to facilities. Recent surveys into birth control practices show that two out of every three French women of childbearing age use some form of birth control, but, in spite of the changes in the law, nearly half still rely on traditional methods.

It is clear that the French people would not in the future accept the reintroduction of negative and repressive policies to prevent the decline in the birthrate. The more positive measures of the *Code de la famille* can be considered as a factor encouraging family building, although it must not be forgotten that other countries with a less impressive array of incentives also underwent a population renewal at the same time. The extent to which such measures may, or may not, influence the birthrate is discussed in Texte 1.3. If government action is to be effective in the future, it is likely, given the present findings on public opinion, that policies must focus on creating a general social and economic climate in which children will not be seen as a factor inhibiting individual choice and personal development.

The deathrate
The level of mortality in France has remained almost static over the past

ten years. In 1976 there were 10.5 deaths for 1000 inhabitants (compared with 12.2 in the United Kingdom), the lowest rate ever recorded in France. The infantile mortality rate had also reached a low level with 12.6 deaths per 1000 live births in 1976 (compared with 14.3 in the United Kingdom).

The overall decline in mortality rates corresponds to a gradual lengthening of life expectancy which has reached 69 years for men and 77 years for women. The very marked difference between the life spans of the two sexes is one of the largest in the world. Several explanations are offered for this phenomenon. The two world wars in the first half of the century and the continued involvement in armed conflict have been more detrimental to the male population. For men in the 15 to 25 age group road accidents now take a particularly heavy toll, and the French roads are amongst the most dangerous in the world. It has been calculated that the disappearance of deaths due to road accidents would increase life expectancy by half a year. The elimination of deaths due to the excessive intake of alcohol would bring about an even greater increase in life expectancy for men. In 1977 France still held the world record for *per capita* consumption of pure alcohol with double the figure for Great Britain. Illnesses associated with smoking contribute to the higher mortality rates for men: approximately 75 per cent of male and 30 per cent of female adults smoke on average thirteen cigarettes a day (compared with 50 and 40 per cent respectively in Great Britain), thereby decreasing their life expectancy by almost three years. The more favourable situation of women may also be attributable to the attention which they have received in their capacity as potential childbearers: compulsory medical examinations during pregnancy in order to qualify for financial benefits, together with the reduction in the number of pregnancies, have brought about substantial improvements in the general standard of health among women at the age when they are most prone to medical problems.

A variable which is as important as sex in producing differences in life expectancy is that of social environment. The style of life and standard of education seem to be more important than the level of income, as primary school teachers and members of the clergy together with top managers and professionals have the longest life expectancy. But if the urban environment is advantageous to those in the more privileged social categories, who show lower mortality rates in towns than in the rural environment, the reverse is true at the other end of the social scale. Deathrates are also higher in the private than in the public sector because of stricter controls on working conditions, hygiene and health care in the latter. Although infant mortality has declined considerably since the Second World War, and France now has the lowest rate in

Europe after the Netherlands, Denmark and Sweden, differences resulting from social variables remain significant: illegitimate children, more frequently born to young mothers, show an infant mortality rate 60 per cent above that of legitimate children, and children born of immigrant parents are also more likely to die during infancy.

If life expectancy varies according to social factors, so do the causes of death: heart disease affects all categories more or less equally, whereas the differences increase along the social scale for cancer, accidents, suicides, tuberculosis and alcoholism. Tuberculosis is a cause of death particularly prevalent in immigrant groups, whereas it has almost been eradicated from the host community. Unskilled manual workers, often immigrants, are more likely than other categories to die as a result of industrial injuries or diseases, and again men are more exposed than women.

Backward agricultural areas where the average age is particularly high, as in the Centre, show an above average mortality rate, as do areas, such as the Midi, which attract the elderly during retirement. In 1977 Brittany held the unenviable record for the highest incidence of cirrhosis (Morbihan) and of alcoholism (CÔTES-DU-NORD), explaining its low life expectancy. Although an urban population is more exposed to the risks of contracting infections, contagious diseases and illnesses associated with pollution, recent progress in the control of such diseases and improvements in hygiene and housing seem to have created some advantages for the urban over the rural population, and the former generally benefit from easier access to high standards of medical care and welfare facilities.

Many of the causes of death mentioned here are at the source of political dilemmas: the risks can in most cases be reduced by limiting individual freedom (strict enforcement of speed limits, compulsory wearing of seat belts, controls on the consumption of alcohol and cigarettes by restricting advertising, increasing taxation and limiting consumption in public places and at work). The government has in the past been reluctant to exercise such controls, but the evidence of the enormous cost to the community, both in terms of human suffering and of the burden on the health and welfare services, has led, for example, to the introduction of restrictive legislation, particularly for road users. The fact remains that it is still cheaper to buy a glass of wine in a café than a coffee, mineral water or fruit juice, and cigarettes are much less expensive in France than in Great Britain. The state plays an ambivalent role: while it benefits from the revenues raised by sales of petrol, alcohol and tobacco, it must also deal with the consequences of their abuse and respond to the pressures exerted by producers, retailers and consumers and to the need to act in the nation's best interest.

Population structure by age and sex

As shown above, age and sex are basic variables in demography and essential parameters in the analysis of the dynamics of a population. The effects of changes in the birthrate and life expectancy on the structure of the population by age and sex can be illustrated by age pyramids such as those in Figure 1.2. The 1946 pyramid shows the disastrous consequences of the First World War for the male population. The 1875-98 generation suffered an overall reduction of more than 20 per cent, and the subsequent decline in the number of births was almost 50 per cent for the 1914-18 generations, as indicated by the indents on both sides of the pyramid. When armed conflict again broke out, the deficient generations had reached childbearing age, and an even deeper

Figure 1.2
Age pyramids for 1946 and 1976

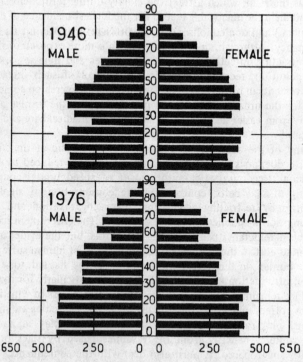

SOURCES: *Population*, XXIX, special issue (June 1974) p.21; *Population*, XXXII, 2 (1977) p.259.

indent might have been expected. In the event, the demographic consequences of the Second World War were less severe than those of the First.
The 1976 pyramid highlights the extent of the population expansion
for the age group 20 to 30 years which is now part of the work force.
The marked feature of the ageing of the population will in the next few
years be offset to some extent as the reduced generations of the First
World War reach retirement age. The dissymmetry at the top of the
1976 pyramid continues to show the effects of the disparity for life
expectancy between the two sexes. Immigration tends to redress the
sex balance for the population of working age, since most immigrants
are young men, but this characteristic is likely to be of a temporary
nature.

The changing age structure of the population, for the three main
stages in the life cycle, has brought about important shifts in the
dependency ratio, namely the number of the young and the elderly
relying on members of the work force to produce and pay for the
goods and services which they need. As already mentioned, over the
past half century greater life expectancy, in conjunction with compulsory retirement, has significantly increased the number of elderly
dependents; the post-war baby boom, together with the reduction in
infant mortality and childhood diseases, longer compulsory schooling
and increasing access to tertiary education, has created many more
young dependents.

Regional differences may accentuate the problems of the dependency ratio. Rapidly industrialising areas, for example in the North
and the Paris Basin, tend to be younger, because a dynamic industry
attracts young workers at an age when they are likely to be rearing
young children, and their demands are primarily for housing, schools
and other child welfare services. Regions in which traditional industries
are in decline are characterised by an elderly population requiring
above all old-age benefits and medical care. Although two-thirds of the
elderly live in the urban environment, the poorer agricultural areas also
have a high proportion of elderly people, since the young tend to leave
the small family farm to seek work in the towns.

The sense of continuity, which in the past brought together different
age groups throughout the life cycle, has gradually been replaced by
sharp divisions between the different stages of life, and each age category
has developed its own culture and its own value-system. In previous
centuries it was a remarkable feat to survive to an old age, and therefore
the elderly were venerated for their achievement and considered as a
repository of the wisdom and knowledge of the whole community.
Because old age has now become commonplace – and the rapid pace of
technological change has meant that the knowledge of the elderly has

lost its relevance – the so-called *troisième âge* has come to be associated with a sense of isolation, uselessness and rejection, which policy-makers and society in general for a long time preferred to ignore.

The continued ageing of the population over the next few years is expected to bring about a further increase in the number of the very old (75 and above), with the related problems of invalidity and chronic ailments, which will impose an even greater strain on medical and social resources. Since life expectancy is much longer for women than for men, two-thirds of the population aged over 65 are women, and because wives generally tend to be younger than their husbands, the number of women left alone increases steeply with age.

As public attention is directed increasingly towards the search for a better quality of life, the plight of the elderly is becoming a subject of concern, and slowly attitudes towards old age are changing. Politicians, for example, have realised that they must win the votes of the elderly, and the sheer weight of numbers, particularly for women, makes such votes crucial. More attention is being paid to the organisation of activities at community level, and the world of commerce has been alerted to the potential of this new category of consumers. In 1977 the first exhibition for the aged (entitled *L'Age et la vie*) was held at La Villette in Paris. It included a film festival, fashion shows and debates. Estate agents, tourist bureaux, newspapers and banks were represented, all eager to take advantage of a new market. In the late 1970s these privileged young old people (*jeunes vieux*), at whom the publicity campaigns are aimed, were only a minority, but their numbers are expanding rapidly, as they are joined by a new generation of the aged composed of former salaried workers who are the recipients of fully paid-up earnings-related pensions (a topic pursued in Chapter 3), and who are demanding a decent standard of living as of right.

If the elderly have been neglected until recent years, this is because the nation has preferred to invest in its youthful population. In relation to the countries of the Third World, where 43 per cent of the population is aged below 15 and three out of every four people are under 30 years old, France's present age structure may not appear particularly unbalanced. But the French situation is characterised within the Northern European context by the fact that the sudden growth of a youthful population took place at a time when the country was still suffering from the effects of the climate of conservatism, defeatism and stagnation, which had prevailed for so many years. Because France had fallen behind her neighbours both economically and socially, and because her population growth was greater, its repercussions were more severe and far-reaching.

Not only were the young to take up more space physically in French society, but, in an age of rapid technological and scientific progress, with access to an ever increasing store of information and exposure to constantly renewed models of behaviour, they were also to make greater psychological demands on society. According to some observers, youth has become a social class to be reckoned with: for example, since the young can now vote at the age of 18, politicians are heedful of their opinions and demands. In the materialistic consumer society of today, the young provide an enormous mass market for goods and culture designed especially for them, but which they do not help to produce, since they spend a longer period in compulsory education.

The considerable improvement in the general standard of living in France since 1945 has brought about an easier life for the young, while, at the same time, the period of dependency has been lengthened. By the 1960s the combination of these factors had led, particularly amongst the better educated, to a questioning of the accepted values traditionally supported by the basic social institutions of family, church and school, and to the rejection of their authority. The events of May 1968 in the schools and universities have been interpreted as a revolt against the adult world. As the post-war generations began to reach working age at the end of the 1960s, they were confronted with the reluctance of employers to accept inexperienced workers and a realisation of the inadequacy of the professional training provided by the educational system. The May explosion can be seen as the expression of the frustration and resentment created by this situation.

More recently the opinion surveys show that a different generation of the young are searching for new social values. At the beginning of 1979, the weekly magazine L'Express, published its findings about the demands of youth: the new generation want a country without concrete, without nuclear power and closer to nature; they are demanding a warm family environment and guaranteed employment; and they are asking for freedom from the threat of concentration camps and military regimes. It is significant that the keyword in official policy documents has in recent years changed from 'quantity' to 'quality' and 'equality', for this corresponds to the aspirations of today's youth. This new policy orientation is reflected in the priority areas selected by the French government within the framework of the International Year of the Child in 1979: particular attention was to be devoted to the opportunities afforded to the young during their free time for self-development, self-sufficiency and security, values closely associated with the quality of life and the quest for greater social justice for all members of society.

Geographical distribution and migratory movements

Population censuses in France since the beginning of the nineteenth century have distinguished urban from rural areas,[1] and it is therefore possible to chart movements between town and country. During the nineteenth and early twentieth centuries, there was a steady increase in urbanisation, followed by a marked acceleration after the Second World War. But just as overall population growth was slow in France in relation to other comparable European countries, migration from the countryside was more limited, to the extent that, in spite of the rapid growth of isolated industrial towns, the rural population was almost the same size at the end of the nineteenth century as it had been at the beginning. Even today France continues to be distinguished by its relatively low level of urban concentration: figures from the 1975 census showed that 72.9 per cent of the French population is urban compared with 81 per cent in the United Kingdom. Nowadays movement from the rural to the urban environment is confined mainly to the working population, and particularly the less privileged social categories, whereas those leaving the work force, and with the means to do so, tend to move in the opposite direction.

Regional disparities
The post-war population expansion accentuated regional differences: although most small and medium sized towns underwent substantial growth, the Paris, Rhône-Alpes and Provence-Côte d'Azur areas benefited most. The burgeoning of conurbations around Paris is the most outstanding feature of the post-war developments and the phenomenon most frequently studied by analysts of population distribution in France. It is explained by the enormous attraction of the capital, which continued to expand throughout the nineteenth and early twentieth centuries, when the country as a whole was undergoing a demographic decline. Since 1962 a saturation point seems to have been reached for the inner city. The latest census figures show that there has been a net decrease in the flow of migrants to Paris together with a reduction in employment opportunities. New building for housing has consequently been curtailed, and cheap housing is being replaced by offices and low density luxury accommodation. The occupational structure of the inner city is being transformed, as the traditional small craftsmen and shopkeepers are forced to leave and are replaced by a social category distinguished by a high average age and an above average level of income, as described in Texte 1.5. This population exodus from the inner city has contributed to the growth of the surrounding area, or Greater Paris. Although the overall density of France is ninety-seven inhabitants to the square kilometre, the average figure masks enormous differences from one area to another and in particular between Paris and the rest of the country. In 1973 Greater Paris had an average density of 800 inhabitants to the square kilometre, compared with fourteen in the Lozère area.

Within Europe it is now the largest city. Today one Frenchman in six is a Parisian, one quarter of the non-agricultural working population is to be found there; Paris accounts for a quarter of all industrial workers and a quarter of those employed in the tertiary sector. Its attraction has been such that only two other French cities have reached a million inhabitants, whereas there are five in the United Kingdom apart from London.

The concentration of demographic and economic resources in the capital is closely linked to its political role over the centuries, and it is only recently that coherent policies have been formulated to encourage the devolution of power to the regions and their economic development. It would seem, however, that the areas where expansion has taken place are often those in which industry was already firmly established, with the result that the dichotomy between the so-called two Frances has been accentuated: the part of France to the north-east of an imaginary line between Le Havre and Marseilles is demographically and economically privileged, and its assets are likely to multiply since it has easy access to other countries in the European Community; on the other hand in the regions of the south-west, the poor part of France, the population is predominantly rural, productive capacity is below that of the north and the Paris Basin, and salaries are generally lower than in the north-east, as is the standard of living.

Immigration

The relative level of economic development of different areas affects internal migratory movements, but it is also an important determinant of the level and nature of migration to and from foreign countries. Fluctuations correlate closely with changes in economic circumstances and with the evolution in relationships between France and its former overseas territories and also its fellow members of the European Community. In 1975 approximately one and a quarter million French expatriates were living abroad (the majority in Europe, then Africa and the United States); although the numbers have increased considerably in the last twenty years, France has remained a country of immigration rather than emigration.

The number of foreigners living in France has been counted since 1851, and the figures show that immigration was already increasing significantly in the second half of the nineteenth century. For the period 1881–1911 it was accounting for approximately half the growth in population size, and between the two world wars, it took place on a massive scale, as already mentioned. Although the economic crises of the 1930s reversed the trend, immigration picked up after the Second World War to reach a maximum between 1954–62 at the time when the rural exodus was also gathering momentum, and the population was expanding rapidly. Between 1962-8, it continued to serve as a means of bolstering up the work force; one third of the new jobs created were at that time filled by immigrants. More recently during the economic recession, the rate has declined: the 1975 census showed that for the first time in twenty years net immigration was almost at zero level, and since then it has declined even further.

Changes in the economic and political conditions in the countries of origin and the attraction of alternative host countries have affected the sources of immigration and its nature: in the nineteenth century Belgians were the most numerous immigrants; from 1921 Middle European immigrants contributed an ever increasing share of the immigrant population; in the immediate post-war years Italians accounted for more than half the total influx; they were succeeded by Spaniards and then Portuguese in the 1960s. In more recent years immigration has been characterised by a greater diversification of the countries of origin and by an increasing proportion of immigrants from countries which are culturally further from France, namely Yugoslavia, Algeria, Morocco, Tunisia, Turkey and Black Africa. Most of these immigrants maintain close contact with their country of origin, for the tendency has been for most workers to migrate to France without their families but to send back a substantial proportion of their earnings to their homeland. For France this has provided an immediate source of labour without the costs of rearing dependants, since immigrants pay the same level of social insurance contributions and income tax as the host community but do not receive the same benefits. Where family migration does take place, it is the more recent immigrants who make the largest contribution to population growth. Those who have been in France for a longer period tend to have fewer children, as they adopt the dominant model of the host community.

Figures published by the Ministry of the Interior show that on 1 January 1976 there were 4,196,134 foreign nationals living in France. They made up 8 per cent of the total population and almost half of them belonged to the work force. About half of them were from Portugal, Italy or Spain and a third from North Africa. Three main regions have been settled, and these account for 59 per cent of immigrants: the area around Paris (with more than 36 per cent of the foreign nationals), Rhône-Alpes (with nearly 13 per cent) and Provence-Côte d'Azur (with almost 10 per cent).

The age and sex distribution of the immigrant population is very different from that of the host community. Few foreigners are aged below 20, mainly because of the age at which migration takes place but also because children born in France may acquire French nationality if one of their parents is French. Immigrant children represent 6.4 per cent of all children in education. The ratio of male to female is just above two to one for the age group 20 to 40. But the structure differs from one nationality to another: since Belgian, Italian and Polish immigration began a long time ago and has declined in recent years, immigrants from those sources have a higher average age; although in general there are more young men than women in the immigrant population, the proportion of the two sexes is very similar for Spaniards, since Spanish women have more often accompanied their husbands and have easily found employment in domestic service; the most recent immigrants from Portugal and North Africa are predominantly male and of working age; in the case of the Algerians there are six men to every woman. Celibacy is particularly characteristic of the recent immigrants and is at the root of many inflammatory situations between the immigrant and host populations.

In 1974 the French government, in an attempt to reconcile the requirements of industry with the need to improve the living and working conditions of immigrants, drew up a new policy on immigration: it imposed restrictions on the entry of foreign workers, except from Common Market countries, in whose case freedom of movement is guaranteed under the terms of the Treaty of Rome. In 1979 further legislation was introduced making it even more difficult for foreigners to enter France, and deportation became almost automatic for any breaches of administrative regulations or in cases of unemployment. In Texte 1.6 Stoléru defends the 1979 policies in the face of the severe criticism which they provoked.

It could still be claimed at the beginning of the 1970s that France had avoided the kind of racism prevalent in Britain and America. In the first half of the century immigration was the only way to compensate for a declining work force. In the post-war years it answered the needs of a rapidly expanding economy, offering an instantaneous source of labour, prepared to accept low pay for jobs refused by the host community and without the social cost of education. Today the living and working conditions of immigrants are sometimes compared to those awaiting the peasants of the Massif Central when they arrived by special trains from Clermont-Ferrand in the middle of the nineteenth century: inferior jobs, low pay, no security, substandard accommodation and a cultural inadequacy reflected in their poor command of the French language and inability to understand the complexities of administrative procedures. A survey carried out in 1973-4 by the INED showed that there was little contact between the French and the immigrant population. Immigrants from Western Europe were most easily accepted followed by Yugoslavs and Turks. Black Africans were not welcome, and North Africans least of all. This may be seen as a consequence of the tension existing between France and Algeria since the Algerian War, which in the early 1960s ended 130 years of close association between the two countries. Since Algerians still constituted the largest category of immigrants in 1976, in spite of legislation introduced by the Algerian government in 1973 to check the flow of emigrants to France, this animosity is likely to continue. Immigrants are generally accepted for their contribution to the economy, but the majority of the population considers that foreigners should be made redundant before French workers and should be repatriated if they have entered the country illegally or are out of work. As the regulations controlling immigration are tightened and unemployment increases, it is unlikely that public opinion will be reversed and that immigration could ever again reach the level it achieved in the past.

Occupational mobility and socio-economic structure

Since the Second World War major changes have taken place in the composition and structure of the working population[2] in France. Although, in absolute terms, the size of the work force has increased since 1946, it has not expanded as much as the potential working population, taken as those aged between 20 and 64 years, due to the factors which have already been mentioned in reference to the dependency ratio. The reduction in the length of the working life has not been compensated for by any marked increase in the number of women in employment, and in relation to the total female population, by 1975 the proportion had scarcely changed since the beginning of the century, although the nature of female employment and the motivation for it have altered considerably (a topic discussed more fully in Chapter 2), as a result of structural changes in the distribution of economic activities.

Economic sectors

In the period 1946–75 the share of the working population in the primary sector (agriculture, fishing, mining) decreased by about 23 per cent, leading first to expansion in both the other economic sectors, and then since 1962 to growth in the tertiary sector. The proportion of the work force in the secondary sector (manufacturing industries, including building and public works) rose in the 1946–75 period by nearly 9 per cent. The tertiary sector (transport, commerce, banking, public and domestic services) grew more rapidly, increasing its share of the work force by 15 per cent. As shown in Table 1.2, in relation to comparable Western industrialised countries, France is still characterised by the importance of its primary sector. It is likely that this sector will undergo a further contraction over the next few years to the advantage of tertiary employ-

Table 1.2

Distribution of the working population in 1976

	Primary %	Secondary %	Tertiary %
France	10.8	38.1	51.1
German Federal Republic	7.1	45.1	47.8
United Kingdom	2.7	40.0	57.3

SOURCE: *Le Nouvel Observateur: Faits et chiffres* (1978) p.153.

ment, whereas the industrial sector is expected to remain fairly stable. This progression is reflected in the decrease in the number of independent workers and the very marked increase in the number of wage earners, who now account for over 80 per cent of the work force for both men and women, particularly in the tertiary sector.

Socio-occupational categories

The classification of the working population in relation to economic sectors represents only one dimension of occupational structure. A multi-dimensional approach can be adopted using the socio-occupational categories which the INSEE exploits in its censuses and surveys, and which have been widely accepted by other research organisations.[3] The objectives of the INSEE system are to classify the working population according to a limited number of broad groupings which are indicative of social homogeneity. These categories provide information about several socio-economic variables: type of work, distinguishing for example between manual and non-manual employment; branch of activity or economic sector; employment status, that is whether self-employed or a wage earner; level of qualification; level of responsibility or, for employers, number of employees. Nine major categories are thus defined and include a number of subgroups: **0** (*exploitants agricoles*) farmers working on their own account, whatever the size of the holding or number of employees, and therefore a very heterogeneous category and usually grouped with **1** (*salariés agricoles*) agricultural labourers; **2** (*patrons de l'industrie et du commerce*) employers in industry and commerce divided into subgroups for industrialists with more than five employees, craftsmen with five employees or fewer, employers in the fishing industry, large (three employees or more) and small (fewer than three employees) retailers; **3** (*professions libérales et cadres supérieurs*) professional workers, both self-employed and salaried, including teachers in secondary and higher education, engineers, and the higher administrative grades employed both in private firms and by the State, all normally with qualifications at university degree standard; 4 (*cadres moyens*) the different categories of middle management and administrative staff, with subgroups for primary school teachers, various assimilated categories, also technicians and medical and social workers; 5 (*employés*) lower grade non-manual workers in offices and commerce, spanning the whole range of white collar activities; 6 (*ouvriers*) manual workers, with subgroups for supervisors and the different grades of skilled, semi-skilled and unskilled workers and apprentices, miners, merchant seamen and fishermen; 7 (*personnels de service*) personal service workers with subgroups for domestic workers, charwomen and other services; 8 (*autres catégories*) a heterogeneous category for artists, the clergy, the armed forces and police; 9 (*personnes non actives*) a miscellaneous grouping for all those who are not members of the work force, including schoolchildren and students, national servicemen, four subgroups of retired workers, and a separate group for housewives, those living off a private income and prisoners. These last two categories (8 and 9) are often excluded from studies of social phenomena since they are composed of such diverse elements.

Since the census elicits precise information about the socio-economic characteristics of the population (see Texte 1.7 for an example of the questions asked), it is possible to assess the different trends in the structure of the work force from one census to another. Table 1.3 shows the proportion of the working population in the grouped INSEE categories in 1975 and the changes which have taken place between 1968–75. As already mentioned, one of the most significant changes over the past fifteen years has been the reduction in the proportion of the population employed in agriculture, but even greater is the decrease for mining, a subcategory of manual workers. The most substantial increases have been for all grades of teachers, for medical and social workers, technicians, engineers, and the other medium grade intellectual and professional workers, explaining the high overall rates of increase for categories 3 and 4 as well as the growing importance of the tertiary sector.

As mentioned above, the INSEE socio-occupational categories are based on criteria such as the level of educational attainment, the degree of responsibility and independence, the type and nature of employment. In later chapters, it will be shown that these same variables correlate closely with income levels and life-styles, including social, cultural and recreational activities, and that they also determine the social status of an individual, defined in terms of the evaluation by society of his general standing or prestige within the community.

This survey of the demographic features of French society has revealed important variations in the life chances of an individual through-

Table 1.3
Socio-occupational categories in 1975

		Total %	Annual change 1968–75 in %
0	Farmers	7.6	–5.6
1	Agricultural labourers	1.7	–6.1
2	Employers in industry and commerce	7.8	–1.9
3	Professional workers, higher administrative grades	6.7	+5.6
4	Middle management and administrative staff	12.7	+4.7
5	Lower grade non-manual workers	17.7	+3.6
6	Manual workers	37.7	+0.9
7	Personal service workers	5.7	+0.9
8	Other categories	2.4	–0.1

SOURCE: *Notice 3, Supplément aux Cahiers français* p.184 (1978) and *Données sociales* (1978) p.48, from the 1975 Census.

out the life cycle due to his social origins: for example, the probability of being born into a particular family environment, of surviving through childhood, and of working in a certain type of employment; the amount of geographical and occupational mobility, or differential life expectancy and causes of death. Although the term has not yet been used, it is clear that the variations outlined are the result of basic social inequalities, and, as will be shown, these inequalities are to a great extent perpetuated from one generation to another. This inequality of condition and heredity of positions, which is not dependent upon any general consensus (as is the case in some systems of social stratification), can be considered as the necessary preconditions for the existence of social classes. It has been suggested that new class divisions, based, for example, on age, may be characteristic of contemporary French society, but this does not mean that traditional class distinctions have necessarily been eroded. Although the authors of the French classification system have not re-organised their divisions into 'social classes', as do their British counterparts,[4] the INSEE occupational categories can easily be grouped into fairly cohesive social classes which share similar work and market conditions. Broad categories can thus be formed combining occupation and status and based on divisions resembling those of the traditional social classes: the upper classes (*bourgeoisie*) INSEE categories 2 and 3, middle classes (*classes moyennes*) INSEE categories 4 and 5, working classes (*classes ouvrières*) INSEE category 6 and peasantry (*paysannerie*) INSEE categories 0 and 1, often grouped with the working classes to form a *classe populaire*.

Just as the social processes and phenomena charted here with reference to demographic features have been considered as factors contributing to major changes in the occupational structure of the population, they can also be seen to engender transformations in the traditional class structure. As a result the relative importance of the different social classes has evolved, and their contours have become less clearly defined. For example, the INSEE figures for farmers and agricultural labourers show that this social class has been reduced to such an extent that some authors talk of their extinction, while others emphasise the extreme diversity within the agricultural community which inhibits class consciousness and unity. As in Great Britain, there has been a gradual movement away from a predominantly proletarian society, even though the category of manual workers in industry, according to the INSEE, still constitutes one third of the working population. Due to improvements in working conditions, particularly in the advanced industries, more and more skilled manual workers are adopting the lifestyles, aspirations and attitudes of the middle classes. The new middle classes see their numbers expand rapidly as the economy is transformed to accommodate the growth of service sector activities. These changes do not however imply that there are no longer enormous inequalities between the very low paid unskilled industrial or agricultural labourer and the company director, professional worker or senior civil servant at the other end of the social scale. As already indicated, situations of advantage or disadvantage tend to be cumulative. The processes whereby these social inequalities are reinforced and perpetuated and their effects on the access of individuals to the various social systems will be examined in detail in subsequent chapters.

Bibliographical guidance

General works presenting and analysing demographic features and trends in France:

P. Ariès, *Histoire des populations françaises et de leurs attitudes devant la vie depuis le XVIIIe siècle*, new ed. (Paris: Seuil, 1971)

J. Beaujeu-Garnier, *La Population française: après le recensement de 1975* (Paris: Colin, 1976)

'La France et sa population aujourd'hui', *Cahiers français*, 184 (1978)

INSEE, 'Principaux résultats du recensement de 1975', *Les Collections de l'INSEE*, D 52 (1977)

E. Sullerot, *La Démographie de la France: bilan et perspectives* (Paris: Documentation Française, 1978)

The problems of the elderly and the young:

A.-M. Guillemard, *La Retraite, une mort sociale: sociologie des conduites en situation de retraite* (Paris: Mouton, 1972)

'Le Troisième Age', *Le Monde: dossiers et documents*, 21 (May 1975)

P. Desgraupes, 'L'enfant cet inconnu', *Le Point*, 304 (17 July 1978) 74-80, 305 (24 July 1978) 71-80, 306 (31 July 1978) 64-9, 307 (7 Aug 1978) 59-65, 308 (14 Aug 1978) 65-72, 309 (21 Aug 1978) 67-72

A. Sauvy, *La Montée des jeunes* (Paris: Calmann-Lévy, 1959)

The geographical distribution of the population and migratory movements:

P. Brongniart, *La Région en France* (Paris: Colin, 1971)

J.-F. Gravier, *Paris et le désert français en 1972* (Paris: Flammarion, 1972)

'Les travailleurs immigrés', *Après-demain*, 204-5 (May-June 1978)

B. Granotier, *Les Travailleurs immigrés en France* (Paris: Maspero, 1976)

'Les immigrés en France', *Le Monde: dossiers et documents*, 29 (March 1976)

Analysis of socio-occupational structure:

INSEE, *Code des catégories socio-professionnelles*, 6th ed. (1977)

J. Marceau, *Class and Status in France: Economic Change and Social Mobility 1945-1975* (Oxford: Clarendon Press, 1977)

G. Vincent, *Les Français 1945-1975: chronologie et structure d'une sociéte* (Paris: Masson, 1977)

Reviews:

Up-to-date information and analysis, including comparisons with other countries, are provided regularly in publications by the INED: the bimonthly review *Population* and the monthly pamphlet *Population et société*, and by the INSEE: *Données sociales* 1973, 74, 78, 81 and the monthly *Economie et statistique*.

Illustrative texts and linguistic exercises

Texte 1.1   La France vieille en l'an 2000

La France est malade. D'un mal mortel, et qu'elle ignore: notre pays souffre *d'anémie démographique*. Il est né chez nous, l'an dernier, 15 bébés pour 1 000 habitants. Seulement. C'est le chiffre le plus bas *enregistré* depuis la fin de la Seconde Guerre mondiale. Ainsi se trouve rejoint le niveau des années les plus noires de notre histoire démographique: la fin des années trente où la natalité était tombée à 14,8 pour 1 000.

Devant ces chiffres, il y a à peu près autant de réactions que de Français: 52 millions et demi. Mais le pessimisme l'emporte largement dans une population déjà accablée par l'excès de la concentration urbaine, avec *son cortège de difficultés et de nuisances*, et à qui les mass media imposent *un surcroît d'angoisse* en lui montrant chaque jour les images d'une planète surpeuplée.

Loin d'être menacée de surpeuplement, c'est la France qui offre en effet la plus faible densité démographique de toutes les grandes nations industrielles, Etats-Unis et Urss mises à part. Et la baisse du taux de natalité – c'est-à-dire *le vieillissement de la population* – va s'y traduire par des conséquences particulièrement graves.

Outre qu'il diminue l'aptitude au changement, *vertu cardinale* des sociétés modernes, le vieillissement freine *la promotion sociale*, exacerbant les conflits de génération. Les jeunes accepteront-ils indéfiniment de *se plier à la loi du nombre* – c'est-à-dire aux règles de la démocratie? Et le poids de la France dans le monde? Au temps de Saint Louis et des croisades, un homme sur 20 était français. Aujourd'hui, la proportion n'est plus que d'un sur 80. En l'an 2000, elle sera d'un sur 120. En 1850, la France était le troisième pays du monde avec 28 millions d'habitants, dépassée seulement par la Chine et la Russie. Dans vingt-cinq ans, demain, la bombe démographique sera beaucoup plus redoutable que la bombe atomique. Or, la conférence sur la population réunie l'été dernier à Bucarest s'est séparée dans *une cacophonie totale*. 'Nous refusons de limiter notre natalité, ont proclamé la majorité du tiers-monde, Chinois et Algériens en tête. Notre salut est dans le nombre de nos bras. Et si les Occidentaux veulent nous aider, qu'ils cessent d'abord de nous piller'

SOURCE: G. M., *Paris Match* (1 mars 1975) pp.34–5 (adapté).

Exploitation du texte

1 Expliquez en quelques mots les phrases/termes en italique.

2 Présentez en vos propres mots l'attitude de l'auteur envers la situation démographique en France et les conséquences qu'il préconise si la baisse du taux de natalité se poursuit.

3 Relevez les termes exploités dans les deux premiers paragraphes qui indiquent cette attitude.

4 Quelle est, d'après l'auteur, la réaction des Français envers les tendances démographiques et comment peut-on l'expliquer?

5 Expliquez le sens et la portée de la phrase: 'Dans vingt-cinq ans, demain, la bombe démographique sera beaucoup plus redoutable que la bombe atomique.'

Texte 1.2   Le seul ennemi: la vieillesse

Que la France ait 40 ou 80 millions d'habitants n'est plus chose majeure; l'important est le chemin qui s'ouvre. Or il est clair, c'est celui de la vieillesse, du vieillissement. Celui-ci n'a pas résulté, jusqu'ici, de l'allongement de la vie, comme on le croit, mais de *l'érosion, à sa base, de la pyramide des âges*.

Le vieillissement, c'est le grand phénomène qui domine de loin notre époque. La ligne suivie nous mène à *un sexagénaire sur quatre personnes*. La proportion des octogénaires, déjà si mal soignés, doublerait. Et le vieillissement provoquera, un jour l'écroulement du système de retraites, *construit puérilement* sur des concepts naïfs.

Plus sérieux encore est l'aspect éthique. Une population qui a basculé est condamnée, incapable d'innover, de réagir. Prise dans *ce lent tourbillon*, elle ne peut que sombrer; or il n'y a pas d'euthanasie pour les peuples. S'imaginer que les pays pauvres accepteront de continuer à élever des enfants pour qu'ils aillent payer les retraites des vieux Européens est déjà une idée de vieux, d'affaibli.

Si le vieillissement, si sûr, est si mal connu, c'est qu'il provoque sa propre analgésie, sa propre anesthésie. *Il engourdit les nations* de telle façon qu'elles n'ont pas conscience de leur état et refusent de se connaître. Faites une expérience: *mettez la question du vieillissement sur le tapis*, dans une conversation, vous verrez le débat se détourner, dériver, s'effacer. Les populations âgées sont dépourvues de cette qualité, bien utile, qui s'appelle le courage, et cet affaiblissement touche aussi les jeunes.

Les maux, partout dénoncés, de la société occidentale, le relâchement de ses tissus, la sclérose de ses organes, le cancer de la violence, etc., dérivent tous de l'affaiblissement causé par cette sénescence sociale. Mai 68 n'est qu'une réaction instinctive contre le vieillissement mais *les jeunes ont eu finalement le dessous*.

Nous pouvons avoir quinze à vingt ans d'euphorie, en cessant de former les jeunes, ces cellules qui sauvent constamment l'organisme. Euphorie mortelle, car jamais plus le retour héroïque vers la vie ne sera possible.

Devant ce mal lent, sournois et souriant, la réaction est déconcertante;

ce sont les milieux progressistes *qui jouent le plus la carte de la vieillesse.* Ainsi ceux qui veulent construire l'avenir refusent de la voir, alors que les conservateurs s'en préoccupent, eux qui songent, avant tout, au passé! Ce paradoxe a des racines historiques mais son anachronisme n'en est que plus accusé. Vieillissement. En outre, les milieux 'évolués' confondent une fois de plus nation, Etat et gouvernement, et s'opposent aux mesures de salut parce qu'elles sont dans les vues (bien timides d'ailleurs) de leurs adversaires. Puérilité tragique.

Fort ancienne aussi est l'idée que tout changera lorsqu'un nouveau régime satisfera les hommes. Aucun précédent historique n'autorise à penser ainsi. Quel qu'il soit, le gouvernement sera *assailli de tant de sommations* à l'égard des promesses, déjà formulées, qu'il remettra la question à des temps dits meilleurs. Je l'ai dit, l'opposition joue à fond la carte de la vieillesse. Qu'on en juge. Au lendemain du duel Fourcade-Mitterrand le Parti socialiste a publié *le montant de son programme*: il propose, pour la vieillesse, 26,2 milliards de plus et pour la jeunesse 0,7 milliard de moins.

Ainsi la bascule vers la vieillesse est fortement accusée, pleinement volontaire. Vivre, survivre n'est plus un objectif. L'état d'esprit collectif sera demain plus détourné encore de la jeunesse.

A l'inverse, les Soviétiques et les républiques populaires luttent pour la vie. Les mesures profamiliales ont eu leur effet, de sorte que la différence qui existait, il y a dix ans, entre Est et Ouest s'est inversée. Ajoutons que les Soviétiques, instruits par l'expérience, prolongent la vie active par tous les moyens, alors que nous cherchons systématiquement à fabriquer *de nouveaux vieux* et *de nouveaux pauvres*.

Il reste aux *défaitistes de la vie* l'argument suprême: 'Il n'y a rien à faire.' Tout s'inscrit contre cette idée, ne serait-ce que la politique des pays de l'Est. Le manque de franchise, c'est-à-dire de réflexion, est ici comme partout. Après avoir affirmé que les ménages renoncent au troisième enfant à cause des difficultés qu'il soulève, ils annoncent que soulager ces difficultés n'aura pas d'effet. *Il est de bon ton*, aujourd'hui, d'affirmer que les allocations familiales n'ont pas eu de résultat. Sans nier l'existence d'autres causes, observons ceci: la France, qui se traînait, de forte tradition, à l'arrière-garde, avait, il y a peu de temps encore, la fécondité presque la plus forte d'Europe occidentale.

Que toutes ces vues soient *à contre-courant* est l'évidence; mais je ne pense pas qu'un Français sur cent, peut-être sur mille, ait réfléchi profondément à la question et cela sans se laisser entraîner par le 'bon ton' et *les formules acquises.*

Si aléatoire que soit la prévision, n'hésitons pas à écrire, à graver ceci: 'Le siècle qui vient ne verra pas un îlot clairsemé de vieux égrotants, savourant tranquillement leurs derniers biens, au milieu d'un océan de pauvreté. . . et de jeunesse.'

SOURCE: A. Sauvy, *Le Nouvel Observateur* (15 mars 1976) p.35 (adapté).

Exploitation du texte

1 Expliquez en quelques mots les phrases/termes en italique.

2 Reformulez en vos propres mots le paragraphe 'Plus sérieux. . . . affaibli' de manière à faire ressortir son sens en termes simples.

3 Expliquez le paradoxe auquel l'auteur fait allusion et son anachronisme.

4 Quelle est la distinction entre nation, Etat et gouvernement?

5 Commentez l'emploi du subjonctif dans les phrases suivantes:

Que la France ait 40 ou 80 millions d'habitants n'est plus chose majeure.
Quel qu'il soit, le gouvernement sera assailli. . .
Qu'on en juge.
Si aléatoire que soit la prévision.

6 Dans quels domaines l'auteur puise-t-il son langage figuré? Donnez des exemples.

7 Expliquez le sens et la portée de la dernière phrase du texte.

8 Résumez en moins de 200 mots les dangers du vieillissement tels qu'ils sont présentés par l'auteur.

Texte 1.3   Le nombre des naissances a diminué en France de cent dix mille en deux ans

Baisse accéléré de la natalité en France depuis deux ans (cent dix mille naissances de moins l'an dernier qu'en 1973), stabilité de la mortalité, immigration fortement ralentie: telles sont les principales conclusions du rapport que l'Institut national d'études démographiques (INED) vient d'adresser aux parlementaires. La population de la France continue de croître, mais à un rythme ralenti (+0,6% par an au lieu de +0,9% en 1970), tandis que la proportion des jeunes de moins de vingt ans diminue régulièrement.

Cette évolution doit-elle inquiéter? Peut-on la corriger? Les comparaisons démographiques entre la France et l'étranger mettent à mal bien des idées reçues et amènent à se demander si la fécondité humaine est gouvernable.

Pourquoi?

Si toutes les femmes en âge d'avoir des enfants continuaient d'avoir le même taux de fécondité que l'an dernier, la population française pourrait commencer à baisser dans quelques dizaines d'années. C'est la première constation que l'on est tenté de faire au vu des chiffres publiés par l'INED. La 'somme des naissances réduites', indicateur conjoncturel utilisé par les démographes pour observer la fécondité sur une année donnée* est en effet passée de 2,9 enfants par femme en 1964 à 2,1 dix ans plus tard et à 1,9 l'an dernier, chiffre le plus bas enregistré dans l'histoire démographique de la France (si l'on excepte les années de guerre). Ce chiffre se situe au-dessous du seuil nécessaire pour *assurer le simple renouvellement de la population* (2,1).

Rien ne permet cependant de penser que la baisse de la fécondité observée depuis 1964 soit un phénomène passager.

En observant l'évolution de la population sur une longue période, on constate que l' 'explosion démographique' d'après-guerre n'est qu'une sorte d' 'accident' dans une baisse continue de la fécondité, commencée en France dans la deuxième moitié du dix-huitième siècle. Ce mouvement accompagne et souvent précède la baisse tout aussi continue de la mortalité.

Cette évolution est-elle grave pour l'équilibre économique et social de la France? Prudents, les démographes estiment que les générations actuelles assureront leur remplacement; mais ils s'inquiètent de l'instabilité à moyen terme du nombre des naissances, en raison des successions de générations d'inégale importance en âge d'avoir des enfants;† cela risque de donner *une pyramide des âges chahutée* et d''introduire des dyscontinuités' dans les investissements nécessaires en matière d'éducation ou d'emploi.

Peut-on modifier la tendance actuelle? L'évolution démographique dans les pays voisins permet d'en douter. On constate en effet une extraordinaire simultanéité des phénomènes de fécondité depuis au moins le début du siècle dans tous les pays d'Europe occidentale.

Les différences d'*appartenance religieuse* et de législation familiale ou sociale ne paraissent pas avoir influencé sur les tendances profondes de la fécondité. Rien ne permet en particulier d'affirmer, comme on l'a souvent fait, que les mesures prises en France à la veille et au lendemain de la guerre en faveur des familles aient joué un rôle déterminant; au mieux, elles ont peut-être contribué à amplifier un mouvement général, la dimension moyenne des familles s'étant située en France à un niveau

---

* '*La somme des naissances réduites*' est l'addition des taux de fécondité des femmes de dix-huit à quarante ans, observés la même année. C'est un indicateur conjoncturel qu'il faut distinguer de '*la descendance finale de la génération*', c'est-à-dire du nombre moyen d'enfants effectivement mis au monde par femme; cette dernière donnée ne peut être connue qu'après-coup. Actuellement, 'la somme des naissances réduites' est de 1,9, mais la descendance finale pour la deuxième génération observée est de 2,35.

† La génération des quinze–dix-neuf ans, qui arrive à l'âge de la fécondité, est nettement moins importante que celle qui précède (vingt–vingt-quatre ans), mais aussi que celle qui la suit (dix–quatorze ans).

supérieur (2,6 enfants) à celui atteint en Angleterre (2,4) et en Allemagne (2,2).

Inversement, si le retard pris depuis trente ans par les prestations familiales sur l'évolution du revenu par tête est choquant sur le plan de la justice, il n'a vraisemblablement pas eu d'*effets sensibles* sur la baisse de la fécondité. Il n'est pas sûr non plus qu'une amélioration des conditions de logement des jeunes ménages ait un effet direct sur le nombre d'enfants par famille. N'est-ce pas d'ailleurs dans une période de reconstruction où l'habitat était autrement précaire qu'aujourd'hui que s'est produite l'explosion démographique?

Pour certains la chute actuelle des naissances est le signe d'une société égoïste qui refuse la vie. Comment expliquer alors que le pourcentage de couples sans enfant n'ait jamais été aussi faible qu'aujourd'hui (6%)? Il est à un niveau tellement bas qu'il ne paraît guère pouvoir diminuer, compte tenu de la stérilité physiologique. Quant à la proportion de couples ayant deux enfants, elle a également augmenté; c'est le nombre des familles de trois enfants et plus, en baisse constante sur une très longue période, qui a le plus diminué depuis 1964.

Ce changement de comportement est, pour l'essentiel, lié à l'élévation du niveau de vie et de culture, et à une plus grande maîtrise de la fécondité par les familles. Radicalement inverser cette évolution impliquerait le retour à une société d'ouvriers agricoles et de manoeuvres, catégories sociales parmi lesquelles on trouve toujours le plus grand nombre de familles nombreuses ou à un ordre politique et moral de sinistre mémoire: le seul pays d'Europe occidentale qui, depuis le début du siècle, ait vu sa fécondité formidablement progresser, au moment où elle diminuait partout ailleurs, est l'Allemagne . . . à partir de 1933. Faut-il, au nom du '*dynamisme démographique*', avoir la nostalgie de ce passé?

SOURCE: J.-M. Dupont, *Le Monde* (22 janv. 1976) pp.1, 30 (adapté).

Exploitation du texte

1 Expliquez en quelques mots les phrases/termes en italique, sauf l'en-tête.

2 Expliquez en vos propres mots la différence entre les deux indicateurs des taux de fécondité utilisés par les démographes (présentés en note), à savoir la somme des naissances réduites et la descendance finale. Pourquoi faut-il deux indicateurs et comment les exploite-t-on?

3 Faites un résumé en moins de 200 mots des réponses que l'auteur donne aux questions qu'il pose dans l'en-tête.

4 Quelle semble être l'opinion personnelle de l'auteur sur les tendances démographiques telle qu'elle se dégage de cet article, et quel est le sens de la dernière phrase du texte?

5 Pourquoi est-ce qu'un taux de natalité instable 'risque d'introduire des discontinuités' quant aux dépenses sur l'éducation ou l'emploi?

6 Comment peut-on expliquer l' 'extraordinaire simultanéité des phénomènes de fécondité' dans l'Europe occidentale?

7 Formulez des phrases à partir des expressions suivantes de manière à en illustrer le sens: au vu des chiffres, à moyen terme, en matière de, compte tenu de.

Texte 1.4   Les perspectives de population

Au cours des prochaines années, le nombre annuel de mariages doit rester de l'ordre de 420 000–430 000; celui des naissances atteindra puis dépassera le seuil des 900 000; celui des décès passera d'environ 550 000 en 1970 à 600 000 vers 1990. Dans l'hypothèse vraisemblable de fécondité basse, avec migrations, l'excédent naturel annuel, de l'ordre de 300 000 en 1970, s'élèvera à 350 000 vers 1975; il baissera à partir de 1980, pour atteindre environ 300 000 en 1990. L'accroissement total, égal à 440 000 en 1970, atteindra, sous la même hypothèse, près de 500 000 à partir de 1975.

La population sera comprise entre 55 et 59 millions au 1er janvier 1985, selon l'hypothèse d'évolution; elle avoisinera vraisemblablement 58 millions à cette date; le seuil des 60 millions sera franchi en 1991–1992.

En répartissant la population en trois grands groupes d'âges (0–19 ans, 20–64 ans, 65 ans ou plus), on constate que la croissance du groupe le plus âgé s'inversera entre 1980 et 1985 (passage dans ce groupe des générations 'creuses' 1915–1919) en sorte que l'effectif des '65 ans ou plus, aura progresse de 7% entre 1970 et 1985 tandis que celui des '20–64 ans' se sera accru dans le même temps de 21% (avec migrations); à la fin du siècle, les '20–64 ans' conserveront une certaine avance. Quant à l'effectif des plus jeunes (0–19 ans), son évolution dépend essentiellement de l'hypothèse de fécondité: dans l'hypothèse de fécondité basse, l'augmentation de l'effectif de ce groupe sera faible (quelques points pour cent) et tiendra essentiellement à l'apport direct ou indirect de l'immigration. Au total, le poids des adultes (20–64 ans) dans la population s'accroîtra; dans l'hypothèse de fécondité basse, si les migrations se poursuivent au même rythme – ou à un rythme légèrement inférieur – jusqu'à la fin du siècle, il retrouvera alors sa valeur de 1955 (57,5%). Dans les mêmes hypothèses, la proportion de personnes âgées (65 ans ou plus) sera alors de l'ordre de 13%; elle retrouvera ainsi la valeur qu'elle avait au début de la décennie 1970. La part des jeunes (0–19 ans) chutera; ils rassembleront vraisemblablement environ 29% de la population en 2000 et retrouveront ainsi le pourcentage de l'immédiat après-guerre.

La population active disponible s'accroîtra de près de 20% (migrations) comprises) au cours de la période 1970-1984, son effectif passant de 21 800 000 à 25 250 000. Elle comprendra moins de jeunes et moins de vieux mais plus de personnes d'âge moyen et, parmi ces dernières, surtout plus de femmes. Au cours de la période 1970-1985, la croissance des ménages et celle de la population active s'accélérera par rapport aux années 1960. Il en sera de même pour la population totale au cours d'une partie de la période.

Une population totale croissant au même rythme que dans les années 1960, avec relativement plus d'adultes, moins de jeunes et moins de vieux; un nombre de ménages augmentant à un rythme supérieur à celui des années 1960; une population active augmentant également à un rythme supérieur, tels sont les caractères majeurs de l'évolution de la population française au cours des prochaines décennies.

SOURCE: A. Nizard, *Population,* XXIX, numéro spécial (juin 1974) pp.281-4 (adapté).

Exploitation du texte

1 En vous servant de l'en-tête du Texte 1.3 comme modèle, rédigez un résumé de la situation démographique en 1985 qui pourrait figurer dans un commentaire de presse.

2 Relevez au moins 10 termes différents exploités dans le texte pour indiquer les variations quantitatives de la population et classez-les selon leur fonction dans le discours, par exemple: verbes - atteindre, dépasser, etc.; substantifs - l'accroissement, etc.

3 Quelle est la différence entre nombre, chiffre, effectif, proportion, valeur, taux, niveau?

4 Distinguez entre les verbes croître, s'accroître, augmenter.

5 Commentez les emplois du temps des verbes dans tout le texte.

6 Dessinez une pyramide des âges pour la population française en 1985 en vous servant des données présentées dans le texte dans l'hypothèse de fécondité basse avec migrations.

7 Traduisez en français les phrases suivantes:
   (i) An annual birthrate of between 800,000 and 875,000 was maintained until about 1973.
   (ii) Between 1963 and 1972 the average age at which men married fell by approximately 1.5 years whereas that for women fell by 0.75 years.
   (iii) In 1971 people of pensionable age made up 16 per cent of the total population, a slightly higher proportion than in 1961.

Texte 1.5   Où sont passés les Parisiens?

Mystère des statistiques et de *l'alchimie des villes*: en vingt ans, Paris a perdu 600 000 habitants et gagné 200 000 logements.

Paris se dépeuple, et pourtant on n'y a jamais construit autant de logements. Paris se couvre de bureaux, mais ne gagne pas d'emplois supplémentaires: le nombre de chômeurs y augmente même au point d'atteindre désormais *la cote inquiétante de 80 000*.

Au total, le Parisien se fait de plus en plus rare, mais il occupe davantage d'espace: c'est la conclusion qu'il faut tirer des résultats, apparemment contradictoires, du dernier recensement national. Plus de logements, moins d'habitants: le paradoxe a, en fait, une double signification.

Paris est une ville plus aérée qu'autrefois et ses habitants y *vivent plus au large*. On y construit plus grand qu'il y a vingt ans et la densité d'occupation des appartements et des bureaux a considérablement diminué. Ainsi, là où résidaient quatre personnes en 1954, on ne trouve en 1975 que deux occupants.

La population parisienne a vieilli et *s'est embourgeoisée*. Dans ce Paris baudruche, qui ne cesse de se dégonfler, les catégories sociales les plus défavorisées – en particulier les jeunes de 25 à 35 ans et leurs enfants – sont en effet les premières à s'exiler. Parce qu'on démolit les vieux logements, qu'on louait 200 F par mois, pour construire à la place – dans le meilleur des cas – des HLM à 600 F, trop chers. Ou parce que les petites entreprises artisanales et industrielles ont cédé la place *aux gratte-ciel pour cols blancs*.

Les quartiers les premiers touchés ont été ceux du centre de la capitale. Certains ont perdu plus de 40% de leur population depuis 1954. Chassé du ventre parisien, le flot migratoire a d'abord trouvé refuge dans les arrondissements périphériques. Puis il a débordé de Paris intra-muros. Non pour se répandre en province, mais, surtout, dans les autres départements de la région parisienne, dont la population a augmenté de 2,5 millions d'habitants. Progression considérable qui, depuis 1968, profite essentiellement à la grande banlieue.

L'exode est tel, d'ailleurs, qu'il devient inquiétant. Il est anormal que le cœur d'une grande cité se vide au rythme actuel. Aussi, certains commencent à *prôner un arrêt* de l'hémorragie et donnent des remèdes: une meilleure maîtrise des sols, un arrêt des destructions systématiques, la réalisation de grandes opérations. Comme dans le 13e , où la rénovation du quartier Italie a permis de renverser le flot.

SOURCE: M. de Saint-Pulgent, *Le Point* (22 sept. 1975) p.69 (adapté).

Exploitation du texte
1 Expliquez en quelques mots les phrases/termes en italique.

2 Résumez en moins de 100 mots l'essentiel des résultats apparemment contradictoires du recensement et les conséquences qui en découlent.

3 De quels moyens l'auteur se sert-il pour faire ressortir les différents contrastes qu'il introduit?

4 Quelles sont les 6 entités territoriales mentionnées dans le texte et comment peut-on les définir?

Texte 1.6 Entre le bouc et l'autruche

A entendre les passions se déchaîner dès que l'on parle d'immigration, on sent se creuser un fossé entre deux attitudes extrêmes.

D'un côté, c'est l'attitude du bouc émissaire: la crise secoue-t-elle notre pays? Le chômage augmente-t-il? Il faut chercher un coupable. Et il est vite trouvé: ce ne peut être nous, c'est donc celui qui est différent de nous: l'étranger. Chargeons-le vite de nos fardeaux et, comme dans la Bible, renvoyons-le dans le désert à Azazel, nom biblique du diable. Ainsi entend-on dire *d'une voix docte* qu'il y a un million trois cent mille chômeurs en France parce qu'il y a un million huit cent mille travailleurs immigrés, comme si c'étaient eux les responsables de la hausse du pétrole.

D'un autre côté, c'est l'attitude de l'autruche: comme les travailleurs immigrés ne sont pas responsables de la crise, il faut se fermer les yeux sur leur existence et avoir la même politique d'immigration qu'avant 1973, lorsque notre économie croissait deux fois plus vite. Ose-t-on dire que ce serait une bonne chose pour le retour au plein-emploi que la population étrangère, au lieu d'augmenter comme elle le fait depuis vingt-cinq ans, commence à diminuer? Horreur! Cette évidence de bon sens *vous attire les foudres* de tous ceux qui, à haute voix, se déclarent garants des droits des masses populaires exploitées et, à voix basse, susurrent que plus il y aura de chômeurs, plus vite la majorité tombera. *Le bec dans le sable et la rose au poing*, nos autruches évitent ainsi de se donner la peine de réfléchir au problème posé.

Je suis de ceux qui pensent que, entre le bouc et l'autruche, il y a une autre attitude qui puisse être à la fois conforme aux grandes traditions d'accueil de la France et aux nécessités du moment.

Pendant encore cinq ans, la démographie sera défavorable au plein-emploi: arrivent sur le marché de l'emploi les classes de jeunes les plus nombreuses. Parmi ces jeunes figurent les jeunes immigrés de la seconde génération, scolarisés en France, souvent nés en France, et auxquels il n'est pas question de dénier le droit d'accès au travail.

La bonne politique de l'immigration doit être le résultat d'un triple effort:

— Interdire toute immigration nouvelle;
— Encourager tout départ volontaire;
— Adapter les renouvellements à la situation de l'emploi.

Enfin, il faut comprendre que l'on peut à la fois organiser dans la dignité le retour d'un certain nombre de travailleurs étrangers tout en continuant à respecter la plénitude des droits de ceux qui restent en France. J'entends dire ici et là: 'A quoi bon s'occuper des immigrés pour leur formation et leur logement... puisqu'ils vont repartir?' Ce langage est absurde. Par rapport au passé, la seule différence est que les quatre millions d'étrangers qui vivent en France, au lieu de voir leur nombre augmenter comme depuis trente ans, vont le voir diminuer de 3 ou 5% par an. C'est dire que de très nombreuses communautés étrangères continueront à vivre durablement en France, pour le plus grand enrichissement de notre vie économique et sociale. Nous devons, non seulement nous garder de tout racisme, mais *mettre tout en oeuvre* pour que ces hommes, ces femmes et ces enfants vivent chez nous, avec nous et comme nous.

Il y va de leur dignité.

Il y va donc de la nôtre.

SOURCE: L. Stoléru, *Le Monde* (15 juin 1979) p.38 (adapté).

Exploitation du texte

1 Expliquez en quelques mots les phrases/termes en italique.

2 Résumez en vos propres mots les trois attitudes envers l'immigration décrites dans cet article, à savoir du bouc émissaire, de l'autruche et de l'auteur.

3 A qui l'auteur fait-il allusion lorsqu'il parle de 'tous ceux qui se déclarent garants des droits des masses populaires exploitées'.

4 Expliquez comment l'attitude de l'auteur peut être et 'conforme aux grandes traditions d'accueil de la France et aux nécessités du moment'.

5 Prenez le rôle du bouc ou de l'autruche et rédigez une lettre au *Monde* attaquant la politique de Stoléru.

Texte 1.7   Le recensement de la population: bulletin individuel

Comment remplir les questionnaires:

Les questionnaires sont la *matière première* du recensement et de leur qualité dépendent la rapidité du *dépouillement* et la valeur des résultats: il est donc, bien entendu, essentiel de les remplir correctement et complètement.

Il faut lire attentivement les questions, y compris les explications ou les exemples en petits caractères, avant de répondre. Aucune question ne doit rester sans réponse, sauf s'il est précisé qu'elle ne concerne pas la personne considérée (exemple: les questions 8 et suivantes dans le cas d'une personne de moins de 16 ans).

Les *bulletins*, lors de leur transformation en *documents mécano-*

graphiques, seront lus par des *opératrices* dont il importe de simplifier la tâche; c'est pourquoi il faut écrire lisiblement, *sans surcharges* ni abréviations (*bannir les sigles* dans la *raison sociale* de l'employeur, par exemple), éviter d'indiquer le *lieu-dit* à la place de la commune, ne pas oublier de préciser le département de naissance, de résidence antérieure.

ACTIVITÉ PROFESSIONNELLE *(Pour toute personne de 16 ans ou plus)*

- Si vous êtes actuellement sans travail et si vous en recherchez, passez directement à la question **17**
- Si vous ne travaillez plus, passez directement à la question **18**

---

(11) PROFESSION PRINCIPALE

Indiquez la profession ou le métier que vous exercez actuellement *(même si vous n'êtes encore qu'apprenti ou si vous travaillez en aidant un membre de votre famille dans sa profession). Une femme ne s'occupant que de son propre intérieur répondra "sans profession".*

Soyez précis. Exemples : mécanicien réparateur d'automobiles, mécanicienne en confection, charpentier en fer, monteur en chauffage central, peintre en bâtiment, dessinateur industriel, ingénieur électricien, viticulteur, chauffeur de poids lourds, sténodactylo, droguiste en gros, etc.

(12) Travaillez-vous, **sans être salarié**, en aidant une autre personne dans sa profession (par exemple un membre de votre famille) ? OUI ☐ 1   NON ☐

(13) Exercez-vous votre profession principale déclarée à la question 11 comme :

- Exploitant agricole (propriétaire, fermier, métayer) . . . . ☐ 2
- Membre d'une profession libérale . . . . ☐ 3
- Employeur ou travailleur indépendant : artisan, commerçant, industriel, etc. . . . . ☐ 4
  (travaillant à son compte, y compris gérants majoritaires de S.A.R.L. et personnes ne travaillant qu'à la commission)
- Travailleur à domicile pour le compte d'une (ou plusieurs) entreprise(s) . . . . ☐ 5
- Apprenti sous contrat . . . . ☐ 6
- Salarié . . . . ☐ 7

(14) POUR LES SALARIÉS :

a Si vous êtes ouvrier, précisez la qualification de votre emploi actuel :

- Manœuvre ou manœuvre spécialisé . . . . ☐ 1
- Ouvrier spécialisé (OS1, OS2,...). . . . . ☐ 2
- Ouvrier qualifié ou hautement qualifié (P1, P2, P3,...). . ☐ 3

b Si vous êtes agent de l'État, d'une collectivité locale ou d'un service public (E.D.F., S.N.C.F., etc.) ou militaire de carrière, précisez votre **grade** :
Exemples : agent d'administration principal, secrétaire administratif, chef de gare de 2ᵉ classe, etc.

c Si vous êtes dans un **autre cas**, précisez votre position hiérarchique :
Exemples : contremaître, chef de culture, chef de rayon, directeur commercial, etc.

(15) SI VOUS ÊTES ÉTABLI À VOTRE COMPTE :
(réponse 2, 3 ou 4 à la question 13)

Employez-vous des salariés ?

Ne comptez pas les gens de maison à votre service. Dans l'agriculture, comptez seulement les salariés permanents.

OUI ☐ Combien ? { 1 ou 2 ☐ 1 / 3 à 5 ☐ 3 / 6 ou plus ☐ 6

NON ☐ 0

---

(16) OÙ TRAVAILLEZ-VOUS ?

a ADRESSE de votre lieu de travail :

N°_____ Rue (ou lieudit) : _____

Commune : _____
(Pour Paris, Lyon, Marseille, précisez l'arrondissement)

Département : _____
Si, au cours de votre travail, vous êtes amené à vous déplacer (cas du personnel roulant de la S.N.C.F., des conducteurs d'autobus, etc.), indiquez l'endroit où vous vous rendez ordinairement pour prendre votre travail (gare, dépôt, etc.).
Si vous ne prenez pas toujours votre travail au même endroit (cas des voyageurs de commerce par exemple), répondez "variable".

b NOM (ou raison sociale) de l'établissement (industriel, commercial, administratif, agricole, etc.) que vous dirigez ou qui vous emploie :

c ACTIVITÉ de cet établissement :
Soyez précis. Exemples : commerce de vins en gros, épicerie de détail, fabrication de charpentes métalliques, filature de coton, transport routier de voyageurs, culture maraîchère, etc.

d Adresse de cet établissement, si elle est différente de celle déclarée à la question 16 a :

N°_____ Rue (ou lieudit) : _____

Commune : _____
(Pour Paris, Lyon, Marseille, précisez l'arrondissement)

Département : _____

(17) SI VOUS ÊTES ACTUELLEMENT SANS TRAVAIL ET SI VOUS EN RECHERCHEZ :

a Depuis combien de temps cherchez-vous du travail ? { moins de 3 mois . . . . ☐ 1 / de 3 mois à moins de 6 mois . . . ☐ 2 / de 6 mois à moins d'un an. . . . . ☐ 3 / un an ou plus . . . . ☐ 4

b Avez-vous déjà travaillé ? OUI ☐   NON ☐ 0

c Quel est votre métier ? _____

(18) SI VOUS NE TRAVAILLEZ PLUS :
(Vous êtes, par exemple, retraité des services publics, retraité vieux travailleur, cadre en retraite, ancien agriculteur, retiré des affaires, etc.)

Quelle a été votre profession principale ? _____

POUR LES PERSONNES DE PASSAGE (voir le cadre C, page 3 de l'imprimé n° 1).

Adresse de la résidence habituelle.

N°_____ Rue (ou lieudit) : _____

Commune : _____
(Pour Paris, Lyon, Marseille, précisez l'arrondissement)

Département : _____

Ne rien écrire dans les grilles ci-dessous.

TA   P   ST   Q   NBS   AE

DLT   CLT   CVLT   NOLT   RT   AP

A _____

le _____ 1975.

Signature du déclarant :

La majorité des questions sont *assorties d'une série de petites cases* placées à la fin des diverses rubriques possibles:
La case qui convient doit être *cochée*; *ne pas rayer les cases* (ou les rubriques) inutiles; ne pas entourer non plus la *mention qui convient*.

SOURCE: INSEE, 'L'Institut National de la Statistique et des Etudes Economiques et le recensement de la population de 1975', *La Documentation française illustrée*, numéro spécial (28 déc. 1974) pp.38-40 (adapté).

Exploitation du texte

1 Expliquez en quelques mots les phrases/termes en italique.

2 Observez les instructions et remplissez ce questionnaire en adoptant le rôle d'un personnage fictif.

3 Faites un résumé des données que ce questionnaire permettra de déduire sur votre personnage fictif.

4 A partir de ces données, à quelle catégorie socio-professionnelle appartenez-vous, et quelle est votre classification selon les rubriques suivantes: métier ou profession individuelle, activité économique, salarié ou à votre propre compte, qualification professionnelle, hiérarchie d'encadrement, nombre de salariés?

5 Quelle est la distinction entre profession et métier; fermier et métayer; ouvrier qualifié et spécialisé et manoeuvre; commerce en gros et en détail; retraité des services publics, retraité vieux travailleur, cadre retraité?

6 Donnez des exemples de professions libérales.

7 Que veulent dire les sigles utilisés dans le questionnaire: SARL, EDF, SNCF?

Exercices de comparaison et d'application

1 Bien que tous les textes traitent du même sujet, il existe des différences importantes quant à la manière de le présenter. Essayez de relever les caractéristiques de chaque texte en vous servant des rubriques suivantes:
  (i)   point de départ (question, constatation, hypothèse);
  (ii) forme et ton (description, présentation d'information ou d'opinion, simple commentaire, critique ou analyse, exposition personnalisée, objective, didactique ou polémique);
  (iii) conclusions tirées;
  (iv) type de phrases (longue, courte, variable, simple, complexe, interrogative, exclamative, ou parenthèse);

(v) choix de vocabulaire (varié ou restreint, simple ou complexe, figuré ou propre, émotif ou neutre, avec ou sans qualificatifs);

(vi) parties du discours dominantes, par exemple, pronoms personnels ou substantifs, structures verbales ou nominales;

(vii) personnes à qui l'auteur s'adresse (grand public, lecteurs avisés, lecteurs spécialisés) et dans quel but.

Faites une évaluation critique de chaque texte.

2 Dans les 7 textes, relevez les locutions adverbiales et les autres moyens exploités par l'auteur pour enchaîner les paragraphes et les arguments.

3 Préparez un débat sur les tendances démographiques révélées par le dernier recensement en présentant différents points de vue, à savoir celui en faveur d'une stabilité démographique, celui qui prévoit la catastrophe si la baisse de la natalité continue et celui qui recherche un accroissement modéré et continu de la population.

4 Ecrivez une dissertation d'environ 1500 à 2000 mots sur un des sujets suivants:

(i) D'après Beaujeu-Garnier, 'la population française apparaît par bien des aspects nettement originale.' Faites une analyse des traits particuliers de l'évolution de la population française depuis 1945.

(ii) Examinez les interventions récentes de l'Etat, soit en matière de contrôle des naissances, soit en ce qui concerne l'immigration.

5 Rédigez un questionnaire sur un des sujets suivants:

(i) un bulletin individuel comportant des questions sur l'état civil (nom, sexe, situation de famille, date et lieu de naissance, etc.), sur les migrations (changement de lieu de résidence depuis le dernier recensement), sur l'instruction et la formation professionnelle;

(ii) l'attitude envers les jeunes, les vieux ou les immigrés et la politique sociale qui les concerne (introduisez des questions vous permettant de dégager l'état civil de la personne interrogée).

2

The Family

During the preparatory phase of the Seventh National Economic Plan for the years 1976–80, a number of working parties were set up to investigate themes such as life-styles, leisure and workers' mobility. The intention behind these studies was to give a new dimension to the National Plans: they were to look further into the future and examine the social and cultural consequences of economic growth in order to ensure more integrated social planning. The first of the working parties to present its findings was the group called *Prospective de la Famille*. Many factors explain the priority given to this report: the amount of attention focused on the family in present-day French society; the concern expressed about demographic trends in relation to the family; and the current debate in the media and literature, exemplified in Texte 2.1, about the institutional functions of the family.

The report, like most of the studies of the family in French society today, stresses the interactive nature of the relationships between the family as a fundamental social unit and society at large, an emphasis reflected in government pronouncements and policy in recent years. As shown in Chapter 1, family building is nowadays determined less by biological than by social variables, such as the general standard of living, the level of educational attainment, the social climate and customs, religious belief, regional traditions and social reforms. It is often suggested that the family is being undermined as a basic social institution due to the reduction in its size and to the intrusion of so many outside agencies, but this claim is countered by evidence that there has been a decline in the level of celibacy and in the proportion of childless couples and that the family is now expected to fulfil different and possibly more demanding functions than those traditionally ascribed to it, an argument supported in Texte 2.2.

Today, as in the past, there is no general consensus, either amongst the public or amongst political parties and religious bodies, about the most desirable conception of the family, nor is there a single model of family structure applicable to all social categories and age groups. Authors writing about the history of the family in France demonstrate how particular models of the family have been dominant at different periods in response to changing economic, political and social circumstances. Although there would seem to be new types of family structure which are becoming prevalent in contemporary France, many features of earlier models can still be identified in present-day society, and it is therefore useful to outline very briefly their salient characteristics before examining in more detail, through an analysis of current trends in marriage, divorce, family building and role allocation, their relevance to the family of today.

The evolution of the family

Four main types of family pattern are documented in accounts of the ways in which the family has evolved in France: those of feudal society, the traditional, *romanesque* and companionship models. Texte 2.3 sets out the main characteristics of the three latter models of matrimony and clearly demonstrates the changes which have occurred in its structure and functions.

Family models in the past

Studies of feudal society in France show that the conjugal or nuclear family was already generally the norm, but that the status of marriage varied considerably according to whether or not there was a family patrimony to protect. From the sixteenth century the so-called traditional model of the family was being adopted, particularly by the bourgeoisie. This conception of the family, which was supported by the Catholic Church, stressed the institutional nature of marriage and the value of its permanency, and family roles were clearly delineated, the father being the dominant figure. Just as divinity sanctified the monarchy, paternal authority was asserted by the church, and marriage was seen as the natural environment in which women could fulfil their altruistic role. As well as being the fundamental unit of production and consumption, the family carried out specific social functions. For the traditionalists marriage was not associated with bonds of affection, and its primary objective was the production and rearing of children.

The abolition of legal privileges by the French Revolution of 1789 did not imply any radical changes in the structure of the family or in the dominant role ascribed to the husband. The Constitution of 1795 reiterated the importance of the family unit with the words *'Nul n'est bon citoyen, s'il n'est bon fils, bon père, bon ami et bon époux'* (Article

4). Napoleon and then the Restoration placed renewed emphasis on paternal authority and confirmed the permanency of the family by prohibiting divorce in 1816. According to Napoleon, wife and children belonged to a husband as a fruit tree and its apples belong to the gardener, and Article 1124 of the *Code civil* stated that those deprived of judicial rights are minors, married women, criminals and the mentally defective. Just as Napoleon formalised and reinforced the hierarchical structure of a bourgeois-dominated society in other areas of social life (his influence in moulding the educational system is commented on in Chapter 4), he codified the traditional family model in order to guarantee the ordered functioning of society.

In spite of Napoleon's attempts to perpetuate the institutional role of marriage, the traditional model was already being adapted and changed in the nineteenth century by the bourgeoisie, as the family began to turn inwards, and the bonds of mutual affection were added to institutional ties. By the second half of the century marriage was becoming more than simply a social act for the bourgeoisie, and the family unit was being transformed. The new conception of the family, known as the *romanesque* model, is distinguished from the traditional family by its less rigid framework. Women and children assume a new status in an environment of intimacy, although the husband continues to act as the main agent for contact with the outside world. The family loses its productive function and becomes a unit of consumption, as the husband supports his family economically by his activity outside the home. Although, for the less privileged members of industrial society, such a model had little relevance in the nineteenth century, they were adopting it by the turn of the century, as social reforms began to improve living and working conditions.

Alternatives to the traditional and *romanesque* models were being preached and lived out during the nineteenth century by the followers of Saint-Simon and Fourier, as well as by Marxists and anarchist groups. They had in common their rejection of the institutional value of marriage and of the constraints which it imposed, particularly on women. In general they favoured union based solely on mutual affection and a more egalitarian distribution of roles within the family.

Whether industrialisation was the cause of the changes which were taking place in family structure in the nineteenth and early twentieth centuries or whether industrialisation and accelerated urbanisation were made possible by such changes is now an academic debate. But it is interesting to note that the family model which has emerged and become dominant in the twentieth century, the companionship, or, as it is sometimes called, 'democratic' model,[1] corresponds closely in several respects to that predicted by Marx and Engels, if the revolutionary social changes they advocated were brought about. Several elements in the alternative patterns sought by the followers of Saint-Simon and Fourier and by the anarchist groups are also discernible in this model.

Family models in contemporary France

The companionship model of the family emphasises the bond of affection almost to the exclusion of institutional ties, and marriage is seen as a formality for social convenience. There is little differentiation according to sex roles, and relative economic independence is expected for both husband and wife. Union is founded on mutual affection and ceases by mutual agreement. Although the primary purpose of marriage is not reproduction, children are considered as a natural and necessary means of confirming the union. They are not, however, allowed to prevent the couple from pursuing other interests which they have in common. The relationships between parents and children are no longer authoritarian, rather, like those between the parents, they are based on companionship.

The changes which have taken place in the family are closely associated with changing social, economic and political structures. Just as the state has increased its control over other areas of social life in the twentieth century, it has also intervened increasingly to reshape the legal framework within which the family evolves and to influence the ways in which the family unit responds to changing social and economic circumstances.

An important feature of the companionship model of the family is its rejection of the institutional framework. It is therefore ironical that the state, while upholding the role of the family as a basic social institution, has played a major part in providing the necessary conditions for the development of such a model. For example, in an effort to stem the population decline, social legislation, initially designed to assist working class families, was extended to afford protection for any child born outside wedlock, or whose mother was widowed or divorced; family benefits were allocated to all social categories, irrespective of marital status, in order to encourage family building and efficient child-rearing. The state thereby sanctioned the dismantling of the marriage institution and introduced a much broader conception of the family unit, with emphasis on personal rather than institutional ties. At the same time old age has come to be treated as a separate area of policy, which tends once more to stress the small conjugal or nuclear family unit as distinct from wider family responsibilities.

The state intervenes in family life even before marriage by imposing compulsory medical examinations on the engaged couple before they are allowed to marry and by laying down the conditions under which contraceptive practices can be adopted. Women are carefully supervised during pregnancy. Babies are born in maternity wards. After its mother has completed her statutory sixteen weeks of maternity leave, the baby of a working woman will often be cared for by a state-approved child-minder or *crèche* before going to a state school. During the early years of its life a child may spend only a small fraction of its waking hours with its parents. By removing income compulsorily through direct and indirect taxation and social security contributions, the state limits the family's consumer choice. It is significant that the number of monetary benefits allocated to the family is decreasing in favour of benefits in kind, including education, health care, housing and communal rec-reational facilities, often leaving little room for individual preferences. In cases where the state takes children into care, the amount of inter-vention is at a maximum, and individual autonomy is completely sacrificed to the conception of social normality as laid down by the law.

Although their motivation and methods may differ, political parties of all persuasions staunchly support the family as a basic social institution and defend the complementary role that it plays in society. In several widely quoted speeches former President Giscard d'Estaing reiterated the contribution made by the family to security and social stability. He depicted it as the haven of peace or a safety valve in the face of a com-petitive and unsettled world in which the individual feels alienated and devoid of responsibility. Debré, a former prime minister, gained a repu-tation for his outspoken views, as illustrated in Texte 2.4, about the importance of government support for the family unit, which he sees as the key to the nation's future.

Critics of the increasing state intervention in all aspects of family life attack the way in which governments abuse their political power and use the family as a tool for social control. For it is debatable whether the progressive takeover by external agencies, ostensibly to relieve the family of functions which it is not capable of performing adequately, or to assist it to operate more effectively, has in reality created a more stable unit capable of fulfilling the specialised functions which are assigned to it.

Whereas the state has in some respects contributed to the consoli-dation of the companionship model of the family, the Roman Catholic Church has continued to act as a restraining influence, upholding the traditional model of the family. Even though the majority of the popu-lation no longer accepts that marriage is a God-given union, it was not until after the Second World War that the Catholic Church confirmed that couples may base their union on love, but it also restated that pro-creation remains the primary purpose of marriage. Recent documents for the guidance of Catholics reiterate the acceptability to the church of a relationship founded on mutual affection, while affirming the social and moral purpose of marriage and its permanency (see Texte 2.5). Far from leading public morals and opinion, the church has tended to follow social change. Although it may bend to accommodate changing attitudes and practices, it exercises a conservative and often repressive influence in its efforts to protect traditional moral values, as demonstrated in recent years by its opposition to divorce, for marriage is still considered as an indissoluble union, or to reform of the legislation on birth control and abortion on the grounds that human life is sacred. A white paper by the Episcopal Commission on the Family, published in 1979, reaffirmed the traditional view of the church on abortion, but in their comments on the documents the bishops were careful to state that they were not attempting to impose their moral standards on non-catholics and that in some cases abortion may be a lesser evil. They remained critical, however, of the nation's political leaders for introducing the new legislation.

As mentioned earlier, there is not a single family model which applies to the whole population at a given time, and it can be shown from a study of marriage and divorce, family building and family roles that the companionship model is by no means universally adopted in contemporary French society. While there are certain social categories whose life-styles and attitudes are particularly well suited to this family pattern, some social groups continue to be influenced by traditional attitudes, such as those of the church, and others, whether for economic or social reasons, are unable or unwilling to conform to such a model.

Marriage

The concept of marriage as an institution has fluctuated considerably over the centuries in response to social change: in feudal society there was no civil ceremony, and cohabitation was accepted as the sign of marriage, the only religious bond being the approval of the clergy. Little or no distinction was made by the majority of the population between children born in or out of wedlock. As the precepts of Roman and Germanic law were adopted in different parts of the country, the conception of marriage came to depend upon geographical origins, Roman law providing for a more formal institutional bond. But social origins were also an important determining factor in attitudes towards marriage: where there was an inheritance to protect, the formal aspects of marriage as a civil contract were given priority. In the traditional and *romanesque* models of the family, marriage was still primarily an economic and social necessity. When, in the nineteenth century, the marriage contract was formulated in the *Code civil*, it corresponded to the requirements of the bourgeoisie, for whom the indissolubility of marriage was a means of ensuring economic survival. It is in essence this contract which is still used today in the compulsory civil wedding ceremony, although significant changes have been introduced in the wording in recent years[2] to confirm the joint responsibility of the married couple in assuring the well-being of their offspring.

Public opinion surveys of attitudes towards marriage in contemporary French society indicate important differences according to social variables, such as age, sex, family origins, level of educational attainment and religious and political convictions. There is, however, almost general agreement that one of the main objectives, if not the primary purpose, of marriage is to guarantee companionship. For the older generations the institution of marriage maintains its value, but for the young marriage is considered as a formality often contracted in response to parental and other social pressures, for it is still easier for a couple to find accommodation, to use credit facilities and to carry out administrative procedures if married.

The number of marriages in any population depends upon the balance between the sexes, or availability of marriage partners of the right age, interests and origins, and on the feasibility and desirability of wedlock in the prevailing socio-economic circumstances. Over the past fifty years there has been a gradual reduction in celibacy, and it is still considered socially abnormal for a man or woman to remain unmarried. As in the past some social categories have higher celibacy rates than others: agricultural labourers have most difficulty in finding marriage partners, which can be explained by their lack of social contact and undesirable social status. Highly qualified women are most likely to remain celibate in order to devote themselves to their careers, whereas highly qualified men have very low celibacy rates, since they are attractive marriage partners and rely on support from their wives in their professional duties. The legal minimum age of marriage for men and women is still different: 18 for men and 15 for women. The average age at marriage is decreasing, as is the age difference between couples. The more highly qualified an individual is, the more likely he is to marry late in life in order to avoid any constraints on his occupational mobility. Workers in agriculture tend to marry later than average, and women brought up in the rural environment are likely to leave the land if they have not married by the age of 25.

Geographical origins affect marriage chances: not only is there a discrepancy between town and country, but also between the north and the south. The north is now favoured by a higher rate of marriage than the south, due mainly to the age structure of the population. In Paris the urban environment is associated with a low level of marriage and at a relatively late age. This can be explained by the socio-occupational and age structure of the capital, referred to in the previous chapter.

In spite of the publicity given to alternative forms of union, such as cohabitation, trial marriage, or communal life, formal marriage remains the norm. The greater life expectancy of today entails the possibility that marriage will last for a much longer period. In a context where the main function of marriage is no longer reproduction and child-rearing, and where the duration of life as a couple has been significantly extended, an assurance is often sought that the relationship is founded on deeply rooted mutual compatibility. Although marriages are no longer 'arranged' and less importance is attached to inheritance and a dowry, the degree of social inbreeding remains very high. Surveys indicate that ultimately there is close affinity between social matching and choice based on emotional attraction. It would seem that individuals seek marriage partners who share common cultural and social interests in the knowledge that a lasting relationship must be based on something more than affection. Trial marriage can be interpreted in similar terms: it offers a means of testing out the stability of a relationship and thereby avoiding disappointment. A survey carried out by the INSEE in 1976 found that couples also tend to consider the first two years of marriage as a period of enjoyment, of trial marriage and of adaptation.

The attitude towards premarital sexual relationships is closely associated with the age variable, and the differences between generations would seem to indicate that new norms are being adopted. Permissiveness increases with the level of educational attainment, and the Paris area is found to be much more liberal in this respect than the rest of France. Parisians are further distinguished by their rejection of the religious wedding ceremony. Fewer than half the marriages celebrated in Paris are given the blessing of the church, as compared with almost 70 per cent in the provinces, but surveys show that a religious union is considered more binding than the civil contract.

Divorce

While greater freedom is advocated by the younger generations prior to marriage, paradoxically the matrionial state is still idealised, to the extent that marital infidelity is thought to cause irreparable harm to the relationship and to justify separation. Where the expectations from marriage are so great and the demands made of it so high, it is not surprising that marriage should frequently end in disillusionment, in spite of the precautions taken. If the compatibility and mutual affection on which union is founded should cease to exist, marriage no longer has a purpose, and separation is more and more often the outcome. In spite of the potential for a long married life, it is estimated that the average duration of a 1974 marriage ending in divorce is nine years. Approximately one in eight of the marriages contracted in 1965 will end in divorce, and the figure for 1974 marriages is expected to be about 17 per cent. France is in this respect slightly behind Great Britain and a long way behind the United States.

Although divorce was not made legal again in France until 1884 by the *Loi Naquet*, when it was argued that a less rigid framework would make marriage more acceptable to the working classes, it was only in 1976 that legislation was introduced to allow divorce by mutual consent and to make it almost automatic in cases of desertion after six years. Previously it had been necessary to prove the guilt of one of the partners, and the resulting verdict was seen as a punishment. Changing legislation has been accompanied by a less hostile attitude by the public at large towards divorcees. Surveys show that divorce is still considered as a final recourse, but it is generally tolerated, except when there are young children. The intention behind divorce does not appear to be the rejection of the marriage institution, since two thirds of men and 55 per cent of women who divorce remarry, and it is often the desire to remarry which prompts legal action.

Variables such as sex, age, socio-economic circumstances and religious belief are important factors influencing the divorce rate. The changing structure of the female working population is affecting petitions for divorce: it would seem to be almost a precondition for divorce, mainly for financial reasons, that the wife should be in paid employment. Whatever the social category, women are more likely than men to petition for divorce. This may be explained by the more compelling constraints which marriage still imposes on women and by the fact that, for most women, the home remains the focal point of their lives, whereas this is less frequently the case for men. Where marriage is the result of social pressures, as when early marriage is due to premarital conception, the divorce rate is relatively high, and the duration of marriage is likely to be short.

Religious affiliation remains an important factor influencing the rate of divorce: there is evidence to suggest that practising Catholics are less likely to divorce than non-Catholics, but it would seem that the absence of religion does not necessarily encourage divorce. Since the Catholic Church now accepts legal separation, practising Catholics tend to prefer this remedy to divorce. The rural and bourgeois categories, for reasons of economic necessity, tend to observe the rule, sanctioned by moral and religious codes, that marriage is indissoluble, whereas for the middle classes and less privileged social categories such norms do not have the same relevance.

Family building

In the same way that the decline in celibacy or the number of remarriages amongst divorcees in recent years serves as evidence to support the theory that the marriage institution is not becoming obsolete, the decrease in the number of childless couples can be interpreted as confirmation of the social acceptability of family building, even if the average family is becoming smaller. Public opinion surveys show that for most French people a childless couple, or an unmarried couple with children, does not constitute a real family and that the intention to have children, more than any other single factor, is a sufficient reason for marriage.

As indicated in Chapter 1, average family size fluctuates between two and three children, and although the variation about the mean extends over a smaller range than in the past, there are still important differences which can be explained in terms of the factors already referred to: age, socio-economic status, political affiliations, geographical origins and religious beliefs. It is particularly the younger generations which are opting for the smaller family model, but those who come themselves from large families are more likely to have several children, as are women with a low level of educational attainment. Women who continue their studies beyond the minimum school-leaving age have fewer children, but those who complete higher education tend to have more children than average.

As shown in Table 2.1, both ideal and actual family size varies from one socio-occupational category to another. Farmers, agricultural workers and low-paid manual workers, particularly recent immigrants, have the biggest families, but they are also the categories who desire a relatively large family, and who use family planning less often than other social categories. Although the figures for actual family size are the same for the lower-grade non-manual workers and the category of professional workers and higher administrative grades, these averages mask the fact that professional workers are the subcategory with the largest family size amongst all non-manual workers and that the INSEE grouping for employees in commerce shows the smallest average family size over all. The high figure for ideal family size recorded for professional workers and the higher administrative grades may be seen as a reflection of their advantageous position in society. Members of this category are not inhibited in their other activities by the presence of children, since they can afford paid assistance, and it is possible that they, more than most other categories, may be aware of the social repercussions of a declining population and of their own self-interest in ensuring their succession.

Political allegiance is found to be related to ideal family size: left-wing voters tend to favour a smaller family size – although they are not necessarily successful in achieving it – than those supporting a govern-

Table 2.1

Ideal and actual family size in relation to socio-occupational categories in 1975

		Ideal (1)	Actual (2)	
0	Farmers	2.72	2.8*	2.94
1	Agricultural labourers	2.60	3.2*	
2	Employers in industry and commerce	2.57	2.19	
3	Professional workers, higher administrative grades	2.65	2.36	
4	Middle management and administrative staff	2.52	2.17	
5	Lower-grade non-manual workers	2.49	2.36	
6	Manual workers	2.58	2.85	

* Estimated.

SOURCES: for col (1) *Population*, XXX, 4–5 (1975) p.701 (figures for 1974); for col. (2) *Economie et Statistique*, 111 (May 1978) p.28 (average figures for the total number of children produced by the generations 1925–9.

ment on the Right. This may be explained by the higher average age and socio-economic status of the latter category, since these factors are normally associated today with an attitude of support for population growth.

Geographical origins still affect family size: the north remains more prolific than the south; a peak is reached in the Ardennes and the lowest point in the Alpes Maritimes. These regional variations are thought to be caused by a combination of factors: traditional customs and attitudes, generally associated with political and religious affiliations, the degree of urbanisation and industrialisation, knowledge about and access to means of birth control, the general standard of living, the age distribution and marital status of the population.

Religious affiliation still affects family size: where both partners are practising Catholics the number of children desired and produced is significantly higher than for couples where religion plays a lesser role, indicating that the traditional attitude of the Catholic Church remains influential. But Catholicism is thought to be less important in encouraging large family size in countries, such as France, Belgium and Italy, where it is the religion of the majority, than in countries where it is a minority religion, such as Great Britain, the Netherlands, Switzerland or the United States.

The general trend in France towards the small conjugal family unit is
reinforced by the decrease in the number of families in which several
generations live together: three generations cohabit in only about 5 per
cent of all households.[3] Although cohabitation with other generations
is rare (it may be used as a temporary expedient in times of difficulty),
the kinship system offers an important supportive network, and the
services provided mutually are considerable, both in economic and
emotional terms. Studies show that at least a third of all children under
the age of 3 are looked after by their grandparents, and that, when they
set up home for themselves, children tend to live near their parents and
to maintain close contact. They act as a lifeline for each other in times
of crisis in preference to community services, particularly in the less
privileged social categories. Since inheritance is postponed due to greater
life expectancy, financial assistance is given increasingly during the
parents' lifetime, often amongst the wealthier categories, to help the
younger generation to set up home. But parents are no longer relied on
for their worldly wisdom or their knowledge of traditional cultural and
moral values, and their experience is generally considered inappropriate
for present-day circumstances. In return for their material support, they
will expect to receive emotional gratification. When parents reach old
age, the support system may be reversed, but whatever the nature of the
relationship its very existence confirms the bond of solidarity between
the generations.

There is evidence to suggest that, in spite of the progressive takeover
of so many of the family's functions by external agencies, it continues
to be the single most important force determining social reproduction.
Each child is exposed within his family environment to a unique set of
values, models and roles which varies according to the social status of
the family. The values presented through formal education, the media
and other social and commercial organisations may compete with or
take precedence over those of the family, but the way in which the
individual identifies with these external influences is still determined in
the first instance by his family origins.

Changing roles within the family

Twentieth-century technological innovations together with changes in
the socio-occupational structure of the work force have created the
necessary conditions for a new orientation of individual roles both in
society in general and within the family. Some of the social repercussions
of these changes have already been commented on: for example, the
problems resulting from the reduction in family size due to a great
extent to the availability of effective methods of birth control; those

associated with the increase in the proportion of elderly dependents due partly to new medical techniques; or those of satisfying the psychological and material demands of a youthful population in a consumer society. It has been shown how the reduction in the number of home-based workers and the rapid growth of the tertiary sector have created an ageing population in agriculture and the small-scale craft and retail trade, and how, at the same time, the expansion of the tertiary sector has made available new employment opportunities for women. One of the most significant changes, as far as the family is concerned – judging from the literary outpouring on the subject and the number of feminist movements which have burgeoned in recent years – is the evolution in the status of women. It is therefore inevitable in any discussion of family roles that attention should be focused primarily on the woman, although any changes in her status will obviously affect the other members of the family unit.

Amongst the phenomena referred to above, there are two major factors which are generally associated with the changing role of women in society and within the family: the greater availability of work outside the home and the extension on a massive scale of effective means of birth control. These two factors are thought to be closely linked, although it is difficult to establish a precise causal relationship between them: the fact that women are more frequently employed outside the home can be interpreted as a possible reason why they are having fewer children, and effective family planning in turn implies that motherhood need not be the only preoccupation of a married woman and no longer requires her to be home-based for much of her married life. Since the reproductive function of the family, and its implications for family roles, have already been discussed, emphasis here will be centred on different aspects of the involvement of women in the work force and its repercussions on the family and on the participation of women in other areas of social life.

Female employment

Evidence of the number of women in paid employment is unreliable. It is sometimes difficult to distinguish between full-time employment and part-time or temporary work: many women in paid employment, particularly in the lower social categories, work as cleaners or home helps, or they sell commercial products on a door-to-door basis with no security of employment or social insurance cover and may not therefore be included in official records. Figures for 1975 fluctuate between 30 and 38 per cent for the proportion of women in the working population, with between 5 and 7 per cent working part time (figures for Great Britain give a level of about 34 per cent in 1976, with over 23 per cent employed part time). At the beginning of the century approximately 36 per cent of the working population were women. Although the proportion of women in the work force at any one time has remained relatively low, it is estimated that only about 10 per cent of women do not at some time in their life enter paid employment. Nowadays only 10 per cent of working women are employed in agriculture, approximately 25 per cent are in the industrial sector, a figure which has remained almost constant over the past half century, whereas the proportion employed in the tertiary sector had reached 65 per cent by 1974.

Age is an important variable determining the propensity of women to go out to work. Variations are clearly related to the reproductive function, and the figures indicate that women tend to interrupt their working life in order to bring up their children. The motivation to do so depends, however, upon the career structure, the desirability of work and the number of children. Estimates of the contribution made by women to the household budget show that in 95 per cent of cases they supplement taxable income by one-third to a half. The opinion is widely held that women should 'supplement' family income (with a *salaire d'appoint*) rather than earn an equivalent amount to their husbands. However, as demonstrated by Giroud in Texte 2.6, the extra money is often vital for the solvency of the family budget, and, as she indicates elsewhere, this additional income plays a major part in fostering consumer demand for non-essential goods and services, thereby encouraging productivity.

Women at the two ends of the social scale tend to be less frequently employed outside the home, but for different reasons. The wives and daughters of men in high-status positions are not obliged by financial circumstances to work, and they tend to assume a female role similar to that described for the *romanesque* family model: the wife stays at home to govern her household and raise her children. On the other hand, women who in their own right achieve high-status positions tend to marry late and do not generally interrupt their career during motherhood: by employing paid assistance, they are able to reconcile work and a family. The wives and daughters of poorly paid industrial workers, for whom employment is most often an economic necessity, are more likely to stop working, if at all possible financially, in order to raise children, particularly if their work is monotonous and physically exhausting. There is evidence to suggest that for women in these social categories child-rearing offers a means of achieving self-fulfilment which will never be possible through work. Since family size is also greater than the average, and income from employment is low, it is often more viable economically to stay at home than to pay for child-minding facilities. The attitude of husbands in these social categories is generally one of opposition to their wives going out to work: employment must be subordinated to the role of housewife and mother. It is a sign of social status if the wife does not need to work. The image of the working woman with a small family is most frequently the norm amongst the wives and daughters of middle- and lower-grade non-manual workers, particularly in the younger generation. Women in this new category (characterised by the *nouvelles femmes* of Texte 2.7) generally work themselves in lower- or medium-grade non-manual employment and expect to derive personal satisfaction and self-fulfilment from a stimulating job; their ideal and actual family sizes are smaller than those for any other categories.

The problem of finding satisfactory child-minding facilities is still a factor inhibiting female employment. Approximately one-third of working women in France have recourse to child-minders. It is important to note that France has more places available in *crèches* than any other European country and that more than 60 per cent of all children aged two to four are attending nursery school, as compared with some 22 per cent of this age group in England. Working class women more frequently than any other category leave their children with members of their family.

Educational qualifications are an important incentive to enter employment, but women from the most privileged social categories are the least likely to exploit their qualifications. Whatever the educational opportunities for women, it remains that two out of every three employees on the minimum wage are women and that, whereas the number of unskilled and semi-skilled male workers has decreased substantially over the past decade, the number of women in these categories has increased significantly, confirming the low-income status of women in employment. Salary differentials for the same positions at the same age still average about 30 per cent. The differences are often explained by the fact that women work shorter hours, rarely do overtime or night shifts and frequently interrupt their careers. Although the 1972 law on equal pay forbids discrimination for work of equal value, but with derisory fines for infringements, it is difficult to legislate against another form of discrimination which is frequently commented on: work done by women is downgraded, and some professions have become feminised and are consequently shunned by men. Within the range of tertiary employment, many positions have come to be considered as particularly 'suitable' for women: for example, 99.7 per cent of nursery school teachers are women, and they make up 75 per cent of the teaching staff in primary schools, 66 per cent in lower and middle secondary schools, 54 per cent in upper secondary schools and 24 per cent in universities; amongst administrative staff in commerce and industry, women are more often than men employed to work as shorthand typists, telephonists and cashiers; many positions in social work have become a female preserve. Women continue to be poorly represented in the higher ranks throughout the professional hierarchy: they rarely achieve headships in secondary schools or full lecturer status in a university; although 51 per cent of state employees are women, they hold 11 per cent of senior positions, and in the *Commissariat à l'Energie Atomique*, considered as the most favourable employer in this respect, only one seventh of female workers reach the administrative grades, compared with one quarter of the men. Women are still not allowed to be ordained by the Catholic Church, which continues to support the traditional view that women cannot act as leaders of men.

Role conflicts

When women work outside the home, they are, according to the results of surveys and other studies, still expected to fulfil their roles as housewife and mother, and there is little evidence to suggest that many husbands of working women 'help' with domestic chores or child care: few husbands in the higher professional grades participate in household tasks, although husbands in the middle grades are more co-operative, particularly in the age group 20 to 24, where about a quarter give assistance to their wives. Men do not however consider housework to be part of their normative behaviour, and, as Texte 2.8 indicates, even 'modern' husbands find it difficult to reconcile their new role in the family with their roles outside it. Men who do participate in the home prefer to confine their attention to playing with children or helping with their education.

A consequence of technical progress is that the chores of the housewife may occupy a smaller amount of time, but, it is argued, many of these tasks have been taken over by male dominated industries and outside agencies, with the result that the contribution of women to the nation's economy has been devalued. Women have therefore become primarily consumers, and the tasks which they continue to perform are not judged according to the same criteria as work done outside the home. The only home-based productive function still valued by society is that of family building and child-rearing. As already mentioned, external agencies are progressively impinging here as well, although it is estimated that it costs the country less to encourage a woman, through financial incentives, to stay at home and look after her own children than it does to provide communal facilities. The fact remains that today only approximately one seventh of a woman's life will be devoted to child-rearing, but attitudes have not yet evolved sufficiently to prevent problems of role conflict. Social pressures are being exerted in two directions: for women who stay at home, there may be isolation and frustration as a result of knowing that the economic and social advantages of employment are being forgone and that the household tasks they are carrying out are considered to be of little intrinsic value and interest; for women who go out to work, there may be the fear that their children are being deprived, the knowledge that they are being exploited by their employers and that their working day is not over when they return home.

This debate became particularly topical in 1978 when it was suggested by members of the government and the clergy that women should be encouraged to leave the work force in order to reduce male unemployment (reactions from some quarters to this suggestion are summarised in Texte 2.6). There are remarkable similarities between the attitudes of the authorities in this instance towards working women and the views frequently expressed about the acceptability of immigrant labour. Both women and immigrants are welcomed into the work force for their contribution to the economy when the indigenous male population is unable to meet the demands of the labour market, or reluctant to undertake specific types of employment in return for low pay. But in a competitive situation, it is often claimed that preference should be given to the native male population, even though it is clear that the cost to employers would be prohibitive, since they would have to offer higher salaries, and it is unlikely that men would be willing to accept the work made available.

Much attention is being paid to the potential for developing part-time employment, which at the moment is much less widespread than in Great Britain. This solution is contested on the grounds that it would only exacerbate many of the problems concerning the inferior status of female employment and absence of promotional structures, unless the principle is extended to and accepted by the male labour force. Instead it is often suggested that a shorter working day and more flexible working hours should be introduced for both men and women.

Women's rights
The increasing publicity attracted by the changing status of women in French society was confirmed in 1974, when, in preparation for the International Women's Year (1975), a Ministry for Women (*Condition féminine*) was established under the control of Françoise Giroud, the former editor of *L'Express*. The appointment lasted for two years during which attempts were made to bring about substantial reforms in the legislation relating to women. When the Ministry was discontinued in 1976, it was argued by the Prime Minister that considerable progress had been made and that to further pursue specifically feminist policies would in itself be a form of discrimination. Feminists retort that positive

discrimination in favour of women is still necessary to help them to reach a position of greater equality, for although both sexes may now be advancing at the same rate, the distance between them is great.

The high point of Françoise Giroud's term of office was her *Projet pour les femmes*, which included 100 reforms to be carried out before the end of Giscard d'Estaing's presidential term. All but some of the most revolutionary proposals were adopted by the government: amongst the latter were suggestions that women should carry out civilian service, as an equivalent to military service, or that a father should have equal claim to family benefits and should be encouraged to look after the children while his wife goes out to work, or that a mother's name should be given to her children. When it is remembered that at the beginning of the nineteenth century women were completely deprived of all legal rights – they could not act as a witness, inherit, buy or sell property or travel without their husband's consent – that women in France obtained the right to vote only in 1945, and that the Women's Liberation Movement dates from 1968, the fact that most of the reforms suggested in the *Projet* have been accepted marks an important change in attitudes. Theoretically women can now sit most of the same competitive examinations as men for higher education, employers cannot refuse work on the grounds of pregnancy, social security benefits have been improved for widows and divorcees, women can now withdraw money from a savings account in their child's name without paternal consent, to give but a few examples. The first government appointed after the 1981 parliamentary elections included a Minister for Women's Rights, and policies were announced for freedom, equality, employment and responsibility for women through positive discrimination.

Although in theory women now have freedom of movement and conscience and access to political rights, in practice they are reluctant to participate in public life and, if they do, are not easily accepted. Few women belong to a trade union, although it is significant that 25 per cent of the *nouvelles femmes* are members, a figure higher than the national average for all wage earners. In the government formed in 1978 only two women were given important cabinet positions (out of nineteen), and these were in areas of social rather than economic life, namely higher education, health and the family. Two other women were appointed to lower grade posts to deal with justice and female employment. Mauroy's second left-wing government included six women with responsibility for national solidarity, women's rights, agriculture, youth and sports, consumer affairs and the family. At a local level the number of women elected to councils has increased in recent years, although less than 10 per cent of councillors are women. For the whole of France nearly 53 per cent of voters are women. They tend to abstain more frequently than men, but nonetheless cast a greater number of the total votes, more often in support of the Centre Right than the left-wing parties. Just as politicians have come under pressure from the growing number of elderly and young voters, the need to catch the female vote has forced them to support policies for improving the living and working conditions of women. The young female population possesses a distinct advantage over the elderly in the knowledge that the nation's future depends upon their willingness to raise a family. It seems more likely that this function may be encouraged if motherhood and employment are made compatible than if they are set up in competition, and this involves not only changes in working and living conditions but also a reversal of firmly entrenched attitudes and conceptions about sex roles.

Sex roles

Much pressure is being exerted by feminist movements to eliminate the social conditioning of children and young people through sex stereotyping in school textbooks, story books, toys and advertising, or by depicting particular careers as more suitable for one sex than the other. Surveys show that parents are still stricter about their daughters' behaviour than they are about their sons', that they still expect boys to pursue their education further, to achieve a higher level of qualification, more often in the sciences than in the arts, to progress further in the career hierarchy and exercise greater responsibility.

It is clear that the major changes in attitudes which are called for, if the role of women in contemporary French society is to continue to evolve in the direction of greater emancipation, cannot take place without corresponding changes in male roles, and it is not therefore surprising to find that associations are being set up to defend men's interests. The legal changes in the status of parents in relation to their children – granting equal rights in many areas to husband and wife – are considered by some critics to be demoralising for men. The takeover of the educational system by women is seen as a threat to male supremacy. More and more husbands in divorce cases are appealing against the decisions of magistrates to give custody of children to the mother. Even though a few men are willing to look after their children while their wives go out to work, men who choose to do so tend to be classed as socially abnormal. There is little prospect of any significant changes in this situation in the near future, although, as shown by Texte 2.8, attitudes are becoming less entrenched. The younger, better educated generations, particularly in the middle classes, are prepared to modify their approach to family roles, but most couples still consider that the sex roles are complementary, and few men are prepared to relinquish their position as head of the family.

Family models and social categories

On the basis of this analysis of the present trends in marriage, divorce, family building and family roles, it would seem that for many social categories the companionship or democratic model of the family is still far from being a reality. Since some features of this model may have their origins in nineteenth century working class values and attitudes towards marriage, reinforced by legislation designed primarily to improve the lot of the working class family, it is ironical that the low-paid industrial workers should now be ill equipped to assume the characteristics of the model.

The companionship model implies that the family unit should be emotionally self-sufficient, that it should be able to control its own size in order to ensure optimum conditions for such a relationship, and that the partners should be able to enjoy their common cultural experience, a difficult task in the context of poor accommodation, monotonous and soul-destroying employment, a limited budget and inadequate education. Manual labourers have the lowest life expectancy, they are most prone to accidents at work, they have the highest rate of infant mortality and of premarital births. They are least able to control family size and have most difficulty in achieving divorce. The working class husband continues to play the dominant role as far as relationships outside the family are concerned, is reluctant to allow his wife to undertake paid employment and opposes her involvement in political or trade union activities. In the home the woman is expected to manage the family budget and bring up the children, tasks which are rarely shared if she does go out to work. Not surprisingly the kinship group or social worker is frequently turned to for emotional or practical support. The fact that these conditions are prevalent amongst a large section of the population would suggest that this behaviour corresponds to an alternative dominant family model. But there is some indication that, as living standards rise, the companionship model does offer an ideal aspired to by couples who hope to improve their social status.

The companionship family model is not easily applicable to the agricultural population, and reference is made here primarily to agricultural labourers and the small farmers who still make up the majority of the rural population. They tend rather to adhere to a more traditional conception of the family. The acceleration of the rural exodus, increasing government intervention and the growth of farmers' co-operatives, together with the progressive industrialisation of agriculture, are gradually producing changes in the family pattern, but it would be premature to claim that the democratic family model has become dominant in the rural environment.

The companionship model also seems inappropriate as a representation of behaviour within the professional and higher administrative categories, who have tended instead to adapt the *romanesque* model to suit their changing requirements in present-day society.

The ideals and realities of the intermediate social groups, and in particular the younger generations of the new middle classes, (the *nouvelles femmes* and *nouveaux pères* of Textes 2.7 and 2.8), correspond most closely to the companionship model of the family. For them marriage is based on mutual affection and attractiveness associated with identity of cultural and social objectives. Extramarital cohabitation is an accepted form of behaviour and considered to offer a valuable means of assessing the potential durability of the relationship. The institution of marriage has thus become a simple formality enacted out of respect for parents, and the prohibitions of the Catholic Church concerning sexual relationships are considered irrelevant. Children are essential to complete the union and provide a source of emotional gratification, a function which they can perform only if they remain few in number, but they are not allowed to prevent the parents from pursuing other common interests. Nor do they prohibit work outside the home for the mother, who does not enter employment simply for financial reasons. The couple share their family roles and consider them to some extent interchangeable. A breakdown in relationships is accepted as complete justification for separation and is possible because the wife is economically independent. But remarriage will follow divorce in order to satisfy emotional demands, for the family remains a refuge from the hostile outside world. Their level of educational attainment is such that they can exploit their economic and cultural advantages to manipulate the social systems and thereby achieve the objectives of the companionship model. Just as it may be claimed that the middle grade non-manual worker represents the average French man as far as demographic changes, socio-occupational structure and the development of consumer tastes are concerned, it may also be posited that he is the main exponent of the companionship model of the family, and that his example will probably be followed by other social categories lower down the social scale in the next few decades, as they move towards the social and economic conditions which are a prerequisite for this pattern of family life.

Bibliographical guidance

General works examining historical and contemporary trends in marriage and the family in France:

A. Armengaud, *La Famille et l'enfant en France et en Angleterre du XVIe au XVIIIe siècle: aspects démographiques* (Paris: Société d'Editions d'Enseignement Supérieur, 1975)

'Finie la famille: traditions et nouveaux rôles', *Autrement*, 3 (1975)

P. Brechon, *La Famille: idées traditionnelles et idées nouvelles* (Paris: Le Centurion, 1976)

Commissariat Général du Plan, *La Famille* (Paris: Hachette, 1975)

P. Desgraupes, 'L'aventure inconnue de la famille', *Le Point,* 148 (21 July 1975) 77-82, 149 (28 July 1975) 58-63, 150 (4 Aug 1975) 65-71, 151 (11 Aug 1975) 61-6, 152 (18 Aug 1975) 61-6, 153 (25 Aug 1975) 66-71

A. Pitrou, *Vivre sans famille? Les solidarités familiales dans le monde d'aujourd'hui* (Toulouse: Privat, 1978)

L. Roussel, *Le Mariage dans la société française: faits de population, données d'opinion* (Paris: PUF, 1975)

N. Tabard, *Besoins et aspirations des familles et des jeunes* (Paris: CNAF, CREDOC, 1974)

Selected works about women in France:

Documentation Française, *Les Femmes: guide bibliographique* (Paris: Documentation Française, 1975)

'Les droits de la femme', *Après-demain*, 214-15 (May-June 1979)

S. de Beauvoir, *Le Deuxième Sexe*, 2 vols (Paris: Gallimard, 1949)

'Vivre au féminin', *Cahiers français*, 171 (May-Aug 1975)

F. Giroud, *Cent Mesures pour les femmes* (Paris: Documentation Française, 1976)

G. Halimi, *La Cause des femmes* (Paris: Grasset, 1973)

I. Journet-Durcat and P. Aulibe-Istin, *La Femme et ses nouveaux droits* (Paris: Michel, 1975)

A. Michel, *Activité professionnelle de la femme et ses nouveaux droits* (Paris: CNRS, 1974)

J. Rabaut, *Histoire des féminismes français* (Paris: Stock 1979)

E. Sullerot, *Le Fait féminin* (Paris: Fayard, 1978)

Reviews:

Various aspects of family building, divorce and the role of women in French society are analysed in the periodical literature, and the following should be consulted for up-to-date information on current trends: *Données sociales, Economie et statistique, Population.* The monthlies

Les Femmes en mouvement and *F. Magazine* analyse issues concerning women in France today.

Illustrative texts and linguistic exercises

Texte 2.1   La malade se porte bien

Vidée du plus charnu de sa substance traditionnelle, dépouillée de ses fonctions par les institutions sociales qui la relaient *bon gré mal gré*, la famille est creuse. Il en reste surtout des préceptes, d'autant plus contraignants qu'ils sont coupés de leurs racines pourries *depuis belle lurette*. Alors, on balaie les débris? Pas question!

Jamais la famille n'a été plus forte! Elle est ou fait semblant d'être le dernier refuge des valeurs affectives chassées de la vie quotidienne, l'îlot de paix dans la guerre, le seul jardin où l'on puisse envisager *l'aléatoire culture de l'Amour et du Bonheur*. Formidable programme, ambition démesurée! La petite famille bourgeoise, que les sociologues appellent '*famille nucléaire*' depuis qu'elle est réduite à un noyau insécable, n'est plus une communauté fondue dans une communauté plus vaste. Elle est un atome à côté d'autres atomes, comme les polypes juxtaposés d'un banc de corail. Et la voilà chargée de nous rendre heureux, nous qui sommes à chaque instant frustrés de tant d'espérances! On en attend l'amour, l'accomplissement sensuel, la communion intégrale, l'ascèse et l'éternité. Bref, l'absolu. Pas étonnant qu'elle s'épuise à la tâche, la famille, et qu'elle ne nous donne pas totalement satisfaction.

On ressent que l'emballage craque. Aplatie d'un côté, puisque les décisions et les responsabilités lui échappent de plus en plus, la famille se gonfle, d'autre part, comme la grenouille de la fable, des idéaux que la société nous refuse. Elle va mal parce qu'elle va trop bien, elle va bien parce qu'elle va trop mal. Pour la droite, la famille d'aujourd'hui souffre d'être 'en avance' sur nos besoins. Pour la gauche, elle est malade d'être 'en retard'. *Quoi qu'il en soit*, les enquêtes et les sondages donnent des résultats incontestables: la famille grince mais elle n'est pas près de se dissoudre, ni même de se transformer radicalement en qui sait quoi.

Ponctuelles, les tentatives d'avant-garde pour briser le moule sont suspectes, car elles ne semblent guère capables de guérir, sinon l'angoisse, du moins la morosité du plus grand nombre. Egalement ponctuelles, les rares réussites familiales indiscutables restent des exceptions et ne sauraient être érigées en maximes universelles. Ainsi, il y a malaise dans la famille mais, par la force des choses, malaise supporté. Un peu comme les embouteillages du dimanche soir.

SOURCE: J.-F. Held, *Le Nouvel Observateur* (8 nov. 1976) p.74 (adapté).

Exploitation du texte

1 Expliquez en quelques mots le sens des phrases/termes en italique.

2 Commentez les phrases suivantes du point de vue grammatical:
le seul jardin où l'on puisse envisager
Pas étonnant qu'elle s'épuise à la tâche, la famille,
les rares réussites... ne sauraient être érigées

3 Faites un résumé en moins de 150 mots des arguments présentés par Held pour et contre la constatation du titre.

4 Quel semble être l'avis de l'auteur quant à la santé de la famille?

5 Relevez les traits linguistiques du texte qui sont caractéristiques du langage parlé plutôt que d'un texte littéraire.

6 Identifiez tous les termes appartenant au langage imagé et commentez les allusions et l'effet qu'ils produisent.

7 Récrivez le texte en éliminant tous les éléments figurés.

Texte 2.2   Rapport général: premier bilan

La famille a perdu, où a vu s'affaiblir, certaines de ses fonctions. Elle n'est plus, depuis longtemps, unité de production: dans une société de type industriel, cela ne peut que la dévaloriser. Sa production principale est autoconsommée et *la valeur économique* de cette production n'est pas reconnue.

Le milieu familial s'est rétréci. Physiquement, parce que *l'espace est chèrement compté*. Socialement, parce que la cohabitation des générations est difficile et parce qu'il est difficile de choisir son lieu de résidence, donc son voisinage. Du coup, la famille a eu tendance à se refermer sur elle-même: appartement, voiture, *éventuellement résidence secondaire*, partout la famille est, elle aussi, *'solitaire dans la foule'*. Elle n'a plus besoin 'd'aller au monde' puisque le monde vient à elle *par la vertu du téléviseur*. Une certaine réaction s'opère cependant depuis peu: en particulier chez les adolescents, qui tendent à sortir de plus en plus de la famille.

Mais la famille s'est renforcée et s'est même encombrée sur d'autres plans. Dans l'augmentation accélérée de l'activité éducative, la famille a eu sa part: elle a, maintenant, *la charge des enfants* jusqu'à un âge de plus en plus avancé, et cela ne lui pose pas que des problèmes matériels. Mais cela peut aussi contribuer à revaloriser sa situation, en particulier pour la mère de famille.

Ses fonctions techniques se sont multipliées. Pour garder le contact avec *l'organisation sociale environnante*, les parents doivent *multiplier les formalités et les démarches,* tenir des comptabilités aussi précises que possible, *manipuler de nouveaux moyens de paiements*, apprendre à *combler toutes les défaillances d'une société trop bureaucratisée*.

La sexualité et la procréation peuvent être vécues de *manière de plus en plus responsable*. Les méthodes contraceptives existant, et étant supposées accessibles, la grossesse imprévue pourrait être de plus en plus mal jugée.

Enfin, et surtout, dans la quête du bonheur individuel qui est l'objectif au moins apparent de toute société moderne, la famille semble, à la majorité, être le moyen le plus approprié pour l'atteindre. Refuge de l'affectivité et parfois refuge tout court face au reste de la société, la famille défend là *un privilège bien redoutable* et certainement excessif.

SOURCE: Commissariat Général du Plan, *La Famille* (Paris: Hachette, 1975) pp.44-5 (adapté).

Exploitation du texte

1 Expliquez en quelques mots le sens et les allusions des termes/ phrases en italique.

2 Faites un tableau présentant les fonctions que, d'après le texte, la famille a perdues et celles qu'elle a acquises, y compris celles qui sont implicites.

3 Quelle semble être l'opinion des auteurs du rapport en ce qui concerne les changements qui sont intervenus et comment peut-on la connaître?

4 Comment peut-on expliquer le fait que les adolescents tendent à sortir de plus en plus de la famille?

5 Formulez votre propre définition de la 'quête du bonheur'.

6 Relevez toutes les phrases qui contiennent un verbe pronominal et reformulez-les en vous servant d'une autre structure verbale.

Texte 2.3   Tableau comparatif des trois modèles d'union matrimoniale

Type d'union Points de comparaison	Mariage traditionnel	Mariage romanesque	Mariage compagnonnage
1 — Fondement de l'union	L'institution	Le sentiment amoureux et l'institution	Le sentiment. La sanction légale du mariage est une commodité sociale ou même doit être écartée
2 — Définition des rôles	Distinction nette définie par l'institution	Répartition plus souple des rôles et des tâches	Tendance à l'indifférenciation des rôles
3 — Personnage fort à l'intérieur du couple	L'homme	Plutôt la femme	Absence de personnage 'fort'
4 — Position de l'enfant	Prolongement naturel du mariage et vecteur de la continuité du patrimoine	Objet privilégié de l'investissement affectif des parents	Tendance à une relation affective moins exclusive avec l'enfant

Type d'union Points de comparaison	Mariage traditionnel	Mariage romanesque	Mariage compagnonnage
5 — Relations avec le monde extérieur	Ouverture sur des communautés na- turelles de faible taille	Fermeture au monde exté- rieur; Intraver- sion. Intimisme	Recherche de com- munautés électives de faible taille ou projet révolution- naire global
6 — Ménage et économie	Ménage = unité de production et de consomma- tion. Coopération de tous les mem- bres à l'entreprise familiale	Ménage = unité de consomma- tion. Rôle écono- mique dominant de l'époux	Indépendance éco- nomique de chaque époux
7 — Stabilité de l'union	Indissolubilité	Relative stabilité	Stabilité liée au seul consensus des deux conjoints
8 — Permissivité des mœurs	Faible surtout pour les femmes	Plus forte, sur- tout pour la pé- riode prénuptiale	Beaucoup plus forte pour les deux sexes
9 — Transmission culturelle	Forte continuité entre les géné- tions	Socialisation des enfants par la famille mais éman- cipation culturelle de plus en plus précoce	Le couple ne re- cherche plus à assurer une conti- nuité culturelle entre lui et ses enfants

SOURCE: L. Roussel, *Le Mariage dans la société française* (Paris: PUF, 1975) p.367.

Exploitation du texte

1 Définissez les termes suivants: une commodité sociale, l'indifférenciation des rôles, Intraversion, communautés électives, transmission culturelle.

2 Décrivez en environ 350 mots l'évolution de la famille du modèle traditionnel au modèle compagnonnage en vous servant des données du tableau et en reliant vos phrases par les locutions suivantes: Dans le passage de... à, Sur le plan de, Dans le domaine de, En ce qui concerne, Quant à, Aussi bien du point de vue de... que de celui de, Il s'ensuit que, Il en découle que.

3 Reprenez le texte que vous venez de rédiger et, en rajoutant des vocables et des locutions évocateurs, essayez de convaincre votre lecteur que cette évolution est positive *ou* négative.

Texte 2.4   Pour un Grenelle des familles

Le taux de natalité de l'année 1978 peut faire rétrograder la France à 20 millions d'habitants en cinq générations!
Et vous ne faites rien, messieurs!

Oh! certes, une grande politique familiale est difficile, mais le pouvoir, si on ne veut pas se contenter de *l'exercer pour les apparences et les mondanités*, n'est jamais facile. Il est agréable de parler d'*un phénomène de civilisation*. Or il se trouve que le rôle d'un pouvoir digne de ce nom est de s'élever contre un phénomène de civilisation si celui-ci aboutit à faire périr les valeurs de cette civilisation!

Oh! certes, une grande politique familiale est coûteuse! Mais on ne fera croire à personne, entendez-vous bien, à personne, que des esprits sains sont *hors d'état* sur les milliers de milliards qui représentent le budget de l'Etat, celui de la Sécurité sociale et ceux des collectivités locales d'imposer les économies permettant de dégager les 20 milliards indispensables pour commencer la réaction.

Oh! certes, l'époque où nous vivons n'est pas favorable. Les loisirs, les vacances, la joie de profiter des bienfaits d'une société, où tant de divertissements amusants, intéressants, attirent hommes et femmes, les incitent à gagner de l'argent plutôt qu'à se priver pour élever des jeunes. Mais à quoi sert d'être l'élu du peuple, à quoi sert d'être enseignant, à quoi sert la télévision, à quoi sert l'Etat, à quoi sert l'esprit civique, si nul ne se mobilise pour éviter la catastrophe?

Revoir, en les ajustant et en les augmentant, les allocations familiales: construire et faire fonctionner crèches, garderies, centres de loisirs pour enfants; donner *à tous égards* et en tous domaines un statut privilégié au père et à la mère de famille de plus de trois enfants; *affecter au fonctionnement* des équipements familiaux et à l'aide aux foyers une part des jeunes, notamment des jeunes filles, *d'un service civil* qu'il devient urgent de mettre en place; oser faire le geste démocratique du vote familial pour augmenter dans toute élection le rôle des pères et surtout des mères de famille; cesser d'éduquer les jeunes uniquement sur la contraception en mettant enfin, l'accent sur la famille; revoir la loi sur l'interruption de grossesse... Les républicains, qui se flattent de la grandeur de la liberté, seront-ils incapables de modifier leur législation — ce que font présentement tous les pays européens communistes?

Tout est important de nos jours. Cependant rien n'est plus important que mettre la politique familiale au premier rang de nos soucis. La nouvelle baisse de l'année 1978 est un signal d'alarme qui sonne à nos oreilles comme *un coup de tocsin*, après toutes les alertes des années précédentes. En 1968, un 'Grenelle' a donné de grandes satisfactions aux salariés. Ce fut d'ailleurs *le premier coup d'envol* d'un élan inflationniste qui porta atteinte aux allocations familiales et à la natalité. Le temps vient d'*un Grenelle familial* qui sera, lui, le coup d'envoi d'une politique d'avenir. Ah! comme il est temps d'agir...

Vous rabâchez, me dit celui-ci. On vous a assez entendu, me dit celui-là. Peut-être. Mais nous sommes un certain nombre à ne pas accepter l'incapacité ou l'inefficacité officielle. Toutes les erreurs que l'on peut faire dans les affaires intérieures ou dans les affaires extérieures seraient atténuées par une forte natalité. Elles deviennent mortelles quand la natalité s'affaisse. Mortelles pour la nation. Mortelles pour la liberté. Mortelles pour les hommes et les femmes. Mortelles pour leurs libertés.

SOURCE: M. Debré, *Le Monde* (14 déc. 1978) p.39 (adapté).

Exploitation du texte

1 Expliquez en quelques mots le sens et les allusions des termes/ phrases en italique.

2 Résumez en moins de 150 mots les arguments présentés par Debré.

3 A qui s'adresse-t-il dans ce texte, comment peut-on le savoir, quel est son but, et y parvient-il?

4 Expliquez comment toutes les erreurs dans les affaires intérieures et extérieures seraient atténuées par une forte natalité.

5 Formulez une liste de 5 questions qui auraient pu être posées à Debré dans une interview afin d'évoquer les arguments qu'il expose.

6 Rédigez une réponse à Debré, sous forme d'une lettre à la presse, attaquant ses arguments.

Texte 2.5   Le mariage

1. L'institution contestée

Autrefois, un jeune homme et une jeune fille qui pensaient unir leurs deux vies savaient à peu près dans quelle 'institution' ils allaient entrer et comment elle modèlerait le visage de leur foyer.

Aujourd'hui, les jeunes couples se trouvent, le plus souvent, devant la perspective ouverte à deux personnes cherchant à vivre en commun sans présumer de ce qu'elles pourront faire ensemble. *Plus affranchis des idées reçues,* méfiants ou critiques à l'égard des formes instituées et moins conscients du *caractère social de l'amour,* un jeune homme et une jeune fille se trouvent *d'emblée* plus enclins à la découverte personnelle et mutuelle de la réalité physique, psychologique et morale; vivant dans *un monde qui prétend bien ne pas sacrifier les personnes à l'institution,* ils sont plus attirés par une histoire à essayer d'inventer *au jour le jour* que par un engagement décisif dont la société serait le témoin et le garant. Un certain nombre considèrent même comme de plus grande valeur de s'éprouver l'un l'autre dans des relations précaires, sans garantie, que de s'engager dans du définitif que souvent ils redoutent, tout en le désirant secrètement.

En outre, les échecs de la vie conjugale sont nombreux. Et peut-être viennent-ils justement pour une part de ce qui est nouveau dans les sentiments, les mentalités et les projets. Hier, on pouvait accepter de moins bien réussir sa vie affective parce qu'*on était soutenu socialement par d'autres valeurs.* Aujourd'hui, on le supporte mal ou pas du tout.

Ce climat et ces dispositions constituent à la fois une chance et un risque pour le développement des relations entre deux êtres. Et l'on ne s'étonnera pas que les uns en espèrent un progrès de l'amour humain dans une société rénovée, tandis que d'autres en redoutent une grave décomposition. Espérance ou crainte, tel est le débat.

2. L'institution appelée par l'amour

Aucune institution ne trouve en elle seule sa propre justification. Elle est au service de *la réalité humaine qu'elle porte*, tout particulièrement quand il s'agit de l'amour d'un homme et d'une femme. Les époux font cette expérience d'une vie qui tend à s'exprimer pleinement dans le moment présent et qui, pourtant, devra se prolonger dans la durée de l'existence. Ce qui arrive une fois entre eux, cette union d'amour, expression de leur désir, inscrit en eux quelque chose qui est une fois pour toutes et qui demeure inscrit dans leur chair et dans leur cœur. C'est cette 'inscription' que l'institution du mariage sauve du temps qui s'écoule. Elle l'affermit et la confirme. Ce qui s'accomplit dans l'union amoureuse de l'homme et de la femme suppose et appelle *un engagement mutuel soustrait aux vicissitudes des choses changeantes*: c'est le mariage, que toutes les sociétés reconnaissent et garantissent *en lui donnant de s'incarner dans une institution*.

Certains voient pourtant dans leur refus de l'institution un amour plus sincère. S'il arrive un jour que leurs sentiments changent, ils se sépareront. Cette attitude, que l'on appelle parfois *le mariage à l'essai*, ne reflète-t-elle pas la méconnaissance d'une dimension fondamentale de l'amour? Il n'est pas d'amour, aujourd'hui, qui ne soit amour pour toujours et pour l'inconnu que sera demain. L'amour est nécessairement aventure et création. Dire à quelqu'un: 'Je t'aime!', n'est-ce pas lui dire: 'Quoi qu'il arrive, tu peux compter sur moi, je ne te lâcherai pas.' Il ne peut y avoir de 'mariage à l'essai' parce qu'il ne peut y avoir d'engagement à l'essai ni d'enfant à l'essai.

SOURCE: 'Amour, famille et société', *Les Grands Textes*, 15, *Supplément à la Documentation Catholique*, 1709 (5 déc. 1976) pp.2–3 (adapté).

Exploitation du texte

1 Expliquez en quelques mots le sens et les allusions des phrases/termes en italique.

2 Faites un résumé en moins de 200 mots de la conception du mariage présenté par l'Episcopat dans ce document.

3 D'après ce texte, quelle est l'attitude de l'Eglise envers l'évolution des mœurs? Comment le sait-on?

4 Expliquez pourquoi il s'agit dans la vie du couple d' 'espérance ou

crainte', et relevez d'autres termes utilisés dans le texte pour présenter
cette dichotomie.

5 Un des buts déclarés des auteurs de ce document consiste à 'Employer
un langage plus proche de la sensibilitié des hommes et des femmes
d'aujourd'hui.' Commentez les moyens d'expression et montrez dans
quelle mesure les auteurs parviennent à ce but.

Texte 2.6   0,0001%

Le chômage est un mal trop grave pour repousser sans examen les
remèdes proposés.
Celui que recommandent conjointement M. le ministre du travail et
les évêques de France consiste à retirer les femmes mariées de leur
emploi. Celui-ci, libéré, reviendrait à un chômeur.

Le ministre et l'épiscopat viennent de recevoir un renfort inattendu
en la personne d'une femme, journaliste, qui veut 'rentrer à la maison'
et qui déclare en substance, dans un livre récent: puisqu'on est si bien à
la maison, restez-y, mes soeurs, et ne perdez pas un seul sourire de bébé,
ah! quelle erreur ai-je commise d'en sortir, folle que j'étais, et quel
tourment si j'ai pu inciter quelques-unes à le faire.

Voilà qui mérite trois roses, monsieur le ministre. *Enfin, on en tient
une qui passe aux aveux.*

C'est délicieux la maison
D'ailleurs, c'est délicieux la maison. Il faut avoir la tête à l'envers pour
quitter tous les jours, *dès le petit matin,* quelque belle demeure parisienne
avec personnel de service, voiture pour madame, résidence secondaire
pour le week-end, hiver à la montagne, été à la mer, et – cela va de soi –
revenus personnels tels que, dans l'hypothèse où l'époux viendrait à
manquer, *le coeur se briserait, mais pas le train de vie.*

L'ennui est que les femmes salariées bénéficiant de ces menus
avantages pourraient toutes rentrer à la maison sans que les statistiques
enregistrant les demandes d'emploi en soient dégonflées de 0,0001%.

Mais on peut aussi, pourquoi pas, regretter d'avoir à quitter *son F 4
avec vue sur courette* quand le sourire de bébé l'illumine.

Pour cette raison ou pour une autre, par goût ou par devoir, deux
femmes mariées sur trois restent à la maison. Très exactement: 7 028 000
sur 11 740 000 *en puissance d'époux.*

Elles sont donc 4 712 000 femmes mariées dites 'actives', les autres
actives (3 200 000) étant veuves, célibataires ou divorcées.

Que font-elles, ces épouses actives, ces voleuses d'emploi, pendant
les heures où elles ne s'activent pas à la maison?

425 000 travaillent dans le secteur primaire, c'est-à-dire l'agriculture.
Pour se distraire, probablement.

785 000 sont O.S. ou manoeuvres. Pour payer le caviar, évidemment.

1 375 000 sont employées de bureau et de commerce, dites d'‘exécution'.

280 000 institutrices, 122 000 employées des services sociaux et médicaux rendent de petits services.

180 000 employées de maison ou femmes de ménage exercent une activité hautement gratifiante.

348 000 sont artisanes ou petites commerçantes.

170 000 sont cadres. Hé! hé! voyez-vous ça!

S'y ajoutent, dans la nomenclature établie pour le dernier recensement, *des poussières*.

Notons en passant que les femmes mariées salariées rapportent ensemble, annuellement, 8 milliards net à la Sécurité sociale, produit de leurs cotisations. *Ne travailleraient-elles pas*, elles bénéficieraient, en effet, des mêmes prestations comme *ayants droit de leur époux*.

En une formule subtile, les évêques de France interrogent: 'Est-il impensable que là où deux salaires ne sont pas nécessaires pour l'équilibre de la vie d'une famille, l'on puisse renoncer à l'un d'eux?'

Il est, comme chacun sait, d'usage courant que dans un couple, les deux époux perçoivent des salaires équivalents. Donc, 'l'un ou l'autre' pourrait, dans un geste de solidarité nationale et humaine, quitter son emploi au bénéfice d'un sans-emploi.

La première jeune femme *qui s'en avisera* et qui se retrouvera dans six mois avec un mari licencié et deux enfants à nourrir – deux et demi, peut-être *si elle a poussé jusqu'au bout l'exercice de la solidarité* – nul doute qu'on lui fournira du travail à l'archevêché.

Mais admettons que ledit mari ait *un emploi en bronze*, qu'il soit fonctionnaire, que rien ne le menace, dans combien de ménages pourrait-on retrancher du budget commun le plus faible des deux salaires sans affecter 'l'équilibre de la vie d'une famille?'

Il n'existe aucune statistique qui permette de répondre.

On sait, en revanche, qu'en divisant la masse salariale par le nombre de femmes salairées, on obtient une moyenne de 2 500 francs par mois. Le même calcul donne pour les hommes 3 800 francs par mois.

Comme il est peu commun qu'une ouvrière soit l'épouse d'un conseiller d'Etat, qu'une vendeuse de grande surface ait pour mari un P.-D.G., qu'une dactylographe, une standardiste, une blanchisseuse de fin, une employée de bureau dite d' 'exécution', une laborantine, une mécanographe, etc. soit la légitime compagne d'un homme dont le salaire dépasse 4 000 francs par mois, les budgets qui pourraient, sans porter atteinte à l'équilibre de la vie de famille, être amputés d'un second salaire, sont en nombre pour le moins limité.

Prêts à se séparer de leur secrétaire?

De surcroît, les hommes en quête d'emploi seraient, pour la plupart, *impropres* à accomplir le même travail, ou *réfractaires* à ce travail et au salaire qui le rémunère, comme ils le sont aux tâches qu'effectuent les travailleurs immigrés.

Et combien de ces seigneurs, pressés de voir les femmes rentrer à la maison, seraient-ils prêts à se séparer de leur précieuse secrétaire pour la remplacer par un cadre chômeur, à supposer que celui-ci *se recycle* d'abord dans la sténographie?

C'est délibérément que l'on s'en tient ici à l'aspect strictement matériel des choses, puisque, pour ceux qui forment le projet de ramener au foyer celles qui n'y sont pas, il semble aller de soi que l'espèce féminine doit être tenue pour une masse de manoeuvre. L'industrie a besoin de main-d'oeuvre? A l'usine. Les services également? Au magasin, au bureau, à l'hôpital, à la poste, à l'école primaire. Il y a surplus de main-d'oeuvre? A la maison. On vous rappellera quand on aura besoin de vous.

On attend avec intérêt le jour où M. le ministre de l'éducation, qui préférerait lui aussi voir toutes les femmes à la maison, *préconisera d'interdire* aux jeunes filles les études supérieures.

Pourquoi donc la collectivité devrait-elle en faire les frais?

Pour regarder bébé sourire, *le bon vieux certificat d'études fera aussi bien l'affaire.*

SOURCE: F. Giroud, *Le Monde* (27 janv. 1979) p.10.

Exploitation du texte

1 Expliquez en quelques mots le sens des phrases/termes en italique.

2 Quelles sont les différentes catégories de femmes mentionnées dans l'article et quelles sont leurs caractéristiques?

3 Résumez en moins de 250 mots l'essentiel des arguments de Françoise Giroud.

4 Sur quel ton cet article est-il écrit? Expliquez comment l'auteur produit cet effet.

5 Soit prenez le rôle du ministre du travail et rédigez une déclaration sur les femmes mariées, le travail et le chômage, soit récrivez le texte de manière à présenter un compte-rendu neutre de la situation qu'il dépeint.

Texte 2.7   Les nouvelles femmes et les Françaises

Disons-le tout de suite, les nouvelles femmes, *loin d'être une faction*, sont à coup sûr l'avant-garde d'un vaste courant. *Porteuses de l'image* de la femme nouvelle, elles sont solidaires des autres sur quelques attitudes profondes — mais elles sont également différentes, car plus décidées et plus conscientes. *Différentes en ce qu'elles sont*, sinon des féministes engagées, du moins explicitement et délibérément ralliées à la cause des femmes. Semblables en ce qu'elles recherchent profondément la même chose: la liberté d'être elles-mêmes, de participer à la vie du monde, d'y prendre leurs propres positions.

Mais il y a plus intéressant encore. Nouvelles ou non, il semble que les femmes prennent la direction, ou au moins l'initiative, de l'évolution globale de notre société. Elles conquièrent peu à peu leur juste place. Et c'est bien. Mais surtout, elles sont en train de donner forme à une femme nouvelle, et peut-être à un être humain nouveau.

L'épanouissement compte plus que l'argent

8 La plus grande satisfaction qu'une femme retire de son travail est:

en %

De s'épanouir, de se servir de ses compétences et de ses qualités	**48**
D'avoir son autonomie financière	**21**
D'occuper une vraie place dans la société, de ne pas être confinée à la maison	**19**
De ne pas se sentir entretenue par quelqu'un	**8**
D'être davantage respectée par ses enfants, son conjoint, les autres	**2**
Sans réponse	**2**

Pour une nouvelle femme sur deux, se servir de ses compétences et faire valoir ses qualités est la plus grande satisfaction qu'elle retire de son travail. Mais avec l'âge, au-delà de 45 ans, la réponse devient plus désabusée. Elles ne sont alors plus que quatre sur dix à penser que le travail peut être épanouissant. . .

9 Imaginons que vous deviez changer d'emploi ou en trouver un. On vous propose trois emplois qui tous trois vous conviennent. Lequel prendriez-vous?

en %

Un emploi extrêmement intéressant et épanouissant mais prenant beaucoup de temps et moins bien payé	**72**

Document continued on following page

Un emploi vous laissant beaucoup de
temps libre mais pas très bien payé **16**
ni très intéressant

Un emploi extrêmement bien payé,
qui prend beaucoup de temps et pas **5**
très intéressant

Sans réponse   **7**

*Sept nouvelles femmes sur dix préfereraient un
travail intéressant et très prenant mais mal payé à
une activité peu gratifiante. L'argent n'est pas
tout, disent-elles. . . .*

On constate en effet, *dans ce suivi des courants socio-culturels,* et dans la typologie (*familles d'attitudes et de comportements repérables*), que, déjà l'année dernière et plus fortement cette année, les femmes sont à la tête du changement.

A travers le millier d'études faites depuis 25 ans, à travers une mesure systématique annuelle, nous avons identifié un certain nombre des 'courants' d'attitudes et de comportements qui donnent mouvement au grand fleuve d'évolution de notre société. Nous avons identifié également les huit ou neuf 'types', ou familles d'attitudes, auxquels peut se rattacher tout individu. Cela va du *'défricheur'* ou de 'l'innovateur' au 'traditionaliste', qui sont *les types de pointe* situés aux extrêmes de ce classement. Les défricheurs et innovateurs, qui préfigurent les attitudes générales de demain, sont ceux que l'on trouve à l'avant des mouvements d'innovation et de découverte de nouveaux modes de vie, et, à l'opposé, les traditionalistes restent principalement attachés aux valeurs anciennes et à leur maintien.

Les résultats 3 SC,* comparant les hommes et les femmes, font apparaître les femmes comme agents de changement, initiatrices de nouvelles attitudes: elles devancent les hommes, en degré d'adhésion et en nombre, sur neuf des courants d'évolution (notamment 'simplification de la vie', 'sensibilité au cadre de vie', 'anti-manipulation', 'rejet de l'autorité', compréhension de soi et des autres, moindre différenciation des sexes).

Ainsi, en regardant évoluer les femmes depuis une dizaine d'années, non seulement dans cette recherche socio-culturelle, mais à travers nombre d'études qualitatives et quantitatives, on les voit sur nombre de points – et cette enquête le confirme – faire une révolution bien à elles, tranquillement. Les femmes *réinvestissent* peu à peu, en adultes, *les vieilles citadelles* des valeurs traditionnelles dont elles n'étaient que les servantes: le sexe est vécu en sujet et non plus en objet; la maternité est vécue en

* *Système Cofremca de suivi des courants socio-culturels.*

épanouissement et en rôle social, choisie et non subie; en leur propre nom, et non en celui du mari, de la famille et du nom à perpétuer. L'immense manipulation sociale des médias et des partis est perçue comme une séduction suspecte, etc. Bien entendu, il s'agit là des femmes de pointe, des 'défricheuses' et des 'innovatrices'. Mais n'avons-nous pas vu que cellesci, comme les nouvelles femmes qui se révèlent, dans notre enquête, *sensiblement de même profil*, sont les pionnières d'une évolution irréversible et tranquille de toutes vers *un tissu social nouveau*?

SOURCE: C. Darré-Jourdan, *F. Magazine*, 9 (oct. 1978) pp. 70, 76 (adapté).

Exploitation du texte

1 Exprimez en d'autres mots les phrases/termes en italique.

2 Relevez tous les termes qui sont exploités pour souligner les aspects positifs de l'évolution tracée dans l'article et cherchez leurs antonymes.

3 Présentez en quelques 200 mots un portrait des 'nouvelles femmes' décrites dans l'article.

4 En vous servant des deux questions tirées de l'enquête comme modèle, formulez d'autres questions qui auraient pu être posées pour permettre aux enquêteurs de rassembler les résultats présentés dans cet article.

Texte 2.8   Papas pas morts

La mort du père. . . *En a-t-on entendu* sur ce thème depuis vingt ans! Peine perdue: la famille tient bon – seule de toutes les institutions à n'avoir pas été sérieusement ébranlée par la crise des valeurs et la contestation. Et, avec elle, la fonction paternelle garde force et vigueur. Elle a plié sans rompre. Elle a changé, c'est tout.

Après 1968, on s'était demandé que les générations montantes laisseraient subsister, *dans leur déferlement corrosif,* des anciennes attitudes, des traditions familiales, en un mot des valeurs de leurs pères. Aujourd'hui, on peut *faire le bilan.*

Les papas modernes ont beaucoup d'ambition, mais peu de réussite. Ils prennent au sérieux leur fonction, mais, sur leur route, les obstacles s'accumulent. Et des projets généreux – partage, attention, disponibilité, etc – *il leur faut faire parfois un deuil qu'ils veulent croire provisoire.* Ils désirent changer la vie à partir de leur vie, mais y parviennent rarement. D'abord, parce qu'ils ne sont pas seuls au monde et qu'il n'est jamais bon de *se marginaliser par rapport aux normes sociales,* même en évolution. Ensuite, parce que, au fond d'eux-mêmes, le passé pèse de tout son poids.

L'IFOP vient de réaliser, pour le compte de la revue *Parents,* une enquête d'opinion qui illustre bien le comportement mi-novateur, mi-traditionnel des 'nouveaux pères'.

Ces papas modernes, chacun autour de soi, en connaît plusieurs. Ils sont pleins de bonne volonté et ne veulent pas *rééditer les erreurs* de leur propre père, supposé ne jamais avoir donné le biberon, suspecte d'avoir sacrifié sa famille à son métier, son bonheur à la réussite. Mais ils sont encore gauches. *Au moindre accroc* du premier-né, c'est l'angoisse, l'inexpérience, l'appel à l'aide. Pour la suite, de même: ils sont sur le front quand tout va bien et se replient en bon ordre quand tout va mal.

L'examen attentif des résultats de ces enquêtes révèle une contradiction qui rend moins agréable qu'on le dit le fait d'être, aujourd'hui, un jeune père. La nouveauté la plus sûre réside dans l'aspiration – chez une immense majorité – à ne négliger aucun aspect de la vie familiale et *à ne pas faire l'économie du sentiment.* Mais la réalité quotidienne s'oppose très souvent – sous peine de marginalisation – à la pratique de ce beau principe. Les papas modernes ne tirent plus leur gloire de leur position de *pater familias* (propriétaire, chef, patron), mais s'efforcent de faire place égale – dans leur vie – au dehors et au dedans.

Depuis quinze ans, on s'est beaucoup intéressé, à juste titre, à l'évolution des femmes. On n'a pas toujours saisi l'effet second de cette évolution sur la condition masculine. Les papas modernes savent ceux qu'ils ne veulent plus être. Ils entrevoient ceux qu'ils voudraient être. En attendant, *ils ne sont pas forcément à la fête.*

SOURCE: B. Frappat, *Le Monde* (17–18 juin 1979) p.9 (adapté).

Exploitation du texte

1 Expliquez en quelques mots le sens des phrases/termes en italique.

2 Expliquez en moins de 200 mots ce que l'auteur veut dire par la phrase 'Elle a plié sans rompre.' Quelle est l'origine de cette phrase?

3 Relevez d'autres phrases au long du texte qui reprennent cette même notion.

4 Formulez 5 questions qui pourraient figurer dans une enquête cherchant à définir le rôle des 'nouveaux pères' à l'intérieur de la famille.

5 Quelles devraient être les caractéristiques des personnes sélectionnées pour participer à une telle enquête.

Exercices de comparaison et d'application

1 Ces 8 textes offrent un échantillon de différentes variétés de langue. Relevez les caractéristiques de chaque texte, et présentez-les sous forme d'un schéma, en vous servant des rubriques suivantes:

Contexte: source (livre, article, discours, etc.), caractéristiques de l'auteur (sexe, âge, métier, etc.), caractéristiques des personnes visées (grand public, lecteurs spécialisés, etc.);

Forme: présentation par paragraphes, syntaxe, vocabulaire;
Contenu: point de départ (hypothèse, constatation, etc.), message (thème), but (convaincre, commenter, etc.), conclusion.

2 Evaluez la manière dont chaque auteur parvient à satisfaire aux exigences du genre de texte qu'il présente.

3 Imaginez un débat dans lequel des personnages tels qu'un homme politique de gauche et de droite, un curé, une mère de famille nombreuse et une jeune femme vivant en union libre, discutent du thème: la famille a encore un rôle à jouer dans la société française contemporaine.

4 Ecrivez une dissertation d'environ 1500 à 2000 mots sur un des sujets suivants:

(i) D'après Brechon, dans la France contemporaine 'la famille n'est pas l'institution de base de la société, elle n'est pas le noyau dur à partir duquel se structurerait le corps social: on ne peut la considérer comme étant le facteur déterminant de la réalité sociale'. A partir d'une analyse des rapports entre famille et société dans la France contemporaine, examinez le bien-fondé de cette description.

(ii) D'après Simone de Beauvoir, 'On ne naît pas femme, on le devient', mais pour Evelyne Sullerot, 'On naît bel et bien femme, avec un destin physique programmé différent de celui de l'homme, et toutes les conséquences psychologiques et sociales attachées à ces différences. Mais on peut modifier ce destin, ou s'en éloigner carrément. Or il se trouve qu'on peut beaucoup plus aisément modifier les faits de nature que les faits de culture.' Examinez ces deux constatations dans le contexte de la société française contemporaine.

3

Social Welfare

All Western industrialised nations are today facing similar difficulties in providing the range and standard of social welfare services expected by the public. There are two main reasons for these problems: the increase in life expectancy and the important decline in infant mortality, which have resulted in longer periods of dependency and created new needs; and the development of a new conception of physical, mental, social and moral well-being, which has come to be considered as a basic social value. Technological progress and political pressures have fostered expectations to a point where every member of society is given to believe that he is entitled to demand and receive the highest standard of protection and care, or of social security,[1] as a basic human right.

Although there is generally agreement about the need for social welfare provision and its permanency as a feature of contemporary societies, the range of services offered, the ways in which they have evolved, are organised and administered, their priorities and their effectiveness in achieving their objectives may differ substantially from one country to another as a consequence of the economic and political circumstances in which they were introduced and the pressures which have been exerted to mould them into their present shape. Provision is made in most Western countries to cover the basic components of welfare, namely health, education, housing and a guaranteed minimum income for households. The areas focused on by social policy may however be extended – as is already the case in Sweden, and it is probable that other countries will follow this example – to cover leisure and recreation, social relations, nutrition, political resources, safety and security. This indicates that, contrary to what might have been expected when social security systems were first introduced, higher standards of living and increased spending power do not lead to a reduction in the demand for and supply of social welfare services.

The social policies adopted in France in the immediate post-war years, and which it has pursued since then, have been influenced by the nation's preoccupation with the demographic issues examined in the first chapter.

Politicians, administrators and researchers continue to emphasise the relationship between social policy and the birthrate, as illustrated in Texte 2.4, but they also devote much attention to the deathrate, the age structure of the population and to migratory movements. Since, as will be shown later, the French social security system, the centrepiece of social welfare provision, depends to a great extent for its finance on income-related contributions, and therefore on the size of the working population, concern is frequently expressed about the long-term effects of the decline in the birthrate, the consequent ageing of the population and any changes in the dependency ratio due to longer education, unemployment and earlier retirement. As indicated in Chapter 1, the size of the work force has, in absolute terms, remained fairly stable since 1945, but the number of beneficiaries and the nature of their demands have fluctuated considerably. Forecasts of future demographic trends and changes in population structure are a valuable source of information about the probable demand for welfare services by different social categories throughout the country, but there are no absolute criteria on which to determine the optimum level of provision or the extent to which demand should be encouraged. Given that it will never be possible to satisfy all needs, however important they are judged to be, the orientation of available resources remains dependent upon the priorities which different governments select, and these are influenced by political ideologies and the pressure exerted by different sections of the community. Many of the factors governing social policy decisions today and many of the difficulties which are characteristic of the French social security system can best be understood by reference to the way in which social security has evolved in France in response to these forces.

The concept of social security

The concept of social security implies that all members of society are exposed to certain definable social 'risks': in more precise terms, the risks concerned are those likely to affect the economic and social position of an individual through loss of income or additional expenditure incurred. The categories of risks generally covered by social security systems are illness, maternity, invalidity, old age, accidents at work, death, family responsibilities and unemployment.

Before the introduction of wide-ranging social welfare services on a national scale, an individual would try to protect himself and his family against hardship and adversity by building up reserves, but most people were unable to provide adequate cover through savings and were helpless in times of hardship. The need for a system of protection beyond that which an individual, or the immediate community, could provide has long been felt, and various mutual aid and collective associations emerged over the centuries to meet this need. Although the systems of mutual aid, based on the insurance principle, were an improvement on savings and charity, they were still only effective for a narrow range of risks and for a small proportion of the population, and more extensive provision became necessary.

During the second half of the nineteenth century some of the most exposed or better organised workers had achieved a certain degree of social welfare through a system of patronage. Employers in the mining industry and the big railway companies, for example, provided medical services and a guaranteed retirement age in order to strengthen and keep their labour force. In 1898 employers were made legally responsible for accidents at work. In the first half of the twentieth century in France and elsewhere the state intervened more and more in the provision of welfare: in 1930 a social insurance scheme was instituted for low-paid workers in commerce and industry to cover health, maternity, death, invalidity and retirement, and in 1932 family allowances were introduced for these same categories by extending schemes already operated by employers. As mentioned in Chapter 1, the first real attempt to formulate a coherent and comprehensive social policy on a national level was the 1939 *Code de la famille*. By the end of the Second World War different sections of the working population were protected to varying degrees for a number of risks through a system of compulsory and voluntary schemes organised on the basis of free enterprise and collective initiative.

The post-war period, both in France and in other highly industrialised and urbanised Western nations, is characterised by the general acceptance that it is the duty of the state to ensure elaborate and compulsory social protection for the whole population in accordance with coherent social objectives. By definition, the underlying principle of social policy is that it should improve the lot of the less fortunate members of society and thereby reduce social inequalities. In the same way that the mutual aid associations were intended to establish solidarity among workers, a generalised system of social security might be expected to extend this principle to the whole of the nation, as suggested in Textes 3.1 and 3.2. But it can be shown that, just as employers who introduced their own schemes to protect their workers prior to 1945 were never motivated solely by philanthropic aims, governments may exploit their role to achieve political objectives which are not necessarily always compatible with social justice or national solidarity.

Social security in France

At the end of the Second World War, the climate was favourable for wide-ranging state intervention to direct the economy and to give a new orientation to social life, as outlined in Texte 3.1. In the crisis which prevailed, it was possible to introduce reforms by order (*ordonnance*) rather than through the normal lengthier parliamentary procedures. The order of 4 October 1945 set out the framework for the new social security system, creating a general scheme (*régime général*) for all wage earners in industry and commerce. But the French government did not, both for reasons of expediency and in response to pressures exerted by different social groups, introduce a single comprehensive and universal system designed to cover the whole population immediately and in the same way for all possible risks, as had originally been intended, and as was achieved in Great Britain when Beveridge's recommendations, made in 1941 for a unified and greatly improved social security system, were adopted as the basis for legislation.

In France, by unifying and extending the insurance schemes already in existence and by introducing the concept of social security, the avowed intention, as expressed by Laroque, the founding father of the French system, in Texte 3.1, was to move towards the principle of national solidarity and offer to everybody – farmers were at the outset considered as a special case – the same access to services and the guarantee of a substitute income when necessary. Emphasis was placed on the ability of the individual to protect himself through his earning power, and any threats to this from illness, accident or old age were insured against, with the notable exception of the risk of unemployment which was not considered a priority, as it had been in Great Britain.

By 1946 the ideals were already being modified: for example, the better paid non-manual workers in commerce and industry, who had been excluded from the state schemes in the 1930s because of their high earnings, and who had therefore set up their own more advantageous schemes, resisted integration into the newly created general scheme (see Texte 3.8). By 1947 complementary schemes, such as the pension fund for the middle and higher administrative grades (*retraite des cadres*), were in operation. From the outset the reluctance to override interest groups, either because of their political influence or the convenience of preserving existing schemes, led to a multitude of different funds. Some were unable to cover their costs and therefore looked to the general scheme for compensation; others, because of their sound financial basis, were able to offer higher benefits than those provided under the general scheme.

Gradually the coverage has been extended, and attempts have been made to harmonise the various schemes, on the model of the general scheme. The 1 January 1978 was fixed as the date on which the same social security cover was to become available to all insured persons and their families and on which everybody was expected to contribute to a social insurance fund. Prior to this date approximately one and a quarter million individuals were still not insured by any of the existing compulsory schemes, including anybody over 21 and still at school, private detectives, piano teachers, widows under 25, concubines, prostitutes, tramps, gypsies and members of religious orders. All the legal compulsory schemes were to be aligned with regard to contributions and benefits for health, maternity, old age and family allowances, and the state undertook to cover the costs incurred by the general scheme in compensating funds which were in deficit. Not until thirty-three years after its inception, could it be claimed that the French social security system provided comprehensive, though not necessarily, as will be shown, equal, cover for all members of society.

Organisational structure

There are two major systems of social welfare which can be exploited to protect individuals against the risks outlined above: national assistance (*aide sociale*) designed to provide a 'social minimum' for every individual in need, and generally administered and financed by central or local government; and compulsory or voluntary wage-related social insurance (*sécurité sociale*), whereby the insured person protects himself and his family, through a system of contributions and benefits, for certain categories of risks. The relative importance of the cover afforded by each of these systems varies from one country to another and may also change over time. The difference between social insurance and private insurance, such as that covering drivers of motor vehicles, is that social insurance contributions are not calculated according to the individual risks involved but on the basis of the ability to pay, at least insofar as contributions are proportional to incomes rather than at a flat rate, and they therefore fulfil a social function (as described in Texte 3.2) through their redistributive effect. In France where social insurance is the main technique used, national assistance acts as a safety net, but it does not come within the organisational framework of the social security system. The original intention was that national assistance should eventually disappear, because it would no longer be necessary once the whole population could protect itself. In other terms, national assistance was expected to eliminate the inequalities of access to the social insurance schemes, and thereafter the insurance principle would be respected. Between 1962 and 1974 the share of national assistance in the total amount paid out in social benefits decreased significantly, due mainly to the reduction in the number of war pensioners, and there should be a further decrease following the extension of insurance cover in 1978. It is likely that national assistance will continue to play an important role for many years to come in protecting the mentally and physically handicapped, the aged and chronically sick, children in need and the destitute who, for a number of reasons, are not adequately covered by contributory schemes. National assistance provides a good example of the principle of national solidarity, a theme which will be investigated further in this chapter, but in relation to total welfare spending, it accounts for only a small proportion of the benefits paid out, approximately 10 per cent in 1974.

The French system of social insurance depends upon a multitude of occupational schemes and funds, which are generally grouped into four main categories, although their relative importance is very different. They are the general, special, statutory and complementary schemes. The so-called general scheme, by far the most important, at present covers approximately 65 per cent of all insured persons, including all wage earners in commerce and industry. Since 1967 the scheme has been organised on the basis of three national funds: health, old age and family welfare, administered by committees comprising representatives of heads of industry and employees in equal proportions. National bodies control and co-ordinate branches at regional and local levels. An important principle has thus been upheld: those concerned, the insured persons and their employers, are responsible for administering their own funds, but the state fixes the scales for contributions and ensures that compensatory mechanisms operate between funds.

As shown in Texte 3.3, which illustrates the complexity of the administrative framework, the general scheme also covers the whole population, with the exception of farmers, for family benefits, and it covers most civil servants, students, war invalids, widows and orphans for health insurance. Categories which are not members of other occupational schemes may elect to be covered by the general scheme for health. Some funds, at present grouped under the umbrella of the general scheme, should eventually disappear; they protect, for example, those who are not eligible for contributory pension rights or who are suffering from the consequences of accidents which occurred before 1955.

Approximately fifteen special schemes cover groups which do not qualify for the general scheme because of the nature of their employment: independent workers, such as industrialists, retailers, craftsmen and professional men and women; and those employed in specified activities, namely agriculture, mining, navigation or the building trade, who were allowed to maintain existing schemes. One special scheme exists only for workers at the *Comédie Française*. These schemes are subject to different systems of funding, and they sometimes offer more generous benefits than the general scheme. They cover approximately 15 per cent of the population but pay out 25 per cent of all benefits.

Statutory schemes cover risks not included in the general scheme for many workers in the public services, for example, members of the armed forces for health, local authority workers for old age, or workers in nationalised industries for these same risks.

Complementary schemes offer their members additional protection for old age and standard cover for unemployment. It must be remembered that, when the social security system was first introduced, there was no compulsory scheme for unemployment, because it was not considered a major risk at that time. Even today unemployment contributions and benefits are still organised separately from the social insurance cover provided by the social security system. Membership of complementary pension schemes became compulsory in 1972 for all wage earners, thus institutionalising private insurance organisations. There are as a result now so many pension schemes that the exact number is not known, and a single individual may belong to several different schemes.

To these four main categories of contributory schemes can be added social insurance funds which are not operated strictly according to the principle of direct contributions in return for benefits. These apply for old age and family benefits and industrial accidents for some groups of public service employees, where the employer is at the same time con-tributor and paymaster. Finally mutual aid associations (*mutuelles*) have continued to exist and provide additional voluntary cover for their members. They tend to make the range of available schemes even more complicated.

In some respects the French system of social security has evolved in the opposite direction from the British one: because of the pressures exerted, many and varied schemes were retained in France in the first instance, and subsequently attempts have been made to reduce the disparities in the cover afforded and to extend it to those who were not previously eligible; in Great Britain on the other hand, the initial system imposed a basic minimum for everybody, and efforts have been made to supplement cover through wage-related benefits. This difference in emphasis is clearly demonstrated by the methods adopted to fund the system.

Financing social security

When the social security system was instituted in 1945, only 53 per cent of the population was covered by social insurance schemes. As antici-pated, the consequence of extending cover over the years has been a steep rise in the cost of providing the services. From a situation in 1949 where social security benefits accounted for less than one tenth of the gross national product, a stage has now been reached where they absorb almost a fifth. Today the proportion of individual income (if the employers' contributions are considered as part of earned income), which is compulsorily withdrawn to pay for social security, has increased to the extent that in France and in many other countries in Western Europe more than one fifth of a family's income is absorbed by contributions to specified social needs.

There are two main ways of financing a social security system: through taxation, whether direct or indirect, and through social insurance contributions from those covered and/or their employers. Most countries combine the two but in varying proportions, a feature commented on in Texte 3.2. The French system of social security, unlike the British, relies most heavily on contributions (*cotisations*) from employers and employees, particularly the former. Within the EEC, France is amongst the countries in which state participation in social welfare spending is relatively low, as illustrated in Figure 3.1. The reliance in the French system on contributions from workers and their employers is an indication of the importance which is attributed to the insurance principle and to individual responsibility.

Because of the constant rise in the cost of providing social welfare, and consequently in the level of contributions needed, this system of finance has important repercussions on the work force and especially on employers. In 1946 employers' contributions were similar to those of their workers, whereas today, they can pay four times as much and up to 50 per cent of the wage. For family benefits and industrial accidents, the technique adopted when the original schemes were introduced has been retained, and the contribution is paid by the employer alone, the rate for accidents being calculated according to the risks involved, as for traditional insurance premiums, although it is still wage-related. Employers' associations argue that their financial burden is so great that they are discouraged from creating jobs and that their competitiveness in international markets is threatened by high labour costs.

Another much-debated feature of the way in which the French system is financed is the ceiling (*plafond*) on contributions. This has been maintained as a concession to the recipients of high salaries, who were reluctant in the first place to be absorbed into the general scheme because they thought they would bear a disproportionate share of the cost. In effect they rejected an important mechanism for redistributing incomes vertically, that is from higher to lower income groups, and by the same token the concept of national as opposed to corporate solidarity (commented on in Texte 3.8). Employers and employees contribute at

Figure 3.1
Financing of social welfare spending in Europe in 1975

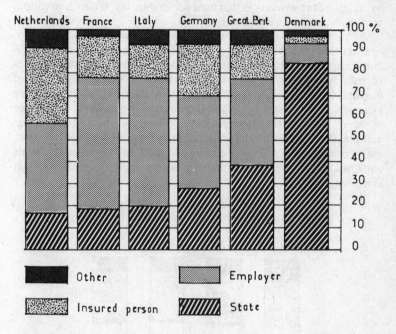

SOURCE: EEC (July 1978), reproduced in *Le Monde* (13 December 1978) p.45.

a lower rate on income above the ceiling. For employers this has served to encourage them to take on workers with good qualifications in return for high wages and to replace workers on lower wages by machines. The ceiling acts as a regressive tax, since low wage earners contribute at the same rate over the whole of their salaries, whereas those earning salaries above the ceiling pay out a smaller proportion of their total earned income.[2] Where both a husband and wife are employed on low salaries, the burden of social insurance contributions is particularly onerous and anti-redistributive, for both must pay contributions, although many of the benefits are no greater than if only one member of the family were contributing.

The 'injustice' resulting from this system of finance is further reinforced by the basis used for assessing contributions (*assiette*). For those whose source of income is their salary, contributions are levied on the whole of their earnings, whereas those who have other sources of income do not pay contributions on the total amount they receive. In some cases the criterion adopted for establishing the basis for contributions by independent workers is that used for income tax, which is notorious for the abuse to which it gives rise.

Although the total amount deducted from income in social insurance contributions as a proportion of salary has changed little since the system was instituted, the distribution of benefits for the different categories of risks has varied considerably in response to changing patterns of demand. As shown by Figure 3.2, the proportion for health insurance increased steadily until 1972, and that for family benefits has decreased in recent years to take account of the surpluses which this fund was accruing. As expenditure on pensions is now rising steeply, contributions are increasing and are likely to continue to do so. In the present economic circumstances, the same will most probably apply to unemployment contributions.

Figure 3.2
Social spending on different welfare benefits

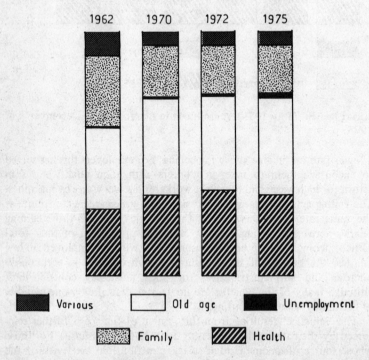

SOURCE: *Données sociales* (1978) p.222.

Social security benefits

It is estimated that on average nearly one quarter of a family's disposable income is derived from social benefits (*prestations*). Clearly some individuals make net gains, while others are losers, at least at some stages in their life cycle. At the national level, there is a measure of redistribution of incomes, as the healthy finance the sick, bachelors support families, and those at work provide an income for the elderly and the unemployed.

Although there is only one contribution under the general scheme for each category of risk, any one such contribution may be associated with more than one type of benefit, reflecting its different functions: benefits may serve to provide a substitute or deferred income, proportional to the amount lost, as for sickness benefits, invalidity and retirement pensions; a fixed-rate payment may supplement income in order to compensate for the additional expenditure incurred in particular circumstances, as is the case for maternity benefits and child allowances; or services may be in kind, such as medical care.

Health care

Insurance contributions for sickness, maternity, invalidity and death are grouped together because they all involve medical care. The intention of medical insurance is to guarantee that an individual, or a member of his family, is able to receive treatment if he falls ill, and that he should not become destitute as a result of poor health.

An important feature of health care in France is that the sick person is not obliged to register with one practitioner, and he is free to choose the hospital to which he is admitted, a point stressed in Texte 3.4. One reason for this is to ensure the patient can relate to his medical advisor, a prerequisite for successful treatment, presupposing of course that members of the public have access to the information necessary to enable them to make such a choice. The degree of choice will also be determined by the medical density of the area of residence: there were 145 medical practitioners for every 100,000 inhabitants in France in 1977, compared with 125 in Great Britain and 160 in the German Federal Republic, but the density in the Paris area was 231 and in Picardy only 101. The rural environment can rarely offer a choice, and specialists, approximately 37 per cent of all doctors in 1976, are concentrated in the main cities. Important regional differences exist for the number of hospital beds, Brittany being the area with the most outdated hospital provision.

Other factors limiting the degree of individual freedom of choice, at least for some members of the public, can be explained by the techniques used for the payment of doctors and reimbursement of patients and by the organisational structure of the hospital system. When the social security system was conceived, the medical profession refused steadfastly to be absorbed into a health service along the lines of the British one, and they agreed to participate only on the condition that they could negotiate their own contracts with the social insurance funds and maintain a high degree of independence, as reiterated in Texte 3.4. Today one third of doctors receive a salary: some are employed under special occupational schemes, such as those organised by mining companies, but more often they work in hospitals, and in recent years there has been a decrease in the number entering general practice due to the more attractive conditions in the hospitals and higher incomes for specialists. Medical practitioners not employed by a special scheme or a hospital, but working by themselves or in group practices (about one fifth of independent doctors), derive their income from consultation fees (*honoraires*), at rates set by the medical insurance funds and reviewed annually. Higher fees may be charged, and agreed by the funds, for medical practitioners with special qualifications. Fees are paid directly to the doctors by patients, with a few exceptions, such as pregnancy, treatment for industrial accidents and in some cases of chronic illness, when the medical insurance fund may take over entirely (*tiers payant*). The direct payment of fees is in strict contrast to the British practice, whereby, except for private medicine, the doctor-patient relationship is never subject to financial considerations. The French system of payment is much criticised (the topic is debated in Texte 3.5), and there is evidence to suggest that it is an important factor inhibiting the low income groups from having recourse to medical care at the first signs of illness.

Patients are reimbursed if their doctor has signed an agreement with a medical insurance fund (as is the case for about 90 per cent of independent medical practitioners), and if his charges fall within the limits set by the fund. In most cases social security does not reimburse charges in full: the patient generally pays about one fifth of the bill, except if he belongs to a private insurance fund, which, in return for additional premiums, covers most of the outstanding amount on agreed charges. The purpose behind the patient's contribution (*ticket modérateur*), when it was first introduced, was to ensure that the provision of medical care was not abused. The rates of refund for prescribed medicines may vary considerably: some very expensive drugs are reimbursed at 100 per cent, accounting for nearly 43 per cent of all reimbursements, and others at only 40 per cent. Dental and ophthalmic treatment is reimbursed on the basis of a standard payment, which may fall far below the actual amount charged. In the case of hospital treatment, the medical insurance fund reimburses the standard rate for a general ward, and a patient who requests a single room must cover the difference. The patient pays only his share of the costs, and the fund pays the remainder directly to the hospital. These regulations apply both to public and private hospitals (*cliniques*), or at least to the 90 per cent of private hospitals which have agreements with the insurance funds. The private sector accounts for approximately one third of all hospital beds, but it does not offer such a wide range of treatment as the public sector and is often criticised for its profit motive, since it tends to concentrate on the most cost-effective types of surgery and is not concerned with research. Private hospitals are undoubtedly instrumental in increasing the number of beds available (1024 per 100,000 inhabitants in 1975, compared with 895 in Great Britain and 1155 in the German Federal Republic), and the problem of waiting lists is almost unknown in France.

Another factor which may discourage the poorly educated members of the public and foreign workers from making effective use of health services is the very complicated procedure for claiming reimbursement of expenses. The formalities involved are described in Texte 3.6. It would seem however that easier access to medical services would not greatly improve the standard of health of the community, and it is estimated that between 2 and 5 per cent of all hospital admissions in France are for the treatment of complaints resulting from the abuse of medicines. There is evidence to suggest that improvements in housing, nutrition and education probably have more impact on health than does medical care.

In spite of efforts made to control the expenditure on health, the continual increase in the cost of providing medical services seems to be a permanent feature of social welfare provision both in France and in neighbouring countries. The figure went up by 50 per cent between 1969 and 1979 and more than twice as much as total social welfare spending. Many reasons are put forward to explain the rising cost: the extension of medical insurance to sections of the population not previously covered; the increase in the proportion of the elderly in the population for whom old age is often a time of ill health; general improvements in medical technology allowing expensive forms of treatment for diseases which in the past would have been fatal; poor management in the hospitals (administrative costs account for about twice as much of the hospital budget in France compared with Great Britain); the increase in medical density and in consultation fees and prescription charges in relation to other consumer spending.

Although there has been an overall increase in the demand for medical services, access to care still varies considerably according to factors such as age, family size and socio-occupational origins. The elderly and the young are by far the biggest consumers. So great is the concentration of spending on medical care that it is estimated that 10 per cent of all patients account for 70 per cent of all expenditure, whereas 40 per cent of the population derive little benefit from the services provided. As shown by Figure 3.3, income levels (which can be interpreted here as a reflection of general standards of living and educational qualifications) determine not only the amount spent on health services but also the way in which it is spent. The low income groups, who are often the most exposed to health risks, receive the least benefit, and their biggest item of spending is hospital care. As income levels rise, doctors' fees quickly take over, and the highest income groups rarely resort to hospital care, and even more rarely do they receive sickness benefits, whereas they are the biggest consumers of pharmaceutical products. It is the middle income groups, particularly in the Paris area, which are the biggest consumers of medical benefits overall, and their rate of spending is found to correlate closely with a level of educational attainment cor-

Figure 3.3

Distribution of expenditure on health in relation to income in 1970

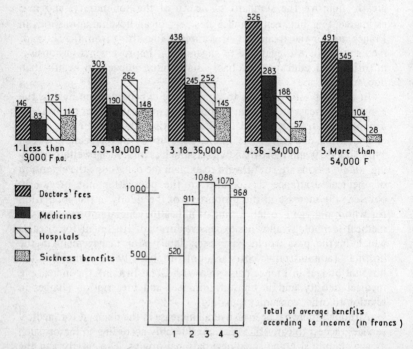

SOURCE: *Le Monde* (7 November 1973) p.38.

responding to the secondary school-leaving certificate (*baccalauréat*).

Although the daily cost of a hospital bed is higher in France than in Great Britain, hospital care accounts for a smaller share of the total health budget in France. Recent reports suggest that the proportion of the budget devoted to pharmaceutical products – still a more imporant item of spending in France than in Great Britain – is no longer increasing so rapidly as in the past. This trend may be explained to some extent by the enormous rise in the cost of hospital care, but also by the stricter controls now exercised over the introduction of new medicines, prices and advertising. It may be a response to publicity campaigns to alert customers to the dangers of drug abuse, thought to be responsible for approximately 15 per cent of all illness. One quarter of all medicines consumed are believed to be self-prescribed (a decrease since 1965). Nowadays the main self-prescribers are the wealthier and better informed social groups, but in the 1960s the low income groups resorted to self-prescription as a means of avoiding doctors' bills, particularly if they were not covered by medical insurance. Approximately 4 to 5 per cent of all medicines are probably prescribed in retrospect: in order to claim reimbursement on drugs bought without a prescription, patients ask their doctor to add the medicine to the next prescription (*ordonnance de régularisation*). The most publicised forms of abuse concern over-prescription by doctors, and it is estimated that 30 to 40 per cent of all medicines prescribed are not used. This is part of a broader problem of doctor-patient relationships and of the function of the pharmaceutical industry. It is a basic principle of the medical profession (reiterated in Texte 3.4) that doctors should be free to prescribe as they choose. In the absence of other reliable criteria, patients may come to judge their medical practitioner by the price and the number of drugs prescribed. For the general practitioner, working on average sixty to seventy hours a week and paid according to the number of consultations, a 'good' prescription offers a quick and easy way of gaining a patient's confidence. The public has been encouraged by advertising to believe that there is a medicine to cure every ill, and the doctor is dependent upon advice, which is hardly objective, received from drug companies, for information about the effectiveness of new products. Recently attempts have been made to persuade doctors to avoid prescribing unnecessary expensive medicines. In addition the number of consultations, prescriptions and sick leaves granted by doctors are monitored, and those with 'unusual' levels, compared with the norm in their area, are asked for an explanation, with the ultimate sanction that their contract with the medical insurance fund could be rescinded if they do not comply.

It is generally agreed that the cost of providing a high standard of health services – and in international terms France is very well placed –

will continue to rise, but the economists are increasingly reminded that health services should not be judged according to the same criteria as other areas of economic activity, and that health is not a marketable commodity subject to the forces of competition, cost-effectiveness and profitability. Nevertheless there are many proposals for rationalising provision and reducing wastage, and recent public opinion surveys indicate that there is general awareness of the necessity to cut spending, particularly on medicines. Most of those questioned favour abolishing reimbursement of charges for minor ailments for all but the low income groups. Other suggestions which have not yet received public approval are that patients in hospitals should be expected to pay fixed daily charges, and that the length of stay should be reduced. It has also been mooted that a new system for paying doctors should be introduced to discourage unnecessary visits, that stricter control should be exercised over medicines, but also over new equipment and techniques, that medical training should foster a more coherent approach to health care, with more emphasis on preventive medicine and a better knowledge about ways of avoiding waste.

Family policy
As explained in Chapter 1, the French preoccupation with demographic problems prompted a whole range of family-orientated social policies dating back to the 1920s. The avowed intention in the *Code de la famille* of 1939 was to encourage family building by providing family allowances at a level which would cover the cost of raising additional children. Whereas other social welfare benefits were only gradually extended to the whole of the working population, family allowances were made payable to all residents in France as early as 1946, when they became part of the social security system and one of the main funds in the general scheme. Since 1946, many other forms of aid to the family have been instituted: they include monetary benefits, such as maternity benefits conditional on medical examinations being carried out at regular intervals during pregnancy, grants and allowances for schooling and housing and privileges for families, such as reduction on public transport, cheap subsidised housing (*habitations à loyer modéré*), income tax relief for family dependents (through the *quotient familial*), as well as services in kind, including child-minding facilities, family social workers, day centres and subsidised holiday camps. Many of the policies referred to in the previous chapter for the improvement of the everyday life of working women can be seen as part of the overall strategy for family welfare.

Within the framework of the social security system, the main thrust of family policy has come from the family allowances provided under the contributory scheme, administered by the Child Allowances Fund. This category of benefits affords an interesting example of the ways in which social policy has evolved in France and of the problems resulting from attributing several functions to a particular form of welfare.

With the exception of housing allowances (and since January 1977 the *allocation logement* is being phased out and replaced by a system of personalised aid based on income and family size, *aide personnalisée au logement*)[3] and the new family supplement, which will be discussed later, all allowances are calculated according to a percentage of a fixed monthly figure based on the price index. It has become customary for the Child Allowances Fund to show a surplus. Unlike other funds the number of beneficiaries has not increased, due to the decline in the birthrate, and the amount paid out in benefits has not been allowed to rise at the same rate as incomes. The surpluses have generally been used to compensate for deficits in other funds, a practice frequently criticised by the administrators of child allowances who argue that the proportion of household income derived from this source, particularly for the low income groups, has fallen substantially over the years.

In 1939, the underlying principle was that aid, based on national solidarity, should be provided for every family, whatever its social class, to ensure that no married couple should be deterred by financial considerations from raising a family. The allowances, like those of the earlier schemes initiated by employers and dating back to 1860, thereby fulfilled a compensatory function in recognition of the service rendered to society. But their overt objective in doing so was to bring about an increase in the birthrate. The fact that allowances are not granted for the first child, even though it is generally agreed that it involves the greatest cost to the family, is an indication that this objective is still given priority. Scepticism has already been expressed about the success of family allowances in carrying out their compensatory function, and despite Debré's convictions (see Texte 2.4), it is doubtful that they can be effective in bringing about a substantial and longlasting increase in the birthrate (as argued in Texte 1.3). More and more this function is rejected as a legitimate aim for a family policy, and there is much discussion about the way in which the two objectives have become confused.

A third function of family policy, which often comes into conflict with the other two, is that of vertical redistribution of income. Many observers in France today maintain that family policy should not be exploited to eliminate social inequalities. The intention of working towards greater 'social justice' is more generally evoked as an appropriate objective for family policy. Basic family allowances are paid out at a flat rate, determined by family size and the ages of the children, in order to bring about a horizontal redistribution of income, that is from those without children to those with a family. It would seem however that flat-rate payments may cause redistribution in favour of the wealthier social categories, since for a given family size, benefits from the family fund sometimes increase as income rises: this occurs when children in high income families pursue their education beyond the minimum school-leaving age, thereby prolonging their entitlement to child allowances, whereas children from low income families tend to leave school earlier. The counterclaim is sometimes made that for families with a higher standard of living, the cost of rearing a child is greater in absolute terms, and, that on a strictly economic basis, they should receive higher allowances. The system of income tax relief can be interpreted as a concession to meet this demand.

Where benefits are paid only to low income groups, an example of positive discrimination, vertical redistribution clearly takes place. This is the case for the new non-contributory family supplement (*complément familial*), which since January 1978 replaces the former single salary, mother-at-home and child-minding allowances, as well as other supplements for low income groups. It is awarded to families with one child under three years old or with three children, whether or not the mother is working, if family resources fall below a certain ceiling. It can therefore be seen either as a payment for looking after children at home or as a means of covering the cost of having them minded. The ceiling is higher if both husband and wife are working, and benefits increase with family size and at the same rate as the monthly basis on which family allowances are calculated. When the family supplement was introduced, it was estimated that the number of beneficiaries would be approximately 2,200,000, almost half the number of families in receipt of family allowances. In that this new allowance replaces other forms of means-tested benefits, it will help to streamline administrative procedures, but since it is directed at such a large proportion of the low income groups, it may be taken as an indication of government commitment to policies designed to reduce social injustices.

Policy for the aged

When the social security system was conceived in 1945, the intention was to create a single insurance scheme for pensions guaranteeing a minimum income to all those over retirement age. As already mentioned, the failure to establish one universal fund for each category of benefits has resulted in administrative complexity and disparate cover for different occupational groups. In the case of pensions, a three-tiered system has evolved (described in Texte 3.7): in return for contributions up to a ceiling, it provides a basic or minimum social security pension; complementary contributory schemes, now compulsory for most workers, provide wage-related benefits on income up to a ceiling, and high wage earners contribute up to a second ceiling, and sometimes above, to obtain more generous pensions. The present three-tiered system operated in Great Britain bears many similarities to that which has been developed in France, but a significant difference between the British and the French systems lies in the techniques adopted to finance contributory pensions. The British opted for a funding technique (*capitalisation*), based on the principle that each individual builds up his own reserves, thereby emphasising personal rather than collective responsibility. When the French social security system was introduced, the funding method was abandoned in favour of a pay-as-you-earn principle (*répartition*), which depends upon the contributive capacity of different generations of workers and upon occupational and national solidarity. When it was first instituted the pay-as-you-earn technique had a number of advantages, but more recently it has been at the source of many of the financial problems facing the pension schemes (see Texte 3.7).

The two main advantages of the method adopted by the French were that benefits could be paid out immediately the scheme came into operation and that, since contributions are a percentage of earnings, they have risen automatically with increases in salaries, enabling proportionate increases in pensions. An important drawback of the pay-as-you-earn principle is that it is vulnerable to change in the age structure of the population. Where schemes cover a broad range of employment, changes in the number of dependents are likely to take place gradually, but where the number of contributors to a particular pension scheme is declining, as is the case for small independent workers and the railways, which were financing 550,000 pensioners for 290,000 workers in 1972, it is impossible for the working population in these categories to cover the cost of the benefits being drawn. Farmers now finance only 18 per cent of their pension scheme, and it is estimated that for every miner there is a widow's pension to be paid. The deficits were met in the past by transfer payments from other funds (*charges indues*), an example of national solidarity, but subject to much criticism by those who feel that benefits from their own schemes could be higher if they did not have to compensate for inadequate contributions elsewhere.

When the basic contributory pension falls below the statutory minimum – as frequently occurs for widows' pensions which are fixed at half the level of a husband's contributory pension – it is supplemented by non-contributory benefits. As more attention has been devoted to the plight of the elderly in recent years, the basic pension (*minimum vieillesse*) for the aged has risen considerably, reaching 11,000 francs a year on 1 December 1978 for the two million or so people eligible to receive it. The old age minimum is now indexed according to the guaranteed minimum income (*salaire minimum interprofessionnel de croissance*), which is at present increasing more quickly than other incomes. As the proportion of the population eligible for the full rates of income-related benefits from contributory schemes grows, the pension supplement will gradually be phased out. The main problem in the future will be how to finance wage-related pensions for an ever-increasing proportion of the population.

Contributory pension rights are now calculated on the basis of the ten best years of earnings, generally to a maximum of 50 per cent of earnings. This can be a source of inflation when salaries, and consequently contributions, are increasing more slowly after a period of rapid growth. The problem becomes more acute in the complementary schemes for incomes up to and above the second ceiling. The present balance between the working and the retired population is relatively stable, as the generations most affected by the First World War (*classes creuses*) are now reaching retirement age, but the situation will deteriorate after the year 2000 as the generations of the post-war baby boom leave the work force, expecting to reap the benefits of their contributions to pension funds. It is significant that, whereas the number of those retiring went up by 18 per cent between 1962 and 1972, the number of pensioners liable for income tax increased threefold. One solution to the budgetary deficits of the social insurance funds has been to levy contributions on some categories of high income pensioners, a practice which is likely to be extended.

It is now generally recognised that any attempt to introduce a lower retirement age would lead to insoluble financial problems for all pension schemes, and interest is centred more on the idea of progressive retirement, which could have financial and psychological advantages, and on general improvements in the living conditions of the elderly: since the majority of those living in housing built before 1949 are elderly people, recent legislation to provide grants for modernisation should help to raise their standard of accommodation; increasingly efforts are made to offer assistance for the elderly in their homes and to discourage institutional care; money is being made available from national assistance to finance the installation of telephones for pensioners with inadequate means of their own. Although the general level of pensions is increasing, a situation has not yet been reached where the benefits distributed can be said to reduce social inequalities. Because of the discrepancies in the schemes offered to different occupational groups, and since some categories of workers can afford additional cover, it is estimated that income differentials are many times greater in old age than during the working life. The fact that the higher income groups are statistically more likely to live longer means that they are able to consume a disproportionate share of pensions and welfare services.

National solidarity

Nowadays there is fairly general agreement and much evidence in support of the theory that, if the same social welfare services are offered to everybody, the best informed and most privileged social categories will gain the greatest benefit. This is demonstrably true in France for benefits which depend upon demand, as in the health service, or for public services such as education, as will be seen in the next chapter. The same applies where welfare payments are made at a flat rate, as is the case for family allowances. Where benefits are proportional to earnings, on the principle to each according to his labour, rather than to his need, the effect is one of cumulative advantage. Only when there is an attempt to give more to the less privileged social categories, through positive discrimination, for example by awarding non-contributory allowances and means-tested benefits, such as the family supplement and old age basic pension, is there any likelihood of bringing about a relative improvement in the living standards of the low income groups and of reducing social inequalities. A social insurance scheme which devotes a major share of its income to wage-related benefits, which sets contribution levels at lower rates for incomes above a ceiling, which affords only partial reimbursement of medical expenses, or is so complicated that not all members of the public apply for the available benefits, cannot be said to give high priority to achieving a more equitable distribution of incomes. As has already been argued, vertical redistribution of incomes is only one possible function which can be attributed to a social security system, but the manifest failure of the French social welfare services on this count is the source of much contention in a society which claims to uphold the principles of social justice.

The social security system has been described as a socialist Trojan horse in the capitalist camp, but it is also considered as a concession made by capitalism to ensure its own survival. No doubt both interpretations were applicable to the French context in the 1940s (as can be deduced from Texte 3.1). The very existence of a social security system in an industrialised capitalist society implies aims other than those of profit, but, as suggested earlier, its objectives are unlikely to be solely altruistic: for example, welfare is expected to ensure the individual's ability to work and therefore his productive capacity, and the system may be used as an argument against granting high wage demands. Whatever its motivation, the role played by the state is ambivalent, and this is particularly so in the French system, where the state acts as arbiter between funds while also exercising considerable control over the budget through its power to adjust the rates for contributions and benefits. At the same time, it must protect its interests as an employer and respond to the pressures exerted by different social groups. By decreeing that a specific proportion will be compulsorily withdrawn from individual incomes, it also dictates the amount of freedom of choice left to the consumer. These role conflicts seem inevitable in a democratic society in which resources will always be limited by what the public is prepared to accept or tolerate as a reasonable intrusion in their lives (as discussed in Texte 3.8).

In a country where the general standard of living is rising, the need for some categories of benefits may become less acute, but the rapid pace of technological, economic and social change in the twentieth century has tended to create new sources of insecurity and new social problems, making even more distant the prospect of self-help. It is extremely difficult for any country to go backwards and reduce the number of benefits, but it is likely that a stage has now been reached where the financial limitations on the continued extension of the social services will lead governments to look for new ways of concentrating aid on the underprivileged social groups. For although nobody is prepared to sacrifice his privileges, the general climate of opinion does seem to be in favour of reducing social inequalities.

Many of the proposals made to improve social welfare provision in France and to set the social security system on a sound financial footing are for piecemeal reform: changes in contribution rates, in the basis on which they are calculated or the level of the ceiling are frequently suggested and implemented; attempts are made to relieve the general scheme of the unjustified expenditure (*charges indues*) by which it is expected to compensate other funds or to pay for medical training, for example; economies are sought by reducing abuse and eliminating waste, or by cutting back on prestigious spending; levies are raised on tobacco, alcohol and petrol to help towards the cost of treating the illnesses they cause. Other suggestions are aimed at reducing the need for welfare services by substantial improvements in working and living conditions, or by greater emphasis on preventive measures, particularly through campaigns against alcoholism, smoking and road accidents.

A more coherent set of proposals has been formulated for a radical reform of the organisational and conceptual framework of the social security system, as described in Texte 3.9 by Dupeyroux. It is suggested that a basic distinction should be made between two categories of benefits according to the two main functions of the social security system, for it is argued that the social insurance principle is not appropriate for all the risks it is expected to cover. One category of benefits should guarantee a substitute or deferred income for professional earnings lost, insuring against the inability to work due to illness, accident, invalidity or old age. In this case, it is considered logical to maintain the triangular relationship between professional income, substitute income and contributions proportional to the first. The second category of protection should guarantee a social minimum for everybody, regardless of earnings, covering medical treatment, family allowances and national assistance. In this case, contributions should be levied according to the ability of every individual to pay and should be based on a progressive taxation system, not only on direct income but also on other sources of revenue. In both cases the ceiling on contributions would disappear.

A severe criticism often levelled against the social welfare services in Great Britain is that the pendulum has swung too far away from self-help and that individuals have come to rely too heavily on the welfare state. This description is probably less applicable to French society, where policy-makers have always stressed the insurance principle, often at the expense of national solidarity. They have also rejected suggestions that health services, amongst others, should be provided free of charge for low income groups, on the grounds that this would create a category of second class citizens living off the state (*mentalité d'assisté*). While reasserting the principle of national solidarity, proposals like those of Dupeyroux avoid this implication. In that they would involve the overhaul of the system of direct taxation and would have to overcome deeply entrenched sectional interests, there is little chance of the scheme being adopted in the near future. It is more likely that the shape of the social welfare services and their priorities in the years to come will continue to depend upon the political ideologies of governments and on their ability to strike a balance between the demands of the various powerful pressure groups intent on preserving their own advantages.

Bibliographical guidance

General works examining the growth of social welfare services and of the French social security system:

Documentation Française, *La Sécurité sociale en France* (Paris: Documentation Française, 1975)

J. Doublet, *Sécurité sociale*, 5th ed. (Paris: PUF, 1972)

H. Hatzfield, *Du Paupérisme à la sécurité sociale: essai sur les origines de la sécurité sociale en France, 1850–1940* (Paris: Colin, 1971)

R. Jambu-Merlin, *La Sécurité sociale* (Paris: Colin, 1970)

Critical appraisals of social policy in France:

J.-M. Belorgey, *La Politique sociale* (Paris: Seghers, 1976)
'Quelle sécurité sociale?', *Courrier de la République*, 107 (July 1974)
X. Greffe, *La Politique sociale: étude critique* (Paris: PUF, 1975)
P. Hermand, *L'Avenir de la sécurité sociale* (Paris: Seuil, 1967)
B. Lory, *La Politique d'action sociale* (Toulouse: Privat, 1975)
'La santé des Français', *Supplément au Monde dossiers et documents* (Nov 1979)
'Perspectives de la sécurité sociale', *Revue française des affaires sociales*, special issue, 2 vols (July–Sep 1976)

Social welfare as a redistributive mechanism:

Centre National de la Recherche Scientifique, *Les Inégalités sociales: situations, mécanismes, actions correctrices* (Paris: Editions du CNRS, 1977)
J.-C. Colli, *L'Inégalité par l'argent* (Paris: Gallimard, 1975)
L. Fabius, *La France inégale* (Paris: Hachette, 1975)
P.-A. Mercier, *Les Inégalités en France* (Paris: CREDOC, 1974)

Reviews:

Up-to-date information about present trends and studies of specific areas of social policy are included in different editions of *Données sociales* and the quarterly publication *Revue française des affaires sociales*.

Illustrative texts and linguistic exercises

Texte 3.1 La sécurité sociale en France

La fin de la guerre de 1939–1945 a été marquée, dans tous les pays qui avaient pris part au conflit, par un large élan de *progrès social*. Après la crise économique des années 1929–1935, après les bouleversements politiques, économiques et sociaux dus à la guerre, après tant d'années d'insécurité, d'incertitude du lendemain, les populations en général, les travailleurs salariés surtout, aspiraient à recevoir la garantie qu'en toutes circonstances chacun serait, à l'avenir, en mesure d'assurer sa subsistance et celle de sa famille. Là est l'origine, au cours de cette période, de la floraison, à travers le monde, *des plans de Sécurité Sociale*.

Cette aspiration générale de la population a trouvé en France un appui dans le climat du moment. Les masses ouvrières, qui avaient pris une part active à la résistance contre l'ennemi et à la lutte contre le régime de Vichy, voyaient dans la victoire militaire et la chute du régime le résultat de leur effort, dans le nouveau gouvernement, leur gouvernement. La Sécurité Sociale, consacrée par les ordonnances de 1945 et les lois de 1946, a été une conquête ouvrière au même titre que les réformes sociales de 1936. Elle est apparue non seulement comme un moyen d'améliorer la situation des travailleurs, mais comme un élément dans la construction d'un ordre social nouveau d'où serait éliminée *l'inégalité dans la sécurité*, l'un des facteurs essentiels des distinctions entre classes sociales.

Ce climat, en même temps que la situation économique de l'époque, et les traditions qui imprégnaient les institutions sociales préexistantes, ont contribué à donner à l'organisation française de la Sécurité Sociale ses traits essentiels.

Le premier s'est marqué dans la tendance à une vaste *solidarité nationale* s'exprimant en une redistribution des revenus dans le cadre d'une organisation d'entr'aide présentât une très grande généralité. Généralité quant aux personnes englobées: c'étaient certes d'abord les travailleurs salariés et leur familles, mais ce devait être par la suite la population tout entière. Généralité aussi quant aux risques couverts: toutes les éventualités pouvant affecter le niveau de vie individuel et familial devaient être prévues, qu'il s'agisse de la maladie, de la maternité, de l'accident, de la vieillesse, des charges de famille.

Un deuxième trait essentiel du plan français de Sécurité Sociale s'est marqué dans son souci de *démocratie sociale*. L'on entendait maintenir dans les organismes nouveaux cet esprit d'entr'aide désintéressée, cette tradition généreuse d'assistance mutuelle qui avait donné depuis un siècle et demi à toutes les institutions sociales françaises *leur physionomie propre*. L'organisation nouvelle devait donc éviter le risque d'*étatisme bureaucratique*. Elle devait être faite d'institutions vivantes, se renouvelant par une création continue, par l'effort des intéressés eux-mêmes chargés par leurs représentants d'en assurer directement la gestion.

La difficulté était de combiner cette préoccupation et celle de la généralité de l'unité du régime, nécessaire pour matérialiser effectivement la solidarité nationale qui était et devait être le fondement du système. Cette unité se heurtait aux *particularismes professionnels et sociaux*, si profonds dans des fractions importantes de la population française. La législation a certes consacré le principe de l'unité de caisse, et posé en principe la disparition progressive des *régimes catégoriels*, dans l'élan de solidarité de la libération. Mais très vite les particularismes ont retrouvé une vigueur croissante, et, au sein de catégories multiples, les résistances se sont affirmées à l'intégration de tous dans une solidarité d'ensemble. Sans doute n'était-il personne qui ne sentît le besoin de la sécurité contre *les risques sociaux*, mais beaucoup répugnaient à admettre leur solidarité avec les membres d'autres catégories sociales ou professionnelles et marquaient leur préférence pour une démocratie se réalisant dans des cadres plus limités, sur la base d'affinités s'exprimant au sein de leurs organisations mutualistes ou syndicales. De ce fait si l'organisation de la

Sécurité Sociale n'a cessé d'évoluer vers une généralisation de plus en plus complète, cette généralisation s'est accompagnée souvent de la juxtaposition de structures autonomes propres aux diverses catégories sociales et professionnelles, rendant plus difficile la réalisation de la solidarité nationale dont l'institution devait être l'expression.

SOURCE: P. Laroque, *Cahiers français*, 172 (sept.–oct. 1975) pp.5–7 (adapté).

Exploitation du texte

1 Formulez des définitions pour expliquer les concepts en italique.

2 Faites un résumé en moins de 100 mots pour présenter l'essentiel des arguments à la manière de l'en-tête du texte 1.3.

3 L'auteur semble adopter une attitude positive envers l'institution de la sécurité sociale en France. Relevez les vocables et les expressions qui tendent à le démontrer.

4 Relevez les termes et les techniques exploités par l'auteur pour assurer l'enchaînement de ses idées à l'intérieur des phrases et d'un paragraphe à un autre.

5 Faites une analyse grammaticale des phrases suivantes:

la population tout entière
qu'il s'agisse de la maladie
une vigueur croissante
Sans doute n'était-il personne qui ne sentît
leur préférence pour une démocratie se réalisant

Texte 3.2   Les célèbres transferts sociaux

Le système traditionnel de garantie contre les risques – appelé assurance – fonctionne bien par *prélèvement* d'un côté (*primes*) et *versements* de l'autre (*indemnités pour sinistres*). Mais, bien que rendant les assurés d'une compagnie solidaires les uns des autres, il n'a pas en lui-même de *caractère social* et il est par nature inégal: d'abord parce que seuls sont assurés ceux qui peuvent payer, ensuite parce que le transfert se fait des non-sinistrés vers les sinistrés, ou si l'on veut, des chanceux vers les malchanceux; sans autre considération.

Mais que l'on proportionne, *les cotisations* – rendues obligatoires – à *la capacité contributive* de chaque citoyen, que l'on calcule *les prestations* en fonction des *besoins* sociaux des bénéficiaires, et l'on construit un véritable système de sécurité sociale, c'est-à-dire de solidarité. Cette solidarité, devoir supérieur que s'assigne la société, est alors naturellement financée par un quasi-impôt (*la parafiscalité sociale*). Et le système égalise autant les chances sociales qu'il est: plus général (tout le monde y est affilié), plus juste et plus sincère dans le prélèvement, plus soigneux dans les prestations sociales. Il illustre ainsi, en quelque sorte, la véritable portée du beau terme de Socialisme, lorsqu'il signifie que la Société fait régner l'équité et la solidarité parmi ses membres.

On peut d'ailleurs classer nos différents pays occidentaux selon la manière dont il répondent à ces besoins nouveaux.

– D'un côté, les pays les plus socialistes, principalement les sociétés nordiques et britannique: Danemark, Suède, Royaume-Uni. Principales caractéristiques: la collectivité y prélève entre 36 et 44% du *produit national brut*, ce qui est beaucoup. Mais au sein de ces prélèvements obligatoires, le prélèvement fiscal tient la plus grande place car il finance une grande partie de la fonction de sécurité sociale, ainsi intégrée dans l'ensemble des fonctions collectives. Corollaire: les 'cotisations sociales' proprement dites ne jouent qu'*un rôle d'appoint* dans le système: 4 à 7,5% seulement du PNB.

– De l'autre côté, la plupart de nos voisins européens qui, avec nous-mêmes, prélèvent globalement à peu près autant que les premiers (de 31% pour l'Italie, à 42% pour les Pays-Bas, en passant par 35% pour la France et l'Allemagne). Mais là, l'ensemble des cotisations spécifiques de sécurité sociale constitue en quelque sorte *un deuxième circuit* concurrent du système fiscal: elles ne représentent pas moins, en effet, de 12% (Allemagne, Italie) à 15% (France, Pays-Bas) du produit national. En d'autres termes: sur 100 francs que verse dans ces pays un citoyen à *la collectivité*, il en affecte plus d'un tiers à la fonction spécifique de sécurité sociale. Et en France, 40 francs, ce qui place notre pays en tête de la parafiscalité sociale.

SOURCE: J.-C. Colli, *L'Inégalité par l'argent* (Paris: Gallimard, 1975) pp.186–7 (adapté).

Exploitation du texte

1 Expliquez en vos propres mots les termes en italique.

2 En vous servant de la terminologie employée dans le texte, expliquez la différence entre l'assurance automobile et l'assurance maladie en France.

3 Présentez sous forme d'un tableau les données exposées dans la deuxième moitié du texte.

4 Utilisez une syntaxe différente pour exprimer les notions présentées dans les phrases suivantes:

Mais que l'on proportionne. . . de solidarité.
Et le système égalise autant. . . prestations sociales.

Texte 3.3 Les régimes d'assurance sociales: étendue et modalités de la protection selon le risque couvert et la catégorie sociale

Catégorie sociale \ Risque	Maladie et maternité		Accidents au travail		Charge de famille	Vieillesse Invalidité Décès	Chômage
	Remboursements de frais	Revenu de remplacement	Remboursements de frais	Revenu de remplacement			
Exploitants agricoles							
Salariés agricoles							
Commerçants, artisans, professions libérales							
Mineurs							
Marins							
SNCF - EDF - RATP - Banque de France							
Personnels militaires							
Fonctionnaires civils							
Agents des collectivités locales							
Autres salariés							(1)
Étudiants							
Grands invalides, veuves, orphelins de guerre							
Non actifs (2)							

(1) Ouvriers du bâtiment, dockers
(2) personnes n'ayant jamais travaillé ou ne pouvant être rattachées à aucune des catégories précédentes.

Légende: Régime général — Employeurs — Régime complémentaire — Travailleurs non salariés — Caisses professionnelles

SOURCE: 'Le domaine de la Sécurité sociale', *Statistiques et études financières*, 6 (1972), reproduced in *Données sociales* (1978) p.215.

Exploitation du texte

1 Faites une description des caractéristiques des différents régimes d'assurances sociales à partir de ce graphique.

2 Expliquez la couverture de la catégorie des agents des collectivités locales pour les divers risques.

Texte 3.4

votre Santé en danger!

L'organisation rationnelle de la SANTE, en France, doit reposer sur la garantie de certaines libertés. DEJA, sous la pression de certains courants d'idées, ces principes ont été remis en cause, contrairement à l'intérêt des malades.

- Liberté de choisir celui qui vous soigne et d'en changer si vous n'êtes pas satisfait.

Les membres de certaines collectivités ne peuvent plus choisir ou changer librement de practiciens: les mineurs, les cheminots, les employés de la R.A.T.P., les bénéficiaires de l'Aide Médicale, etc...

- Liberté pour votre praticien, de choisir le traitement qui vous convient.

Tous les médicaments ne sont pas remboursés. Certains le sont inégalement. Le remboursement d'un millier d'entre eux vient d'être arbitrairement abaissé de 70 à 40%...

- Liberté de choix entre l'hôpital et la clinique.

De 1970 à 1977, le prix de journée de médecine des hôpitaux (exemple Assistance Publique) a été relevé de 300% et celui des cliniques de 141%. Cette situation compromet une gestion normale des établissements privés, dont déjà certains ont dû fermer leurs portes, et mène à un monopole hospitalier public plus coûteux.

- Liberté d'entreprise dans l'industrie du médicament.

Le blocage arbitraire des prix a déjà entraîné la disparition de 5.000 médicaments bon marché! Le prix des spécialités de remplacement, compte-tenu des régles actuelles (et contrôlé par la S.S.) est 3 à 4 fois plus cher. Les difficultés économiques qui en résultent et les contraintes imposées par l'Administration limitent les investissements de recherche et ont amené la disparition de plus de 2.000 sociétés, privant ainsi les malades de progrès dans les moyens de guérir.

- Liberté d'élire les gestionnaires de la Sécurité Sociale, afin de pouvoir contrôler le plus gros budget national dont dépend notamment votre santé.

Depuis 1968, les assurés sociaux n'ont plus le droit d'élire les administrateurs de la S.S. Seuls cinq syndicats, dont la majorité obéit le plus souvent à des consignes politiques, ont le monopole de défendre vos intérêts et les 4/5ème des assurés sont écartés de la gestion des Caisses dont ils supportent le déficit.

- Liberté de discuter librement des accords entre le Corps Médical et la Sécurité Sociale.

En l'absence de «convention» entre le Corps Médical et la Sécurité Sociale, la loi prévoit que les assurés sociaux sont remboursés près de 10 fois moins, bien qu'ils payent des cotisations égales. Ainsi, on oblige le Corps Médical à accepter des conditions d'exercice souvent contraires à vos intérêts de malades.

Ces libertés dépendent des Pouvoirs Publics:

c'est un problème politique

Votre vote en mars 78, peut donc modifier la manière dont vous serez soignés.

SOURCE: Union Nationale pour la Défense des Assurés Sociaux, *Le Monde* (26 oct. 1977) p.10 (adapté).

Exploitation du texte

1 Expliquez en quelques mots le sens des termes/phrases suivants:
praticiens, les cheminots, la R.A.T.P., l'Aide Médicale, Assistance
Publique, clinique, convention.

2 Analysez l'organisation typographique de ce texte en commentant
son effet.

3 A qui les auteurs de ce texte s'adressent-ils, comment le sait-on, quel
est leur but et y parviennent-ils?

4 Rédigez un reportage de presse critiquant les arguments présentés
dans ce texte.

Texte 3.5   En votre âme et conscience!

Le 'paiement à l'acte' du médecin est-il immoral, *susceptible d'accroître
indûment la consommation médicale* et coupable de réduire l'action
médicale à une action purement curative? Ou bien est-il le seul moyen
qui subsiste encore, pour le patient, de contrôler le pouvoir médical et
d'équilibrer la relation médecin-malade, en ôtant *sa toute-puissance de
bienfaiteur* et en le rendant dépendant, personnellement, de ses patients?

JEAN DE COULIBŒUF – Hors du paiement à l'acte par le patient lui-
même, *le médecin devient un fonctionnaire ou un apôtre*: deux êtres
parfaitement inaptes à la fonction médicale.

JEAN GUYOTAT – Le paiement à l'acte diminue *l'endettement affectif*
par rapport au médecin et un certain degré de contrainte morale donc.
Cependant, cet endettement n'existe que si ce malade est suivi personnellement pendant un temps suffisant. Le problème se pose moins en
milieu hospitalier, par exemple. A mon avis, le système français actuel
paraît être le meilleur car il permet de répondre à toutes les variétés de
demandes. Autrement dit, l'idéal me semble être que soit conservée
pour tout médecin qui le désire la possibilité d'un mode de fonctionnement public et d'un mode de fonctionnement privé. Mais *le remboursement à l'acte* n'est pas entièrement satisfaisant, surtout parce que *sa
valeur n'est cotée qu*'en fonction du degré de spécialisation et du coût
des appareils. La consultation est insuffisamment remboursée, ce qui ne
permet pas au médecin de répondre valablement aux aspects psychologiques de la demande de son patient.

FRANÇOIS GREMY – Le paiement à l'acte du médecin invite à multiplier
les actes et à choisir les actes remboursés au taux le plus élevé. C'est en
ce sens qu'il devient immoral. Les actes de prévention n'étant pas
remboursés par la Sécurité sociale, *l'action curative devient seule possible.*
L'expérience ne semble pas confirmer l'hypothèse que le pouvoir médical
est diminué par le paiement par le malade, le prestige étant directement

lié à l'importance des *honoraires*. *Le paiement à la fonction* par des collectivités publiques (municipalités, Assistance publique, *mutuelles*, etc.) semble être la solution.

SOURCE: N. Bensaid, *Le Nouvel Observateur* (31 janv. 1977) p.57 (adapté).

Exploitation du texte

1 Expliquez en quelques mots le sens et les allusions des expressions en italique.

2 Faites un résumé en moins de 100 mots des arguments présentés dans le texte en réponse aux questions posées dans le premier paragraphe.

3 A votre avis, le système français actuel de rémunération des médecins est-il le meilleur? Justifiez votre point de vue en vous servant de comparaisons avec le système britannique.

Texte 3.6 La constitution de votre dossier d'assurance maladie

Certaines formalités administratives vous paraissent parfois fastidieuses. Elles sont pourtant indispensables.

De nombreux dossiers ne peuvent être payés parce qu'ils ne sont pas identifiés.

Pour éviter ceci, veuillez suivre ces quelques conseils:

TOUTE DEMANDE DE REMBOURSEMENT DOIT COMPRENDRE

- la feuille de soins;
- les ordonnances;
- les vignettes collées à l'emplacement prévu à cet effet sur la feuille de soins
- et pour tout changement survenu dans l'état-civil de votre famille (mariage, naissance, décès), une fiche d'état-civil établie par la mairie ou par votre caisse sur présentation du livret de famille.

Si vous êtes salarié, vous devez joindre:

- l'attestation annuelle d'activité qui vous a été délivrée par votre employeur. Le volet de l'attestation destiné à la Caisse Primaire d'Assurance Maladie doit être joint à votre première demande de remboursement postérieur au 1er Avril. L'attestation n'est valable que pour les prestations en nature (remboursement des soins).
- A défaut les bulletins de paie des trois mois précédant les soins.
- S'il y a lieu un récépissé d'inscription comme demandeur d'emploi délivré par l'Agence Nationale pour l'Emploi et le bulletin de paie précédant cette inscription
- Pour tout enfant âgé de plus de 16 ans, le 1er dossier postérieur au 30 Septembre de chaque année doit comporter un certificat de scolarité ou de contrat d'apprentissage.

Document continued on following page

En cas d'arrêt de travail ou de prolongation d'arrêt de travail pour maladie.

● Envoyez dans les 48 heures, la formule d'avis d'arrêt de travail ou de prolongation, remplie et signée par le médecin;

● Faites remplir par l'employeur l'attestation indiquant la période d'arrêt de travail, même si le travail n'a pas été repris et envoyez-la au plus tôt à votre caisse en vue du règlement.

En cas de soins spéciaux (ex: cures thermales — prothèses — placement en établissements spécialisés, etc. . .)

● Faites parvenir au contrôle médical de votre caisse, la 'demande d'entente préalable' dûment remplie par votre praticien (ou auxiliaire médical).

La feuille de soins peut être utilisée pendant 15 jours. Si, pendant cette période vous consultez plusieurs fois le même médecin, présentez-lui la feuille établie le premier jour pour qu'il n'ait pas à vous en délivrer une nouvelle.

● Si le malade est un ayant-droit (épouse, enfant) vous devez indiquer son nom, son prénom, sa date de naissance, son lien de parenté avec l'assuré mais aussi sa profession. S'il n'a pas d'activité professionnelle, indiquez néant.

● N'oubliez pas de signer votre feuille de soins.

Toute feuille non signée est retournée à l'assuré.

LISEZ ATTENTIVEMENT ET REMPLISSEZ CORRECTEMENT
TOUTES LES RUBRIQUES DES IMPRIMES QUI VOUS SONT REMIS

SOURCE: Supplément au *Guide Assurance Maladie*, (Paris: UCANSS, 1977) pp.1-2 (adapté).

Exploitation du texte

1 Expliquez en quelques mots le sens des termes/phrases suivants: la feuille de soins, les ordonnances, les vignettes, état-civil, livret de famille, les prestations en nature, un récipissé d'inscription, un ayant-droit, néant.

2 Résumez en moins de 200 mots et à la troisième personne la procédure à suivre pour se faire rembourser et pour recevoir des indemnités en cas de maladie.

3 A qui faut-il s'adresser pour se procurer les différents documents qui doivent être transmis à la Caisse?

4 A votre avis, ces formalités administratives sont-elles 'fastidieuses'? Dans le cas d'une réponse positive, commentez les conséquences éventuelles pour le malade.

5 Sur quel ton est-ce que cette procédure est présentée? Quel semble être le rapport entre les auteurs et le malade?

Texte 3.7 Votre retraite en danger

Les multiples régimes de retraite français sont très complexes. C'est un fait connu. Ils ne sont plus sûrs. C'est un problème nouveau.

'Vous avez 45 ans, il serait temps de penser à votre retraite.' C'est le langage surprenant qu'un agent d'assurances tient à Mme Danièle B., cadre d'une entreprise parisienne. Il veut la convaincre de prendre une assurance vie. D'abord, Mme B. ne comprend pas: mais à quoi servent les cotisations que ses employeurs et elle-même paient régulièrement depuis vingt ans?

'Fausse sécurité, répond son interlocuteur. Le complément que permet d'obtenir l'assurance vie n'est donc pas un luxe. C'est une nécessité.'

Récemment, le Premier ministre lui-même affirmait: 'On ne pourra pas, dans ce pays, continuer à concevoir un système d'avantages sociaux à partir du *mécanisme de répartition.* Il faudra bien, comme dans d'autres pays, en venir à des mécanismes de *capitalisation.*' Un avant-goût des difficultés qui se profilent à l'horizon de 1985.

Croyant accumuler des droits, les Français accumuleraient-ils surtout des illusions? Leur inquiétude est d'autant plus vive qu'ils ne comprennent rien, plus rien à leur système vieillesse, source des revenus de 10 millions d'entre eux. Sa complexité croissante les déconcerte. En 1977, un sondage révèle que 80% des salariés ignorent tout de leurs droits à la retraite.

Explorer le système de retraite des salariés, c'est déjà partir à l'aventure. Attachez vos ceintures, puisque ce système ressemble à une fusée à trois étages! Premier étage, le plus simple, le plus rudimentaire, si l'on peut dire: la retraite de la Sécurité sociale ou *pension de base.* Elle concerne tout le monde et peut aller jusqu'à 50% du salaire moyen des dix meilleures années de la carrière, *dans la limite du plafond de la Sécurité sociale,* fixé actuellement à 4 000 Francs par mois, ou 48 000 Francs par an. Concrètement, qu'est-ce que cela signifie? D'abord que, dans le meilleur des cas, elle ne dépassera pas 2 000 Francs, la moitié du plafond. Ensuite, qu'elle sera de la moitié du salaire réel lorsque celui-ci est inférieur au plafond. Et c'est le cas de la grosse masse des rémunérations. Par exemple, pour un salaire de 3 000 Francs, on aura 1 500 Francs de retraite Sécurité sociale.

Surtout, il s'agit là d'un maximum. Pour avoir droit à une retraite pleine, entière, il faut la prendre à 65 ans et avoir cotisé pendant les trente-sept ans et demi réglementaires (150 trimestres). Lorsqu'on ne répond pas à ces deux conditions, la pension est réduite en proportion. Sauf s'il est ancien combattant, prisonnier ou déporté, inapte au travail ou manuel effectuant des travaux pénibles, le salarié qui décide de 'décrocher' à 60 ans, âge d'ouverture des droits à la retraite, se verra appliquer un taux de 25%. Quant au conjoint d'un retraité décédé, il n'a droit qu'à une pension dite 'de réversion', limitée à 50% de la pension normale. Une disposition particulièrement contestable.

Deuxième étage de la fusée: *les retraites complémentaires.* Résultant d'accords entre le patronat et les syndicats, elles ont été étendues progressivement, à partir de 1961, jusqu'à être pratiquement généralisées en 1973. Désormais, les cadres et les travailleurs agricoles en bénéficient comme les autres salariés. Au total, une quarantaine de régimes – pas moins – dont l'Arrco (Association des régimes de retraites complémentaires) assure la coordination et l'harmonisation.

Calculées le plus souvent selon *un système de points*, ces retraites complémentaires représentent, pour une cotisation de 4% (le minimum), 20% du salaire d'activité des non-cadres: pratiquement la moitié du régime général, le tiers des prestations totales de retraite. On peut donc atteindre un total de 70% du salaire.

Troisième étage, enfin, particulièrement 'sophistiqué': le régime de l'Agirc (Association générale des retraites des cadres), créé, *paritairement*, lui aussi, dès 1947. Il fonctionne également selon un système de points. Ses ressources proviennent d'une cotisation prélevée sur la part du salaire qui dépasse le plafond de la Sécurité sociale, jusqu'à un second plafond quatre fois plus haut: 16 000 Francs par mois, ou 192 000 Francs par an. Ainsi les cadres cotisent-ils trois fois: au régime général des salariés et à l'Arrco jusqu'au premier plafond et, au-dessus, à l'Agirc. Quatre fois, même, pour les cadres supérieurs, auxquels certaines possibilités sont offertes au-delà du second plafond. Pourtant, selon une estimation de *la C.g.c.,* la retraite globale des cadres n'atteint que 60% du dernier salaire dans les cas heureux.

Comment trouver son chemin dans *le dédale des régimes spéciaux*? Il n'y a pas de formule miracle pour calculer le montant de la retraite. Sécurité sociale, Arrco et Agirc en sont conscientes: elles rivalisent d'initiatives pour permettre à chacun d'estimer ses droits.

SOURCE: M. Jacques, *L'Express* (10–16 juillet 1978) pp.28–30 (adapté).

Exploitation du texte

1 Expliquez en vos propres mots le sens des termes/phrases en italique, sauf l'en-tête.

2 Résumez en quelques phrases les grandes lignes des 'trois étages de la fusée' présentés dans le texte.

3 Examinez le bien-fondé des constatations de l'en-tête, à savoir que les multiples régimes de retraite sont très complexes et qu'ils ne sont plus sûrs?

4 Pourquoi l'auteur décrit-il le droit à la pension 'de réversion' comme une 'disposition particulièrement contestable'?

5 Expliquez pourquoi certains cadres peuvent cotiser quatre fois pour leur retraite.

6 Formulez une dizaine de questions qui pourraient être posées dans un sondage sur les retraites en France.

Texte 3.8 Le cadre et la 'mamma'

Pour aborder *le tracassin complexe* de la Sécurité sociale, le pouvoir s'est présenté avec des idées simples. *La 'Sécu' crie famine?* Qu'on la nourrisse! Comment cela? Eh bien, *en ponctionnant*, quoi de plus naturel, *ses bénéficiaires!* Mais alors, ponctionnera-t-on tous les bénéficiaires? *Que nenni!* Plutôt les cadres, comme d'habitude.

La Sécurité sociale est aujourd'hui *une opulente 'mamma' familière*, envahissante, dispendieuse, complaisante, qui allaite de son sein innombrable tous les Français. La sécurité qu'elle dispense, ce n'est pas rien. Cette 'mamma' nationale a supprimé – ne l'oublions jamais – ce scandale de l'homme civilisé: la mort du pauvre par incapacité de soins. Elle a introduit une des seules égalités possibles, celle des citoyens devant la maladie.

De tout cela, les cadres français acceptent le principe. De surcroît, par éducation économique, ils renoncent pour la plupart à ce *fantasme poujadiste* et imbécile qu'il existerait, pour combler un déficit, *de l'argent*, si je puis dire, *'gratuit'*. L'argent gratuit, ils savent que *la planche à billets* qui le fabrique, fabrique en même temps une baisse du niveau de vie. *Voyez les Anglais!*

Mais avant de se laisser 'tondre', les cadres se posent certaines questions, *et la moutarde leur monte au nez*.

1. La première question consiste à se demander si, avant de trouver des recettes, on ne pourrait pas diminuer les dépenses. Chacun a dans l'esprit des exemples d'abus révoltants. Médecins laxistes distribuant *des certificats de complaisance* et *des poudres de perlimpinpin* à profusion. Hôpitaux mal gérés où l'on ne sait plus ce qui coûte le plus cher des lits vides ou des lits occupés. Cures thermales *à gogo*, etc. Sur tout cela, on nous promet contrôles et sanctions, comme on nous les promet depuis dix ans. Il serait temps qu'on intervienne avec brutalité, et que le Français, ainsi, renonce à son record du monde, celui de la consommation de médicaments par habitant.

Hélas, trois fois hélas, il ne faut pas *se leurrer*: tous ces abus ne représentent qu'une part relativement faible (sauf pour les hôpitaux) des dépenses de la 'mamma'.

2. La deuxième question est politique. Les cadres constatent que s'il y a égalité des citoyens devant la maladie – et donc égalité de ce que la Sécurité sociale leur rembourse – eux, en tout cas, vont débourser plus que les autres. Ils savent à leurs dépens que les hauts revenus, par le système de la progressivité de l'impôt direct, contribuent déjà, plus que les autres – ce qui est légitime – aux dépenses de la nation. Alors, ils se demandent si l'accumulation – à deux niveaux – de cette disparité des contributions ne va pas produire une dose d'égalitarisme insupportable. Au point où nous voici rendus, quelques intrépides se disent même: pourquoi ne pas faire supporter la sécurité sociale par l'impôt direct, de préférence *perçu*, comme les cotisations sociales, *à la source*. Ce serait sans doute aussi lourd, mais à la fois plus juste et moins douloureux.

3. La troisième question est de savoir si seuls les salariés, et *en l'occurrence* les cadres, vont devoir *'trinquer'* une première fois devant l'impôt, et désormais une seconde fois devant les cotisations sociales. Savez-vous, à considérer leurs cotisations sociales, que 97,1% des agriculteurs n'auraient qu'un revenu égal ou inférieur au SMIC? Enorme farce. . .

Quand toute une collectivité triche, il est clair que le non-tricheur, *celui dont les salaires sont transparents*, est vite dépouillé. Dans la crise mondiale où nous sommes, c'est pourtant du cadre français, de ses capacités d'invention et de responsabilité que notre nation aura le plus besoin. Il ne faut pas le rendre fou. *Ou absent.*

SOURCE: C. Imbert, *Le Point* (18 déc. 1978) p.41.

Exploitation du texte

1 Expliquez en quelques mots le sens et les allusions des termes/ phrases en italique.

2 Résumez en moins de 200 mots les différentes étapes des arguments développés dans le texte.

3 Relevez les expressions et les traits linguistiques plus propres au langage parlé qu'à un style littéraire.

4 En vous servant du texte 3.4 comme modèle, récrivez ce texte à la manière d'un document publicitaire provenant du syndicat des cadres.

Texte 3.9   Sécurité sociale: adapter la nature des ressources à celle des dépenses

On s'apercevra en effet, notamment en confrontant les prélèvements sur les salaires et sur les gains professionnels non salariaux, qu'il faut faire une distinction absolument fondamentale entre deux types de prestations sociales, correspondant respectivement aux deux fonctions de la Sécurité sociale: garantie du revenu professionnel ou garantie d'un minimum social.

Les premières sont des prestations de remplacement, destinées, par définition, à compenser la perte, provisoire ou définitive, totale ou partielle, du revenu professionnel: indemnités de maladie, rentes d'invalidité, pensions de vieillesse, *prestations en espèces* en cas d'accidents du travail. Il s'agit alors, par un mécanisme d'assurance plus ou moins déformé, d'étaler sur les périodes d'activité et les périodes d'inactivité les gains acquis pendant les premières.

Tout naturellement cet étalement doit être financé par un prélèvement sur le revenu garanti: la relation triangulaire entre revenu professionnel, revenu de remplacement, cotisation assise sur le premier est d'une parfaite cohérence. Peu importe que cette garantie soit assurée par un régime légal ou un régime complémentaire: le problème du plafond est ici, somme toute, relativement secondaire. Aussi secondaire le problème de la sous-évaluation du revenu professionnel, notamment par les professions non salariées: cette sous-évaluation se répercutant sur le montant des prestations, le fraudeur sera pénalisé. Tant pis pour lui.

Avec les autres prestations – prestations 'en nature' de l'assurance maladie, prestations familiales, allocations de base pour personnes âgées indigentes – changement total de décor! En effet, *tout rapport logique entre ces prestations et le revenu professionnel des intéressés disparaît complètement*: leur financement par des prélèvements assis sur ce revenu professionnel a diverses explications historiques, mais n'est plus aujourd'hui qu'*un anachronisme aberrant*. De toute façon, l'idée d'assurance à laquelle certaines organisations de cadres entendent toujours se référer pour l'assurance maladie ne permet d'établir aucun lien entre la contribution et le revenu professionnel: personne n'a jamais songé à établir un tel lien entre ce revenu et, par example, les primes d'assurance automobile. Et *cette idée d'assurance devient carrément inepte* pour les prestations familiales ou pour les allocations de vieillesse subordonnées à une condition d'indigence.

En réalité, ces prestations du deuxième type traduisent une autre conception de la Sécurité sociale: il ne s'agit plus de garantir un revenu professionnel, mais de garantir un minimum social par l'attribution de prestations de base, à caractère alimentaire et de le garantir à tous.

Ces prestations alimentaires exprimant donc une solidarité nationale à l'endroit des malades, des enfants, des vieillards indigents, etc., la contribution de chaque citoyen à ces politiques nationales de la santé, de la famille, du troisième âge, doit être établie en fonction de ses capacités contributives, et *deux questions relatives à* l'imposition *sont alors inéluctables*: pourquoi un plafond qui la rend dégressive pour les hauts revenus? Pourquoi l'asseoir sur les seuls revenus professionnels?

Si, en effet, les salaires constituent la quasi-totalité des revenus des salariés, de récentes études ont montré qu'il en allait très différemment pour les professions non salariées: le revenu professionnel est loin de représenter la totalité des revenus de ces catégories: et la différence échappe à toute imposition sociale. Or, contrairement à ce que nous avons vu à propos des prestations prenant la forme de revenus de remplacement, *la sous-évaluation n'entraîne ici aucune pénalisation*: si ce n'est celle du voisin... et l'alignement des cotisations perd toute signification réelle.

Pour cet ensemble de raisons. Il convient donc certainement de conserver le revenu professionnel comme assiette des contributions pour les prestations de remplacement: en revanche, pour les autres, il faudra demander moins aux cotisations professionnelles et *s'engager* expressément, serait-ce à pas mesurés, *dans la voie de la fiscalisation. L'éternel problème du plafond sera alors, enfin! dépassé.* Et si l'on veut mettre nos structures sociofiscales à l'heure européenne, en nous inspirant des exemples que nous fournissent nos voisins les plus dynamiques, c'est à l'impôt sur le revenu – malgré tout le plus démocratique, si l'on voulait bien procéder à certaines réformes toujours remises – qu'il faudra faire appel de façon de plus en plus systématique. Sans complexe.

SOURCE: J.-J. Dupeyroux, *Le Monde* (21 sept. 1976) p.22 (adapté).

Exploitation du texte

1 Expliquez en quelques mots le sens des phrases/termes en italique.

2 Résumez en moins de 200 mots les éléments de la 'distinction absolument fondamentale entre deux types de prestations sociales' proposée par l'auteur et les réformes qu'il suggère.

3 Expliquez comment le système proposé par l'auteur apporterait une solution au problème de la sous-évaluation du revenu professionnel.

4 Pourquoi est-ce que 'tout rapport logique entre les prestations "en nature" et le revenu professionnel des intéressés' disparaîtrait?

5 En quoi les structures sociofiscales françaises ne sont-elles pas 'à l'heure européenne'?

Exercices de comparaison et d'application

1 Reprenez les rubriques suggérées dans la première question des Exercices de comparaison et d'application du Chapitre 2 pour résumer, sous forme d'un tableau, les caractéristiques de chacun de ces textes.

2 Comparez les traits que vous avez relevés avec ceux qui ressortaient pour les textes du chapitre précédent.

3 Imaginez un débat sur les avantages et les inconvénients des services sociaux en France et en Grande Bretagne, y compris le rôle joué par le secteur privé dans les deux systèmes.

4 Ecrivez une dissertation d'environ 1500 à 2000 mots sur un des sujets suivants:

(i) 'Instrument d'équilibrage des risques en matière de maladie et d'accidents, instrument de réduction des inégalités sociales, instrument de la solidarité entre les générations, instrument de la compensation – au moins partielle – des charges familiales, la Sécurité sociale est étroitement dépendante de la démographie, à la fois dans ses ressources et dans ses dépenses.' (*Démographie et Sécurité sociale*) Commentez dans le contexte français.

(ii) Maintenant que les besoins fondamentaux sont plus ou moins satisfaits, la santé fait partie de ce qu'on considère comme un droit. Examinez le bien-fondé et les conséquences de cette conception de la santé dans le contexte français.

4

Education

Government offices of statistics closely monitor fluctuations in the birthrate and subsequent changes in the age structure of the population so that the potential demand for goods and services can be forecasted. In the field of education one of the most important consequences of a falling birthrate is that the number of children of school age decreases. Since a smaller family size is considered a permanent feature of present-day population trends in France, ministers of education are no longer giving priority in their budgetary recommendations to major school building programmes or to the massive recruitment of teachers, as they did throughout the 1950s and 1960s. Instead they are seeking to ensure that demands created by changes in the distribution of the school population are satisfied: the expectations are that more very young children will require places in nursery schools; families with young children are likely to move to areas of economic expansion in order to find employment; more young people may be induced to stay longer in education, in order to gain better qualifications and to avoid unemployment. The present respite can also be used to look for ways of improving the quality as well as the quantity of the services provided and of solving some of the problems which have become endemic in the French educational system.

Many of the perennial topics of discussion in the education debate are common to other Western industrialised nations. They concern the general principles and underlying objectives of education, the organisational structure of the system and of school life, its cost both to the nation and to the individual, the role of the private sector, the recruitment and training of teachers, syllabuses and teaching methodology, access to education at all levels and the system's effectiveness as a social service. Although France has reached a stage of economic, social and political development similar to that of her European neighbours, there are still many fundamental differences both in the nature of the problems with which it has to contend and in the solutions adopted. Attention here will be concentrated mainly on the peculiarities of the

French system and on the issues which have been most frequently debated over the past decade.

Principles and objectives

According to the Education Act of 11 July 1975, of which extracts are presented in Texte 4.1, every child has the right to free schooling, and attendance is compulsory between the ages of 6 and 16. The stated aims of schooling are threefold: to encourage personal development by providing education suited to each child's abilities and by stimulating his cultural awareness, to train him for adulthood and to prepare him for his role as a responsible member of society.

The objectives of higher education, which operated independently from the Ministry of Education from 1974 to 1981, are set out in the Higher Education Act of 12 November 1968 (*Loi d'orientation de l'enseignement supérieur*): to pursue the search for knowledge, to promote learning and to offer the opportunity for education in its widest sense. Universities and other institutions of higher education are, like schools, expected to serve both society in general, by training administrators and professionals, and the individual, by helping him to develop his abilities and by preparing him for his chosen career. The right of all workers to continue education and training throughout life is guaranteed by the Act of 16 July 1971 and restated in that of 17 July 1978.

The avowed objectives of the French educational system today differ little from those presented by Condorcet in 1792 when he proposed democratic principles intended to serve as a basis for organising education (quoted in the essay questions at the end of this chapter). Condorcet suggested that, if these aims were achieved, the equality proclaimed by law could become a reality. Education is now a universal social service, and the educational system has undisputedly become a major socialising agent collaborating and competing with the family to offer instruction, protection and recreation. Nearly two hundred years have elapsed since Condorcet formulated his educational ideal, but it is by no means certain that his precepts, or the objectives set out in the education acts referred to above, have been generally adopted, for there is still no general consensus about the role of education in society. The main political parties[1] have held, and continue to hold, such divergent views about the latent and manifest functions of the educational system that a change of government is likely to lead to radical reforms (see Texte 4.2). There is no agreement between providers (teachers and administrators) and users (pupils and their parents) either about the services which should be offered or the means of making them most effective.

Organisational structure

The administrative framework of the French educational system of today owes its most salient characteristics to Napoleon I. During the First Empire (1804–15), a rigid centrally controlled structure was created, imposing uniformity of teaching standards, syllabuses and examination patterns throughout the country. It was administered by a single decision-making body responsible for recruiting teachers, approving national diplomas and dictating the content of teaching programmes and teaching methods. Napoleon instituted a binary system: the state offered a high standard of secondary and tertiary education as a means of training the officers, civil servants and scientists required to organise the efficient running of the machinery of the state and thus serve its interests; for the masses, elementary education was provided by poorly trained teachers, often in church schools, with the intention of guaranteeing their docility and unquestioning acceptance of the moral precepts laid down by the state. The foundations were prepared for a two-tiered centralised structure, in which the church was relegated to a subordinate role. Most of the reforms which have been formulated, and sometimes implemented, since the beginning of the nineteenth century, and particularly those in recent years, have been drawn up in an attempt to solve the problems resulting from centralised control, from the disparities between elitist and mass education and from the uncertain status of religious and private schools.

Administrative framework and budget

Education at all levels is now under the control of the Minister of Education, who appoints inspectors to act as intermediaries between him and the schools, ensuring that his instructions are carried out efficiently. For administrative purposes, France is divided into twenty-five areas (*académies*) each headed by a rector, who supervises and co-ordinates the different sectors of education and is responsible to the minister. At the national level eight directorates are responsible for the various stages of education as well as general administration, staffing, finance, building and equipment. Local authorities provide and maintain school premises and equipment, but every building programme must be approved by the rector and may be financed from central government funds.

Since 1968 the universities are autonomous: they can organise their own teaching programmes, formulate their own constitutions and decide how to spend their budget. However this independence is limited, for it is the minister who determines the amount of money to be allocated to each institution and who approves diplomas, and employers generally accept only nationally recognised qualifications. The share of the national budget devoted to education (18.8 per cent in 1976) is greater than for any other single item. The amount spent on education grew very rapidly in the 1960s and then increased more slowly during the 1970s, as the size of the school population fluctuated. Although education in state schools has for a long time been offered 'free' of charge, it is only in recent years that this principle has been extended to cover textbooks and school transport. It has moreover been necessary to make available financial support for low income families to ensure that normal schooling can take place for every child, and in 1979 it was estimated that some 2.3 million families were eligible for such a grant. University fees are only nominal and cannot therefore be seen as a factor prohibiting access to further education. Few university students are however in receipt of a grant to support them through higher education (about 11 per cent of students in 1975-6), and approximately one third of all students live with their parents (more than 55 per cent of students in Paris). Grants are awarded on the basis of family income and the number of dependents, but at a level which is considered inadequate to live on, and it is estimated that more than half of all students work more than twenty hours a week to support themselves.

Opinion is divided about how much the nation should be expected to spend on educating its young. Doubts are expressed about whether the money is being used wisely and fairly, for, as will be shown, not everybody derives the same benefits from the educational system.

Private education

When, under the Third Republic, school attendance was made compulsory for children aged 6 to 13 by the Education Act of 1882, the neutrality of state education in respect of religious, philosophical and political matters was asserted, and the separation of church and state in 1905 confirmed the secular nature of education. After a period of uneasy relationships, legislation was introduced in 1959 with the *Loi Debré* to allow religious bodies as well as other private organisations to co-exist with public institutions and to receive state aid, subject to their acceptance of state control of teaching standards. Private institutions can now choose between two types of contract with the state: a contract of association, under which the state covers running costs and pays teaching staff, who must hold the same qualifications as teachers in state schools and observe the same regulations, curricula and examinations patterns; a simple contract, under which the school is responsible for meeting its own running costs and enjoys more flexibility in the teaching programme, but whereby approved teachers may be paid by the state. In both cases school inspectors ensure that the regulations on matters such as attendance are observed and that the teaching conforms with moral and legal requirements. It can include religious instruction, whereas no such provision is made in the state schools.

In 1975−6 more than 16 per cent of all schoolchildren were in private schools. The proportion in the final years of secondary schooling was particularly high, with more than a fifth of the total; slightly more girls than boys were in the private sector, and the numbers for the west of France were far above average, corresponding to a relatively high level of religious observance. Investigations into the socio-occupational origins of children in private education in the third and fifth years of secondary schooling demonstrate that the categories of employers in industry and commerce, of professional workers and farmers are over-represented.

It must be remembered that for more than a century and a half the state has provided boarding facilities (approximately 8 per cent of pupils are boarders), and one of the primary purposes of the private sector has not therefore been to answer this particular need. Fees in the state boarding schools are low, whereas in private schools they may vary substantially depending upon whether the school has a contract with the state − as is the case for 98 per cent of all Catholic boarding schools but not for most of the non-denominational schools − and upon the prestige which they enjoy. Since the state system in France has offered education of a high academic standard, the private sector has not fulfilled the role of training an elite, although a few private schools have acquired a high reputation, for example, the Ecole Alsacienne or Collège de Sainte-Barbe, competing with the most prestigious *lycées*, such as Louis-le-Grand, Henri IV or Janson-de-Sailly. In the past children were generally sent to private schools because of the religious convictions of their parents (90 per cent of all private schools are denominational, but between 1960 and 1975 the number of clerical teachers they employed fell from 50,000 to 10,000 and now represents only one tenth of teachers in private education). There are many other reasons which are today prompting parents to opt out of the state system. Many private schools have shifted their emphasis from religious instruction to academic attainment, and, since they have generally continued to be smaller than the state schools, they have been able to maintain contact with parents, uphold discipline and avoid the problems of strikes and the demoralisation of staff which beset the state schools. The teaching framework has been more flexible, and experimental methods have been more easily adopted in some of the progressive schools. Far from being phased out, the private schools are gradually increasing their intake and would seem able to offer a viable alternative to the state sector.

It is unlikely that the struggle for control of education will ever again rouse the same level of animosity between warring fractions as in the nineteenth century (*querelle scolaire*), but there was a hint that the old strife had not been entirely forgotton, when, in the campaign leading up to the general elections of 1978, the issue was raised by the left-wing parties. A report drawn up in 1976 by Mexandeau, a Socialist member of parliament, restated that the private sector of education would be nationalised if the Left came to power. The government retaliated by adopting a series of proposals designed to assist private education: loans were offered to private schools to help them comply with the requirements of the Haby Reform, and the working conditions and status of teachers in private education were made equivalent to those in state schools. However the interest of the electorate was not aroused, and the Socialists decided not to exploit the issue further in order to avoid alienating some of their supporters. During the 1981 presidential and general election campaign Mitterand confirmed his commitment to a unified, rather than uniform, secular state education service but made it clear that any changes affecting the private sector would be subject to negotiation with those concerned.

Reforming the system
The history of French education since the Second World War is one of reform and counter-reform, as piecemeal attempts have been made to implement the proposals of the Langevin-Wallon Commission, set up in 1944 to investigate how the educational system might be democratised. Their report of 1947 constituted a blueprint for far-reaching change and suggested how all the proposals that Condorcet had made a century and a half earlier could become realities. The reforms the report recommended were to be introduced over a period of five years, but more than thirty years later the programme has still not been completed. It would seem that every new minister of education must justify his period of office by conceiving a reform by which he will be remembered and which may bring the system one step nearer to the Langevin-Wallon ideal: Billières tried to introduce the common core (*tronc commun*) in the first year of secondary schooling in 1957; Berthoin reviewed the length of schooling and the provision of a counselling service in 1959; Fouchet reformed vocational training in 1965; Faure overhauled the university structure in 1968; Guichard tackled technical education in 1971; Fontanet gave his name to reforms of teaching methods, educational guidance and 'the 10 per cent'[2] in 1972-3.

The most significant attempts at reform in the 1970s were those of Haby, and they afford an interesting example of the process of change within the educational system. Haby was appointed as Minister of Education in 1974, the sixteenth minister in as many years. He was an educationalist rather than a politician, the son of a manual worker, who had first become a primary school teacher and then, after successfully completing a university education, had been a headmaster, university teacher, school inspector and rector. On taking office, he stated that he would pursue the reforms already set in motion by his predecessor, but he was soon formulating different proposals, and before his plans had completed the design stage, Haby had to contend with a wave of strikes. The opposition came particularly from the left-wing *Fédération de l'Education Nationale* (grouping about twenty-four unions, including the Communist-controlled *Syndicat National de l'Enseignement Secondaire* and the Socialist *Syndicat National des Instituteurs*), from the Communist-affiliated parents' association, *Fédération Cornec* and the pupils' organisation, *Syndicat National des Lycées et Collèges.*

Haby's personal acquaintance with the teaching profession did not however ensure an easy passage for his proposals. After long discussions with representatives of parents, teachers and pupils, resulting in modifications or outright rejection, gradually some of the proposals outlined in the 1975 Haby Reform have been instituted. They concern all stages of schooling. At primary level the age for school entry was lowered to 5 years (in effect the vast majority of children already started school at this age), and parents were given the right to appeal against the decision that their child should repeat a year. Haby's suggestion that the first year of schooling should be extended over two years for slow learners was rapidly abandoned in response to the opposition which it provoked. At secondary level the common core was consolidated, as indicated by the introduction of the term, *collège,* replacing the former *collège d'enseignement général* and *collège d'enseignement secondaire,* symbolising the unity of the first level of secondary education and confirming the comprehensive principle instituted in 1963. Greater autonomy was granted to teachers in organising programmes by the setting of objectives rather than rigid syllabuses. Streaming was abolished, and instead remedial groups were set up. At the upper school level a name change signified the intention to improve the status of technical education: the *collège d'enseignement technique* became the *lycée d'enseignement professionnel,* whilst the former *lycée technique* was absorbed into other types of *lycée.* The reintroduction of a school-leaving examination in two parts has been repeatedly postponed and should now take effect in the 1980s.

When in 1976 the *Société Française d'Enquêtes pour Sondages* undertook a survey of teachers' attitudes towards the Haby Reform (the results of which prompted the comments made in Texte 4.2), it found that only 1 per cent agreed that the proposals offered a solution to the basic problems of the educational system, 10 per cent felt that they might bring some improvements, whereas 57 per cent thought the Reform would not solve any of the underlying problems, and 25 per cent claimed that it would make the situation worse. The almost automatic and spontaneous rejection of any government measures has become a standard feature within the reform process in a society where the teaching profession is deeply suspicious of any action which attacks the school system without first seeking to change society. The fate of any reform has come to depend upon the willingness of teachers to collaborate with central administration, as aptly summarised in the frequently quoted axiom: the minister proposes but teachers dispose (*le ministre propose et les enseignants disposent*' from the proverb *l'homme propose et Dieu dispose*'). But teachers are not the only opposing force with which the minister has to contend: parents are becoming an increasingly powerful pressure group, as illustrated in Texte 4.3 in a description of the situation facing Beullac at the beginning of the school year soon after he replaced Haby in 1978.

The teaching profession

The negative reaction of members of the teaching profession to any government measures which might affect the structure of the educational system, or their own function within it, reflects the profound dissatisfaction felt by many teachers with their status and working conditions. At secondary level in particular teachers are demoralised and feel that they are just a cog in an enormous machine. For many young people, especially women, teaching is the only suitable opening, but compared with other public service employees, teachers in primary schools are poorly paid: they earn less than a local policeman and about the same as a skilled manual worker. They have seen their standing in the community diminish, as described in Texte 4.4, for the expansion of the school population and changing social values have created problems of discipline, communication and conflicting objectives, and the move towards a comprehensive system has highlighted status differences within the hierarchy of the teaching profession.

Teachers undergo different types of training according to the level of education they wish to enter. For primary schools theoretical and practical training, lasting for two years, is provided in one of the 150 or so *écoles normales*. Entrance is by competitive examinations after the school-leaving certificate. Successful applicants are provided with residential accommodation or a grant to cover subsistence, and they must commit themselves to teach for eight years in return. From 1980 the period of training is due to be extended to three years, the first year being probationary in order to assess the suitability of applicants. The teaching degree awarded at the end of the training period will have the same status as a university degree, and this reform may be seen as an attempt to revitalise primary school teaching. In the 1950s the sudden and massive increase in the population of primary school age made recruitment of teachers a priority. Anybody with the secondary school-leaving certificate could be appointed, and large numbers of women were attracted into teaching. Now that the number of children has stabilised, recruitment has become more selective, and an attempt is being made to redress the sex imbalance. In spite of the laws prohibiting sexual discrimination, a much higher proportion of male than of female applicants is being accepted for places in the *écoles normales*. The role of primary education in determining the life chances of an individual is becoming a focal point in the ongoing debate about the democratisation of education, and it seems likely that a concerted effort will be made in the next decade to ensure that primary school teachers are better equipped to carry out the task demanded of them.

At secondary level in the *collèges*, some teachers of general subjects are experienced former primary school teachers, who were absorbed into secondary schooling either when the comprehensive system was introduced or when the school-leaving age was raised to 16 in 1967. Other teachers of general subjects are recruited by special regional training centres. Most permanent specialised teachers at secondary level hold the CAPES (*certificat d'aptitude au professorat de l'enseignement secondaire*), gained by competitive examinations open to graduates, comprising both written and oral examinations, followed by a year of supervised teaching experience. In 1974 there were eight candidates for every place and the number of posts has decreased since then. The success rate varies from one subject to another depending upon the current demand: in 1974 only 2 per cent of candidates in philosophy were awarded the qualification, and 19 per cent for mathematics. Unqualified teachers may hope to find temporary posts, but they have no security of employment and are generally given the most difficult classes in return for a lower level of pay.

For the best students the *agrégation* is the highest teaching award. Originally it was instituted to ensure the recruitment of the most competent students for posts in the *lycées*. The *agrégation* is a competitive examination designed as a test of academic performance rather than teaching ability. Successful candidates are eligible for posts as tutors in universities, but should they decide to teach in a school, they are granted privileges commensurate with their high status: they teach for a maximum of fifteen hours a week, whereas teachers holding the CAPES are scheduled for eighteen hours, teachers of general subjects for twenty-one and primary school teachers for twenty-seven; the *agrégés* can state their preferences for the classes they teach and the way in which they are timetabled, whereas less qualified teachers have little opportunity for choice.

In the past university tutors and junior lecturers (*assistants* and *maîtres assistants*), who completed a state doctorate and were considered acceptable for a tenured post by the autocratic Universities Consultative Committee had to wait for an indefinite period of time until a suitable position became vacant, enabling them to join the ranks of the most privileged section of the teaching profession (some 10,000 lecturers and professors in 1978–9). In 1978 the minister decided to eliminate untenured teaching posts (there were three times as many temporary as permanent teachers in French universities) for those who, after a period of five years, had not completed their research qualification. For those already employed on a contract basis for more than five years, it was proposed that, instead of teaching only five hours a week, teaching duties would be extended to fifteen hours. Predictably the proposals were greeted by a hostile reaction, since they were seen as a threat to the employment opportunities of untenured staff and as a further infringement of the universities' autonomy. In 1979 the minister announced that academic staff would in the future be recruited by competitive examination in order to ensure a fairer system.

The appointments procedure for teaching posts at all levels of the educational system in France is very different from that operated in Great Britain. They are not advertised in the press, and the headmaster of a school, or the head of a university department is not involved. The newly-qualified school teacher will be nominated for a post with little regard for his own preferences and will be expected to hold it for at least three years. As he accumulates years of experience, these will be taken into account, as will his personal circumstances and the marks he has been awarded by school inspectors and administrators, when he requests a transfer. Such a system has advantages: the ministry can ensure that schools with a bad reputation are allocated well qualified and experienced teachers, although it is likely that those with good ratings will try to obtain a transfer (it is significant that almost one quarter of secondary school teachers applied for a transfer in 1979); nepotism may also be prevented. There are however many disadvantages: it is not easy for a headmaster to build up a team of teachers with complementary interests and ideas; teachers may not like the school to which they are appointed, it may be some distance from their home, and they have limited control over their career structure. Even in universities appointments and promotion are subject to ministerial approval, and the individual has little opportunity for choice.

The functions which a French school teacher is expected to fulfil are much more limited than those of his British counterparts, for non-teaching duties are carried out by administrative staff. Discipline outside teaching hours is the responsibility of the *surveillants* under the direction of the *censeur* and his *conseillers pédagogiques*, who are full time permanent appointees. The *surveillants,* who work for a maximum of thirty-two hours a week, or twenty-eight hours if they also carry out administrative duties, are recruited amongst the student population for a maximum of seven years, provided that they sit their university examinations at least every two years. The last two stipulations became necessary since large numbers of students were exploiting this possibility for relatively well paid and undemanding work, instead of pursuing their studies or finding permanent employment. For *bona fide* students, posts as *surveillants* may afford an important source of income during their university career, and this can be seen as a means whereby the state avoids paying higher grants to students. Important consequences of such a system are that teaching staff have fewer opportunities than in Great Britain for contact with their pupils, and that older children have no chances during their school life to exercise responsibility in the running of the institution, considered a valuable part of training in the British system. On the other hand it can be claimed that teachers in France are able to devote their undivided attention to their teaching duties.

In the post-war period the teaching profession has become increasingly militant in defending its rights and privileges, often, it is argued, at the expense of the interests of the children it should be educating. The profession is highly politicised, as testified by the number of teachers who won seats in the 1981 general election (one third of all those elected to the National Assembly and of all ministerial appointees, including the Prime Minister, were teachers, and more than three quarters were Socialists). Whereas less than a quarter of the working population belongs to a trade union, nearly three quarters of teachers in the public sector are members of the many teachers' unions. It is not therefore surprising that most government policies for education have in recent years automatically provoked a conflict of ideologies, as argued in Texte 4.2, or that in many respects the working conditions of French teachers still compare very favourably with those in neighbouring countries.

The different stages of schooling

As the Haby Reform progressively comes into effect, the division of schooling into three distinct stages will be confirmed. It will comprise a primary level and two secondary levels. In 1975-6 approximately 11 million children were attending schools in France (excluding nursery schools). In the ten year period 1965-75, the only level at which numbers declined was in primary schools, as changes in regulations made it possible for more children to progress more quickly into secondary education and the falling birthrate began to affect the size of the school population. The most rapid growth has been at the upper school level of secondary education as more children have stayed on longer at school. Primary schools still account for the largest proportion of schoolchildren, for the most favourable staff-pupil ratios and for the largest number of school buildings, although they are considerably smaller than for other types of school.

Nursery and primary schools

The number of children attending nursery schools, for at least part of the week, has increased steeply in recent years. From 1980 all children aged 3 or above should have a place in a nursery class, if their parents so desire, and the number of children enrolled for each class should not exceed thirty-five. As intimated in Texte 4.1, one of the intentions of nursery schooling is to seek to eliminate the disadvantages resulting from an underprivileged home background, but it has been found that the social categories which derive most benefit from early schooling are those whose school performance is in any case above average. There is evidence to suggest that early schooling may consolidate advantage in such a way that progress through the school system can be predicted at this stage. Nursery schooling might, it is claimed, be a more effective compensatory mechanism if it were offered only to underprivileged groups.

The role of the nursery school is to stimulate the child's interest and to anticipate and remedy learning problems arising from physical, mental or social handicaps, so that he will adapt more easily to formal instruction in primary school. As shown in Figure 4.1, primary schooling is divided into three stages, during which the basic skills of reading, writing and arithmetic are taught according to a set programme. Importance is also attached to developing the child's artistic sensitivity and physical prowess. Both moral (as exemplified by the moral precepts listed in Texte 4.5) and civic instruction remain an essential component of the curriculum.

Figure 4.1
Nursery and primary school education

Age range	Level	Normal length in years
3 – 5	*Ecole maternelle*	0 – 3
5 – 6	*Cours préparatoire*	1
↑	*Cours élémentaire*	2
10 – 11	*Cours moyen*	2

SOURCE: author's own data.

For those who do not achieve the objectives set for each stage of primary education, there is the possibility of repeating a year. The rates vary significantly from one social category to another: in the first three years of primary school the child with a father in the middle or higher administrative grades will have only one chance in ten of repeating a year, whereas for agricultural and manual labourers the chances are one in four and one in three respectively for the first year of schooling. As the pressure on numbers has been reduced, children considered capable of doing so have been allowed to enter primary school at the age of 5 (a practice which is gradually being extended to all children), thereby compounding their early advantage. At the end of the primary school stage, it is estimated that only about 25 per cent of the pupils are progressing according to schedule, and the practice has been that children are not generally allowed to move on to secondary school until they have achieved an acceptable standard.

Secondary schools

At secondary level in the *collèges* a comprehensive system has been instituted to postpone any decisions which might prejudice future choice, and streaming has been abolished, although remedial teaching must be provided for those who need it. As indicated in Figure 4.2, all pupils follow a common curriculum in their first two years at the *collège*. This comprises French, a modern language, mathematics, economic and human sciences, handicrafts, art, music and physical education, with the intention, outlined in Texte 4.1, of providing a balanced education suited to life in present-day society. The core subjects are continued in the following two years, but other subjects are introduced, allowing a choice between more academic studies (including a second foreign language and additional science subjects, Latin or Greek) and a vocational orientation, with the possibility of sandwich periods in industry. Since some pupils will reach school-leaving age

Figure 4.2
Secondary school education at collèges

Age	Class	Cursus	
11 – 12	6ᵉ⎱ 5ᵉ⎰	Common core	Remedial
15 – 16	4ᵉ⎱ 3ᵉ⎰	Common core + options	Vocational training
		Brevet d'études du premier cycle	*Certificat d'études professionnelles*

SOURCE: author's own data.

before completing four years of secondary education, they are given the opportunity to pursue an intensive vocational training course in a specialised centre leading to a professional qualification (*certificat d'études professionnelles*). For those completing their education at the age of 16 after the standard four years of *collège*, there is the possibility of sitting a general examination in six subjects (*brevet d'études du premier cycle*), awarded on the basis of an overall pass mark.

Despite the intention that a single type of school should provide a basic guaranteed level of education to all children alike (*'un savoir minimum garanti'* in the words of Giscard d'Estaing), many reservations (see for example Texte 4.6) are expressed about the ability of the *collège* to fulfil this objective. When the comprehensive system was adopted in 1963, as in England, it involved the reorganisation of existing buildings and personnel as well as new purpose-built schools. Teachers with very different training and experience were sometimes brought together in a single institution, and the quality of equipment and teaching could vary considerably from one area to another. When there is more than one school within a catchment area, parents may be given a choice. Their ability to take advantage of the choice, and to be insistent if they feel that a particular school is likely to produce better results, is found to depend upon their own educational background and knowledge of the system. Although in theory streaming is not permitted, some institutions have managed to group children according to the age at which they enter secondary school or the grades they have been given at primary school. The intention behind remedial teaching is that pupils should be reintegrated into the normal curriculum as quickly as possible, but it does tend to stigmatise children who need to resort to it, and the wealthier parent can avoid such a situation by arranging private tuition as an alternative. From an early stage the ability to select

Figure 4.3
Secondary school education at lycées

Age	Class	Cursus	
		Lycée d'enseignement général et technologique	*Lycée d'enseignement professionnel*
15 – 16	2ᵉ	Core + options	Vocational training
16 – 17	1ᵉʳᵉ	Core + options	*Certificat d'aptitude professionnelle/Brevet d'études professionnelles*
17 – 18	*Terminale*	Options	
		Baccalauréat* /Brevet de technicien	

* For which the major options within each category are:

A Philosophy and arts
B Economics and social sciences
C Mathematics and physics
D Mathematics and natural sciences
E Mathematics and technology
F 1 – 11 Science and technology
G 1 – 3 Economics and business administration
H Computer science

SOURCE: author's own data.

subject combinations which will not preclude later choices is only one of many factors determining progress through the school system.

As shown in Figure 4.3, the second stage of secondary education is organised in two types of institution: three year courses are provided in the *lycée d'enseignement général et technologique,* leading to the school-leaving examination (*baccalauréat*); two year courses in the *lycée d'enseignement professionnel* lead to vocational qualifications (*certificat d'aptitude professionnelle, brevet d'études professionnelles*), although it has been found that most students take three years to complete the course.

The first two years of the longer *lycée* course are based on a common core, in pursuance of the objectives set out in Article 5 of Texte 4.1, and comprising French, mathematics, science and technology, economic and social studies and one foreign language. Different syllabuses are followed according to the weighting given to each subject and the options selected. These include other languages, additional mathematics, technology, engineering, economics and management. In the final year

Table 4.1

Sample coefficients for the baccalauréat

	A5	B	C	D	E
Physics with chemistry			5	4	4
Mathematics		3	5	4	5
Philosophy	4	2	2	2	
History and geography	3	3	2	2	
French (written)	3	2	2	2	2
(oral)	1	1	1	1	1
Natural sciences				4	
Foreign language 1	3	3	2	2	2
Foreign language 2	2				
Mechanics					4
Technology					3
Economics		4			
Total	16	18	19	21	21

SOURCE: author's own data

there are between twenty and thirty possible combinations of subjects for the *baccalauréat*, grouped to give the range shown in Figure 4.3. A system of coefficients, illustrated in Table 4.1, is operated to ensure that the major and minor subjects assume different levels of importance, for the final mark depends upon an overall assessment.

When the *lycée* was created with the intention of training the nation's elite, its pupils were drawn from a narrow social group, and the education it provided, emphasising general culture rather than specialised knowledge, suited the needs of this social category. True to this tradition, and in spite of a much more heterogeneous population, the *lycée* curriculum still ensures that every pupil studies a wide range of subjects and that he proves his proficiency in all of them in the *baccalauréat*, and this examination remains the major preoccupation of the *lycée* pupil. At the beginning of the century, approximately 1 per cent of any age group would hold the *baccalauréat*; by 1977 the proportion had risen to 25 per cent. Although without it many doors are barred, the *baccalauréat* is no longer the passport to a successful career as it was in the past.

While holders of the *baccalauréat* (*bacheliers*) have become more numerous, other forms of elitism have emerged, for not all categories of subjects will give access to the same career opportunities. As indicated in Texte 4.6, the most prestigious *baccalauréat* is C, with high coefficients for mathematics and physics. Successful candidates are more likely than the holders of any other *baccalauréat* to be accepted at one of the most sought after institutions of higher education, namely the *grandes écoles*. The various F categories, with high coefficients in science and technology, tend to lead either to short courses in higher education or directly to employment. In theory all the *baccalauréats*, which are national diplomas, should be of equal difficulty, but the less prestigious *baccalauréats*, tend to have the higher pass rates. Such is the importance attached to some combinations of subjects that parents may prefer to see their children repeat a year, or pay for private tuition in their weaker subjects, rather than encourage them to follow less demanding courses, for which they may be better suited.

Age, sex and social origins are found to determine both the choice of subject combination for the *baccalauréat* and the likelihood of passing it. Pupils who take the examination at an age below the average are more likely to pass: more than 86 per cent at the age of 17 compared with fewer than 34 per cent at the age of 22. More girls than boys sit for the *baccalauréat*, but they tend to choose the A category (73.5 per cent) rather than C (34.7 per cent). In 1976 more than 22 per cent of candidates were from families with a father in the professional and higher administrative grades and nearly 19 per cent in the middle grades, whereas the sons and daughters of manual workers accounted for barely 15 per cent and the agricultural category for under 8 per cent, confirming that the advantages detected in the early years of schooling have been perpetuated. Children from the lower socio-occupational categories who do remain at school after the age of 16 are more often orientated towards the study of technical subjects and the less prestigious *baccalauréats* thereby limiting their opportunities in higher education.

Higher education and continuing education

It was estimated that 80 per cent of those who qualified with the *baccalauréat* in 1979 continued their education at tertiary level. Approximately 20 per cent of any age group pursues higher education, a proportion above that for Great Britain but lower than in the United States. There is no rigidly imposed limit on the length of university studies, and at any one time there are more than a million students in the different types of higher education in France.

Universities

In the absence of any selection procedures such as those used in Great Britain (although quotas have been imposed for a number of years for medicine), universities have traditionally accepted anybody with the *baccalauréat*, which is a university title. The result has been that staff-student ratios in France are amongst the poorest in Northern Europe and that the failure rate is more than 57 per cent, compared with 13 per cent in Great Britain. It is estimated that more than half of French students leave university without any qualification. Many of the basic problems which provoked the explosion of May 1968 have not been solved. The *Loi d'orientation* created new teaching and research units (*unités d'enseignement et de recherche*), replacing the former faculties, which were expected to stimulate interdisciplinary studies, but they have often reproduced the former cleavages. As already mentioned, universities were given administrative autonomy, but the minister still controls the financial allocation and approves national diplomas and appointments. Participation has generally been a failure, as students show little interest in electing representatives, and academic staff often grudge spending their time over administrative matters, with which they are usually unfamiliar. There are now three times as many universities as in 1968 (Paris has fourteen universities), due to the creation of new institutions and the division of existing units. While the number of students has more than doubled, there has been little progress in creating better relationships between the universities and society, in clarifying the functions of the universities, or in improving the quality of teaching by reducing overcrowding. The debate about the role of universities in providing vocational training has become even more acrimonious, as unemployment increases, and the universities have tended to serve as a means of postponing entry into the job market.

In 1973 a new general diploma (*diplôme d'études universitaires générales*) replaced the former literary and scientific diplomas awarded after two years of study (*premier cycle*) (see Figure 4.4). The aim was to provide a short university training course, making it possible to leave university at this stage with a qualification. In the event the new diploma of which there are two main categories – one corresponding to the more traditional disciplines of law, economics, arts and sciences, and the other with a more modern orientation, including economic and social sciences, applied mathematics and applied language studies – have not been accepted as adequate qualifications by employers, and students who complete the course successfully generally continue their studies.

The second level of university education (*second cycle*) consists of one further year of study leading to the award of a degree (*licence*) or two more years leading to a masters degree (*maîtrise*), which is of a standard equivalent to a British honours degree. As for the DEUG, students generally complete modules (*unités de valeur*) based on assessed work and examinations. A reform of the *second cycle*, formulated by Soisson in 1975 and which his successor Saunier-Séïté tried to

Figure 4.4
University education

Cycle	Length in years	Qualification*
1	2	*Diplôme universitaire d'études générales*
2	1	*Licence*
	2	*Maîtrise*
3	1	*Diplôme d'études supérieures spécialisées*
		Diplôme d'études approfondies
	3 maximum	*Doctorat de troisième cycle*
	unlimited	*Doctorat d'état*

* Main qualifications only.

SOURCE: author's own data.

implement in 1976, was intended to introduce a vocational element into university training. Universities were invited to put forward proposals for the courses they wanted to introduce, and an inter-university committee, including representatives from industry and commerce, met to approve them. Despite the problems of unemployment awaiting many graduates, the strikes which the reform provoked were the longest the universities had known.

The third level of university education (*troisième cycle*) allows for a higher degree of specialisation, leading to doctorate qualifications and vocational diplomas. There is more room for flexibility, the number of students is relatively small, but many are engaged in other professional activities, while carrying out their research, often in the capacity of a university tutor. Although the conditions are more conducive to study at this level of university education, for the vast majority of French students university life is generally impersonal and bewildering with few opportunities for contact with academic staff. There is no certainty that the courses being followed will lead to a qualification acceptable to an employer, and the chances of successfully completing any course are strictly limited. Right from the beginning of their university career students know that, even though they have been awarded the prized *baccalauréat,* a university degree is only second best, for their fellow pupils who have been granted places in one of the *grandes écoles* have a guarantee that at the end of their studies they should have no problems in finding worthwhile employment.

Grandes écoles

The *grandes écoles* are a feature of the French educational system which has no equivalent in any comparable Western country. Whereas the universities have been described as a car park, the 200 or so *grandes écoles* are seen as the nursery for the nation's leaders. Students are selected by competitive entrance examinations, for which they are trained in specially designated classes in about 200 of the most highly reputed private schools and *lycées* in the country for two or three years after the *baccalauréat*. Some of the *grandes écoles* are under the control of the Ministry of Education, for example the *Ecole Nationale d'Administration, Ecole Nationale Supérieure d'Ingénieurs*, the *Ecoles Normales Supérieures* or *Instituts Nationaux de Sciences Appliquées*. Others are sponsored by bodies such as chambers of commerce, for example the *Ecole des Hautes Etudes Commerciales*, while others are controlled by different ministries, for example the *Ecole Polytechnique* by the Ministry of Armed Forces.

The function of the *grandes écoles* is to train the higher administrative grades in industry, commerce, the civil service and armed forces for their role as the nation's decision-makers. Two-thirds of the 100 largest companies in France today are managed by former students of the *grandes écoles*, and they are present in even greater proportions in the civil and diplomatic services. Not all the *grandes écoles* enjoy the same prestige. The most sought after places are at the *Ecole Nationale d'Administration* (described in Texte 4.7), which was founded by Debré in 1945 when he was in charge of administrative reforms in De Gaulle's provisional government, but it had originally been planned by the Popular Front Government in the 1930s. The intention in creating the ENA was to democratise and 'deparisianise' entry to the civil service, while also providing a more modern and specialised training by the state for its own civil servants. Entrance to the ENA is extremely competitive, and most candidates (nearly 80 per cent of successful applicants) have first undergone training at the Paris *Institut d'Etudes Politiques*, formerly the *Ecole Libre des Sciences Politiques*, a private institution created in 1871 and superceded in practice by the ENA. Every year the ENA recruits about 150 students for two and a half years of training, two thirds from the open entrance and one third from the civil service. The position achieved in the final examination determines the choice of appointment, and the spirit of rivalry is maintained throughout the course, as an individual's whole career may be influenced by a quarter of a mark in the final assessment. The school trained a president, Giscard d'Estaing, and most of his cabinet ministers in 1977 were former students of the ENA. They were also well represented in the opposition parties (Joxe, Chevènement, Rocard). The most prized positions on leaving the ENA are with the *Conseil d'Etat, Cour des Comptes*, or *Inspection des Finances*, followed by the diplomatic and prefectural services, and it is common after a few years in the public service to transfer to equally prestigious positions in the private sector by a process known as *pantouflage*.

Although the ENA was expected to democratise access to the highest positions in the administration, and hence indirectly in the social, political and economic life of the nation, it has – after first being shunned by the most privileged social categories – now been taken over by the Parisian elite. Studies show that few students have undergone previous training outside the capital, and almost 80 per cent are drawn from the Paris area, although only half were born in Paris. The higher social categories provide about three quarters of the students, whereas only 2 per cent are from manual categories and only 6 per cent are women.

One of the most important characteristics of the *grandes écoles*, particularly the ENA, is that they give the elite their legitimacy, and not even the left-wing parties suggest that they should be abolished, although a number of the school's own students do. While the number of students at the universities has been increasing in an uncontrolled way since the war, the numbers in the *grandes écoles* have remained almost static, and their students have continued, albeit perhaps not so easily as in the past, to find satisfying employment.

Institutes of advanced technology

The first *instituts universitaires de technologie* were established in 1960 in an attempt to solve the problems resulting from the absence of vocational training in the universities. Initially sixty-six IUTs were set up with a capacity to train nearly 68,000 students, but in 1976 they had only about 45,000 students, and the Minister for Higher Education, who had herself at one time been the principal of an IUT, decided to reduce the number of posts and the allocation of teaching hours. Unlike the universities, the IUTs offer intensive vocational training over a two year period, they include industrial placements, and failure rates are lower (approximately one-third). They were expected to meet local needs, but is is claimed that they have often been sited with more regard for political than for economic considerations.

For many years industry did not recognise the qualifications gained at the IUTs, even though between 10 and 20 per cent of the teaching students receive is provided, at least in theory, by industrialists on secondment. When they were first created the IUTs were welcomed enthusiastically, but during the early 1970s they entered a period of crisis and seem to have encountered the same negative response as other areas of technical education, which is still considered as the poor relation in the French educational system.

Many attempts have been made to elevate the status of technical education: since 1971 teachers in secondary technical education have been granted the same professional status as their colleagues in the *lycées*, new diplomas have been introduced, but openings rarely match the level of qualification offered. It is argued that just as the *grandes écoles* ensure the reproduction of society's elite, technical education produces workers with enough knowledge to ensure the smooth running of the industrial machine but insufficient status to contest their position in the social hierarchy.

Continuing education

In 1976 nearly two million workers were undergoing some form of professional training. In 1978 a law was introduced to ensure the right of every individual to take leave for this purpose under sponsorship from his employer and the state, and many specialised training schemes have been instituted in an effort to reduce unemployment amongst the young. In some circumstances employers are expected to pay salaries for a period stipulated by law, and the state takes over this responsibility after a given length of time, when employees are following approved courses.

Another alternative form of education is that provided by the *Centre National de Télé-enseignement*, developed in 1959 from the former correspondence schools. Students can follow courses leading to qualifications such as the *baccalauréat*, professional diplomas and the *agrégation*. Between 160,000 and 180,000 students are enrolled at any one time at the six autonomous centres, each with its own teaching and administrative staff employed by the state. The service is free (the enrolment fee is nominal) and available to anybody who for whatsoever reason, whether it be illness, military service, imprisonment, family obligations, is unable to pursue a normal education.

Adult education is also offered in evening classes, which are given free of charge, but they have become less popular as the system of study leave has been extended. It is significant that in some centres half the students are aged below 25 years, and this would seem to indicate that additional qualifications are sought by young people who have failed school examinations or have found their training inadequate to guarantee them employment and opportunities for promotion.

Equality of educational opportunity

There is no shortage of data demonstrating that some social categories are better able than others to exploit the educational system and achieve the highest rewards that it offers. Parents who know how to take advantage of the system will ensure that they live in an area where good schools are available, that their children start school at an early age, work their way through primary schooling without repeating a year, make the right choice of subjects at secondary level, select the most suitable *baccalauréat* and stay on at school to prepare for the entrance examinations to the *grandes écoles*. If problems arise, private coaching, or a private school, may offer a solution. Parents may also exert pressure on teaching staff to convince them that a child is capable of undertaking a particularly difficult course of study. For the child with parents who do not know how to manipulate the system, a later start at nursery school will often be followed by reading difficulties, repeats, a late move on to secondary school with the need for remedial teaching, the 'wrong' choice of subjects and the likelihood of leaving school at the age of 16 ill-equipped for professional life.

Research has shown that the extension of free compulsory schooling to every member of society, longer schooling and the introduction of a comprehensive system have all failed in their stated objective of ensuring greater equality of educational opportunity and individual occupational mobility. It has been demonstrated that the difference in the chances for the son of a manual worker compared with the son of a member of the higher administrative grades of entering a university is one to eleven, whereas the salary differential between the two is much smaller. Education is found to be five times more discriminatory than income. As the value of qualifications is reduced, the more privileged categories seek higher qualifications in such a way that the greater the amount of education provided, the greater the benefits they derive from it, without there being any change in the social distance between them and the less privileged categories. It would seem that rather than acting as a compensatory mechanism, the educational system tends to compound the initial advantage of the privileged social categories, as summarised in Texte 4.8.

In the context of such deep-seated problems, the attempts at reform in recent years, ostensibly to improve access to education for the less privileged social categories, have proved to be no more than cosmetic. Their lack of success may be due less to the nature of the reforms or to their intentions, than to the steadfast opposition by which they have been greeted, testifying to the resistance to the process of change, particularly within the teaching profession. The passions roused by the introduction of a comprehensive system in Great Britain and moves to phase out private schools have rarely reached the same level of animosity as those betrayed in the ongoing struggle waged in France between the Minister of Education, the teaching profession, parents and pupils. Although many of the incidents regularly reported in the press (see Text 4.3) at the beginning of each school year are localised, they are generally provoked by a ministerial decree, which leaves little room for flexibility and initiative in individual establishments. It is possible that a less centralised system, as advocated by President Mitterrand, could offer a framework for more democratic structures, although, as demonstrated in the universities, greater autonomy does not necessarily lead to greater stability or encourage participation in the administrative process. There is little evidence to suggest that the series of reforms and counter-reforms which have characterised the post-war years have yet produced a system capable of fulfilling all the functions attributed to it or of reconciling the needs of all providers and users.

Bibliographical guidance

Historical surveys and analyses of current trends in the French educational system:

E. Cahm, *Politics and Society in Contemporary France (1789–1971): A Documentary History* (London: Harrap, 1972)

J. Majault, *L'Enseignement en France* (New York: McGraw-Hill, 1973)

J. Minot, *L'Entreprise éducation nationale* (Paris: Colin, 1970)

J. N. Moody, *French Education since Napoleon* (New York: Syracuse University Press, 1978)

M. Ozouf, *L'Ecole, l'Eglise et la République, 1871-1914* (Paris: Colin, 1963)

Discussion of some of the main issues in the education debate:

C. Baudelot, R. Establet, *L'Ecole capitaliste en France* (Paris: Maspero, 1971)

P. Bourdieu, J.-C. Passeron, *La Reproduction* (Paris: Editions de Minuit, 1970)

R. Boudon, *L'Inégalité des chances: la mobilité sociale dans les sociétés industrielles* (Paris: Colin, 1973)

J. Capelle, *Education et politique* (Paris: PUF, 1974)

J. Cornec, *Pour l'Ecole libre* (Paris: Laffont, 1977)

P. Gerbod, *Les Enseignants et la politique* (Paris: PUF, 1976)

D. L. Hanley, A. P. Kerr and H. H. Waites, *Contemporary France: Politics and Society since 1945* (London: Routledge & Kegan Paul, 1979)

'Les enseignants', *Le Monde: dossiers et documents*, 51 (May 1978)

G. Snyders, *Ecole, classe et luttes des classes* (Paris: PUF, 1976)

Syndicat Général de l'Education Nationale, CFDT, *L'Ecole en lutte: action, effectifs, emploi, conditions de travail* (Paris: Maspero, 1977)

Studies of the different stages in education:

G. Vincent, *Le Peuple lycéen* (Paris: Gallimard, 1974)
N. Bisseret, *Les Inégaux ou la sélection universitaire* (Paris: PUF, 1974)
J. de Chalendar, *Une Loi pour l'université avec le manuscrit inédit d'Edgar Faure* (Paris: Desclée de Brower, 1970)
A. Touraine, Z. Hegedus, F. Dubet and M. Wievorka, *La Lutte étudiante* (Paris: Seuil, 1978)
M.-C. Kessler and J.-L. Bodiguel, *L'Ecole Nationale d'Administration*, 2 vols (Paris: Fondation Nationale des Sciences Politiques, 1978)

Reviews:

The main source of up-to-date information and analyses of current trends in education is the monthly publication *Le Monde de l'éducation*.

Illustrative texts and linguistic exercises

Texte 4.1   Loi no. 75 - 620 du 11 juillet 1975 relative à l'éducation

Art. 1er. – Tout enfant a droit à *une formation scolaire* qui, complétant l'action de sa famille, concourt à *son éducation*.

Cette formation scolaire est obligatoire entre six et seize ans.

Elle favorise l'épanouissement de l'enfant, lui permet d'acquérir *une culture*, le prépare à la vie professionnelle et à l'exercice de ses responsabilités d'homme et de citoyen. Elle constitue la base de *l'éducation permanente*. Les familles sont associées à l'accomplissement de ces missions.

Pour favoriser l'égalité des chances, des dispositions appropriées rendent possible l'accès de chacun, en fonction de ses aptitudes, aux différents types ou niveaux de la formation scolaire.

Ces dispositions assurent la gratuité de l'enseignement durant la période de *scolarité* obligatoire.

L'Etat garantit le respect de la personnalité de l'enfant et de *l'action éducative* des familles.

Titre Ier L'enseignement

Art. 2. – Les classes enfantines ou les écoles maternelles sont ouvertes, en milieu rural comme en milieu urbain, aux enfants qui n'ont pas atteint l'âge de la scolarité obligatoire. A l'âge de cinq ans, tout enfant doit pouvoir, selon le voeu de sa famille, y être accueilli, ou à défaut, être admis dans une section enfantine d'une école élémentaire.

Sans rendre obligatoire l'apprentissage précoce de la lecture ou de l'écriture, la formation qui y est dispensée favorise l'éveil de la personnalité des enfants. Elle tend à prévenir les difficultés scolaires, à dépister les handicaps et à compenser les inégalités.

L'Etat affecte le personnel enseignant nécessaire à ces activités éducatives.

Art. 3. – La formation primaire est donnée dans les écoles élémentaires suivant un programme unique réparti sur cinq niveaux successifs; la période initiale peut être organisée sur une durée variable.

La formation primaire assure l'acquisition des instruments fondamentaux de la connaissance : expression orale et écrite, lecture, calcul; elle suscite le développement de l'intelligence, de la sensibilité artistique, des aptitudes manuelles, physiques et sportives. Elle offre une initiation aux arts plastiques et musicaux. Elle assure conjointement avec la famille l'éducation morale et l'éducation civique.

Art. 4. – Tous les enfants reçoivent dans les collèges une formation secondaire. Celle-ci succède sans discontinuité à la formation primaire en vue de donner aux élèves une culture accordée à la société de leur temps. Elle repose sur un équilibre des disciplines intellectuelles, artistiques, manuelles, physiques et sportives et permet de révéler les aptitudes et les goûts. Elle constitue le support de formations générales ou professionnelles ultérieures, que celles-ci la suivent immédiatement ou non ou qu'elles soient données dans le cadre de l'éducation permanente.

Les collèges dispensent un enseignement commun, réparti sur quatre niveaux successifs. Les deux derniers peuvent comporter aussi des enseignements complémentaires dont certains préparent à une formation professionnelle; ces derniers peuvent comporter des stages contrôlés par l'Etat et accomplis auprès de professionnels agréés. La scolarité correspondant à ces deux niveaux et comportant obligatoirement l'enseignement commun peut être accomplie dans des classes préparatoires rattachées à un établissement de formation professionnelle.

Art. 5. – La formation secondaire peut être prolongée dans les lycées en associant, dans tous les types d'enseignement, une formation générale et une formation spécialisée.

SOURCE: *Journal Officiel de la République Française* (12 juillet 1975) pp. 7180–1.

Exploitation du texte

1. Formulez une définition des termes en italique dans l'article ler de manière à faire ressortir les différences de sens.

2. Exprimez en moins de 200 mots l'essentiel des buts esquissés dans cette loi pour chaque niveau de l'enseignement et commentez l'enchaînement des étapes.

3. D'après ce texte, quels devraient être les rapports entre famille et Etat dans le domaine de l'enseignement.

4. Comparez les dispositifs de cette loi avec les principes de Condorcet présentés dans les sujets de dissertation.

5. Relevez les phrases qui indiquent que le législateur se préoccupe de l'individu.

6. Quels sont les traits linguistiques qui font de ce texte un document légal.

Texte 4.2   Impossibles réformes

D'où vient donc que des mesures, dont certaines vont dans *le sens souhaité*, soient unanimement rejetées? Avant tout du divorce profond qui existe – et se creuse probablement de plus en plus – entre le 'corps universitaire' (c'est-à-dire l'ensemble des maîtres et des étudiants de tous les ordres d'enseignement) d'une part, la majorité politique et le gouvernement d'autre part. L'idée 'qu'il n'y a rien à attendre de ce régime', parce qu'il est le gérant d'une société qui méprise globalement l'école est si profondément enracinée que ce n'est pas l'examen de telle ou telle mesure particulière plus ou moins positive qui pourrait faire changer l'état d'esprit. Ce qui vient de ce gouvernement (comme de ses prédécesseurs) ne peut être que suspect, et viser de façon plus ou moins sournoise à la mise au pas de l'école et à son asservissement à la rentabilité et à l'utilitarisme capitalistes.

Les raisons objectives d'alimenter cette amertume ne manquent pas: *considérant le terrain comme perdu*, le pouvoir a, depuis longtemps, renoncé à *prendre des gants*, et son attitude oscille entre l'indifférence et l'autoritarisme. On demeure aussi stupéfait devant l'improvisation, le manque de sérieux et de préparation de certaines propositions. Mais l'unanimité du corps universitaire dans le refus permet de parer des vertus de l'opposition politique des comportements et des intérêts parfaitement contradictoires. Conservateurs et révolutionnaires; *mandarins de tous grades*, syndicalistes progressistes et étudiants révoltés; *nantis* et futurs chômeurs, trouvent des accents identiques pour *vilipender* le gouvernement et ses réformes.

Dans la France coupée en deux, qui attend chaque consultation électorale pour compter les dixièmes de point qui séparent ses deux moitiés, les choses sont désormais claires: aucune réforme de l'enseignement ne peut avoir l'assentiment des enseignants. Conséquence logique de cette situation; seul un gouvernement de gauche pourra espérer bénéficier de la confiance suffisante des maîtres et des élèves pour entreprendre *une réforme véritable*. A ce moment-là seulement un vrai débat pourra s'engager sur les problèmes de fond: la démocratisation, la sélection, l'adaptation des études aux débouchés professionnels, les relations entre l'école et la monde économique, les responsabilités des enseignants, la limitation des coûts de l'enseignement . . . La gauche au pouvoir pourra alors compter les appuis dont elle dispose dans le 'corps universitaire'. . . Elle risque d'avoir des surprises.

SOURCE: F. Gaussen, *Le Monde de l'éducation*, 16 (avril 1976) p.5.

Exploitation du texte

1. Expliquez en quelques mots le sens et la portée des termes/phrases en italique.

2. Exprimez en vos propres mots les phrases suivantes :-
Viser de façon plus ou moins sournoise . . . utilitarisme capitalistes.
Mais l'unanimité du corps universitaire . . . contradictoires.

3. Résumez en moins de 150 mots le tableau esquissé dans le texte du corps enseignant et commentez la conclusion exprimée dans la dernière phrase du texte.

4. Expliquez en quelques phrases ce que l'auteur entend par les 'problèmes de fond'.

5. Rédigez une lettre à la presse de la part d'un enseignant critiquant les mesures proposées par Haby ou de la part d'un parent d'élève critiquant l'opposition systématique des enseignants aux projets de réforme.

Texte 4.3   Les parents aux créneaux

Ce devait être *la rentrée scolaire* la plus paisible depuis dix ans et nous l'avions écrit. Le secrétaire général de *la Fédération de l'éducation nationale* et le ministre de l'éducation multipliaient les sourires réciproques. Le Syndicat des instituteurs négociait une réforme de la formation des maîtres, vieux débat qui débouchait enfin. L'atmosphère, dans les *'appareils'*, était à la négociation et à *la décrispation*. Et chacun d'écarter, d'un geste las et méprisant, les *'bavures'* de la rentrée qui ne manqueraient pas de se produire ici ou là.

Et puis, jour après jour, les petites nouvelles qui tombent de tous côtés. C'est d'abord une pluie fine. Ce n'est pas encore un orage. Ici on manifeste, là on porte des pétitions au rectorat. Plus loin on occupe. Grèves scolaires, grèves d'enseignants se succèdent.

Comment apprécier l'ampleur réelle du phénomène ? Certes les exemples abondent, mais ne faut-il pas, *en regard*, dresser aussi la liste des écoles, des collèges, des lycées où tout paraît normal, où les élèves étudient et où les professeurs enseignent ? Entre l'indifférence hautaine devant les 'bavures' et l'affolement il y a une troisième attitude qui consiste à tenter d'abord de comprendre.

Les causes immédiates des mouvements actuels sont, principalement, de deux ordres : insuffisance du nombre de classes dans le primaire, effectifs jugés excessifs dans le second cycle des lycées. On note, en revanche, que les revendications sur les constructions scolaires, ou sur la sécurité, sont très rares. Signe des temps : la qualité de la vie dans les classes devient l'objectif prioritaire.

Quand on examine de près la manière dont se déclenchent les

mouvements et dont ils se terminent, on ne peut manquer d'être surpris par le fait que, dans la majorité des cas, les parents sont en première ligne. On peut avancer à cet égard deux hypothèses qui, d'ailleurs, ne s'excluent pas :

— Des administrateurs (directeurs d'école, principaux de collège, directeurs de lycée) las de batailler contre l'administration dont ils dépendent lancent la balle dans le camp des parents : 'A vous de jouer'. Sous-entendu : 'Si vous occupez mon école, je ne m'en plaindrai pas.' Il y aurait ainsi des 'séquestrés' volontaires . . .

— Les parents d'élèves de 1978 n'ont plus la passivité des anciens qui laissaient les enseignants *guerroyer* contre le 'pouvoir' pour obtenir des améliorations. Nombre de parents d'élèves de maternelle ou du primaire avaient vingt ans en 1968. Certes, ils sont installés dans la vie professionnelle et familiale, mais ils gardent de leur passé le sentiment que la révolte – sinon la révolution – permet d'obtenir des résultats concrets. Dans l'intérêt passionné que ces jeunes parents portent à la qualité de la vie de leurs enfants, ils rejoignent une autre catégorie de parents : ceux des classe moyennes qui ne supportent pas l'idée de voir se dégrader – si peu que ce soit – la qualité de l'enseignement offert à leurs enfants. Ainsi, les premiers apportent-ils aux seconds les méthodes d'organisation qui leur permettent d'exprimer leur anxiété. On a observé dans plusieurs cas une 'jonction' entre des jeunes parents intellectuels et des employés d'origine modeste avec pour plate-forme commune la défense des enfants.

A ces deux catégories ne manque jamais le concours de militants – politiques et syndicaux – qui ont vite fait de *structurer un mécontement*. Au ministère, on insiste sur la carte de France des 'bavures' et on note que les municipalités communistes sont les plus agitées. Et l'on fait remarquer, à juste titre, que les grèves d'enseignants sont lancées par les syndicats de la FEN proches du P.C.

Mais la politique n'explique pas tout. On avait bien senti depuis quelques années que l'école devait de plus en plus compter avec les parents. Mais on l'avait oublié : M. Beullac et certains syndicalistes paraissaient, au début de cette année, s'en soucier *comme d'une guigne*. Or, les parents *montent aux créneaux* et beaucoup d'entre eux ne paraissent pas se contenter des organes consultatifs, mis en place il y a dix ans dans les lycées et il y a un an dans les écoles.

La chronique des 'bavures' ne doit pas trop faire sourire, même s'il ne faut pas dramatiser les méthodes utilisées par certains parents. Les mouvements auxquels on assiste à la rentrée – mais en cours d'année aussi – attestent l'importance qu'une partie de la population attache à l'école. Ecole décriée, école ennuyeuse, école inutile, école qui 'fabrique des chômeurs', école de classes : oui, mais école défendue par ceux qui y mettent leurs enfants. Si la rentrée ne se passe pas si bien, c'est que l'école ne se porte pas si mal. Ou du moins l'idée qu'on s'en fait.

SOURCE: B. Frappat, *Le Monde* (5 oct. 1978) p. 16 (adapté).

Exploitation du texte
1. Expliquez en quelques mots le sens des termes/phrases en italique.
2. Résumez en moins de 150 mots les raisons pour la participation des parents aux revendications.
3. Expliquez les allusions des deux dernières phrases du texte.
4. Commentez l'emploi des verbes dans le premier paragraphe.
5. Relevez les phrases qui témoignent du ton d'ironie exploité par l'auteur.

Texte 4.4 Le Socle

René Haby fut au fond, le dernier ministre de l'Education nationale *dans le style Jules Ferry.* En 1977, il faisait diffuser *une brochure ronflante* : elle proclamait que l'enseignant doit représenter un 'modèle' pour l'enfant. Ah, cette vision de *l'instituteur apôtre et militant civique*! Ce *quasi-concurrent du curé,* ce *Sur-moi idéal* devait enseigner ce qu'il savait ET ce qu'il était.

On peut être plus modeste et moderne. On doit être plus précis. Des instituteurs, nous attendons qu'ils apprennent aux enfants à lire, à écrire, à compter. Qu'ils leur enseignent les éléments de base de différentes disciplines. Peut-être aussi qu'ils apprennent aux enfants à apprendre, un peu à raisonner, beaucoup à être heureux. Nous voulons des maîtres, comme disent joliment les gosses. Pas des Maîtres.

Seuls enseignants polyvalents, à l'extérieur, les instituteurs paraissaient oubliés par les ministres de l'Education nationale – 28 seulement depuis 1945. 17 depuis 1958! A l'intérieur, le corps des instituteurs était envahi par *les ratés,* réels ou supposés, d'autres professions. L'instituteur est *presque le manoeuvre* de l'Education nationale. Parfois, *l'agrégé* regarde avec condescendance le *certifié.* Qui se rattrape sur l'instituteur titulaire. Qui *déverse son trop-plein d'inquiétude sur les suppléants* – de 15 à 35% des effectifs. L'instituteur fait deux fois plus d'heures de cours ou de présence que son collègue du secondaire. Oublions ceux du supérieur, penseurs privilégiés ou chercheurs indispensables. L'instituteur (l'institutrice encore moins) a rarement une deuxième activité rémunérée ou glorieuse. Sa promotion parallèle passe par une candidature politique ou l'animation d'une association socioculturelle. Il ne fait pas partie du jet-set universitaire.

Même si son espérance de vie est, comme celle des prêtres, une des plus fortes de France, il est très fatigué. Bien fait, l'enseignement est un métier épuisant. Faire travailler une trentaine d'enfants demande un maximum d'énergie, d'attention.

Sur le plan du statut social, les instituteurs se voient plus proches d'un employé de banque ou d'un ouvrier que d'un cadre. Pourtant, ils sont plus 'considérés' qu'ils ne le pensent. Moins qu'ils ne le voudraient, bien sûr, comme la plupart des groupes professionnels. Toutes les catégories de la Fonction publique réclament des augmentations. Pour les instituteurs, ne devrait-on pas, avant tout, *accélérer le déroulement des carrières*? En France, le maximum des rémunérations n'est atteint qu'après vingt et un ans; en Finlande, après douze ans. Notre éventail n'est sûrement pas assez souple.

L'instruction primaire, socle ultime de tout enseignement, est aujourd'hui décisive pour tous les autres. Acceptera-t-on de *faire éclater la grille de la Fonction publique*? Superbe question pour un référendum auquel participeraient tous les fonctionnaires parents. On doit donner aux instituteurs des moyens, et cesser de leur demander, avec une nostalgie passéiste, d'être des surhommes ou des surfemmes

SOURCE: O. Todd, *L'Express,* (28 oct.-4 nov. 1978) p. 65 (adapté).

Exploitation du texte

1. Expliquez en quelques mots les phrases/termes en italique.

2. Faites ressortir en moins de 200 mots la distinction entre 'maîtres' et 'Maîtres' en comparant les caractéristiques de l'instituteur d'autrefois avec celles de l'instituteur de nos jours, tels qu'ils sont présentés par l'auteur.

3. Comment peur-on expliquer cette évolution?

4. Pourquoi l'instruction primaire serait-elle le 'socle ultime de tout enseignement'?

5. Relevez les expressions et les arguments qui donnent un ton ironique au texte.

6. Faites le portrait de l'instituteur tel qu'il pourrait être en l'an 2000.

Texte 4.5 Morales

Le travail est le pain nourricier des grandes nations.
Ne rien faire, c'est déjà mal faire.
Le travail abrège les journées, allonge la vie.
Je dois mes succès dans la vie à ce que j'ai toujours été en avance d'un quart d'heure.
Etre homme, c'est être responsable, c'est connaître la honte en face d'une misère qui ne semblait pas dépendre de soi.
Celui qui instruit est un second père.
Maître et élèves ont un maître commun: l'affection.
Les amitiés nées à l'école éclairent la vie, comme l'aurore éclaire un beau jour.
J'ai contracté envers l'école une dette dont je ne m'acquitterai jamais.
C'est la cendre des morts qui créa la Patrie.

L'enfant à tout âge doit honneur et respect à ses Père et Mère.

C'est sur les genoux d'une Mère que se forme ce qu'il y a de plus noble au monde, l'âme d'un honnête homme.

Le couteau ne vaut rien contre l'esprit.

Tout particulier qui persécute son frère parce qu'il n'est pas de son opinion est un monstre.

Pour aimer et servir mon frère, je ne m'embarrasse pas de son culte.

Le parc national protège contre l'ignorance et le vandalisme des biens et des beautés qui appartiennent à tous.

La marche nettoie la cervelle et rend gai. Enterrez vos soucis et vos boîtes de conserves.

La faiblesse a peur des grands espaces. La sottise a peur du silence.

Ouvrez vos yeux et vos oreilles. Fermez vos transistors.

SOURCE: Extraits d'un Cahier du jour d'un élève en cours moyen 2 en 1978-9.

Exploitation du texte

1. Relevez les qualités recherchées dans ces morales.

2. Commentez cet enseignement dans le contexte de l'école primaire telle qu'elle est dépeinte dans le texte 4.4.

3. Analysez la syntaxe de ces phrases.

4. Rédigez des morales qui pourraient être apprises par des enfants de 10 ans dans une école primaire en Angleterre.

Texte 4.6   Sélection clandestine

Au cours des trente dernières années, le système français d'instruction a connu une transformation si profonde que l'on peut parler de révolution.

La distinction entre l'enseignement primaire et l'enseignement secondaire, qui datait de la fin du siècle dernier, a disparu. Les petites classes des lycées, antérieures à la 6e n'existent plus. Les lycées achèvent de perdre les classes du premier cycle, *de la 6e à 3e*. Les C.e.s., *collèges d'enseignement secondaire,* reçoivent les jeunes de toutes les classes sociales. Les réformateurs obéissaient, semble-t-il, à l'idéal de l'égalité des chances.

Il va sans dire que la généralisation des C.e.s. n'aboutit pas et ne peut pas aboutir à des établissements de qualité équivalente. Les C.e.s. des grandes villes attirent les enseignants plus que ceux des petites villes : ils comprendront, en moyenne, de meilleurs pédagogues.

En même temps que cette révolution administrative, une autre révolution, moins connue, résulte de la différenciation *des sections du baccalauréat*. Une section, C, l'emporte sur toutes les autres, à tel point que, dès la classe de seconde, la majorité des meilleurs élèves se détachent des autres. La section qui correspond à celle qui s'appelait latin-grec, et qui conduisait *éventuellement à l'Ecole normale supérieure* (lettres), recrute malaisément. Le grec ne conserve, dans le second degré, qu'*une présence fantomatique*. Les mathématiques règnent et la culture que l'on appelait celle des humanités devient rare et marginale. La section lettres de Normale supérieure semble condamnée à une rapide décadence, faute de candidats, faute de débouchés pour ceux qui en sortent. Il n'y a plus d'emploi pour eux dans les universités, à la suite du recrutement massif d'assistants et de maîtres assistants, dans les années qui précédèrent et suivirent 1968.

La tradition élitiste de l'enseignement français se prolonge par *des canaux non officiels*. Quand une classe réunit des élèves de niveau trop différent, nombre de professeurs concentrent leurs efforts sur ceux qui apparaissent capables ou désireux d'apprendre. *Le brassage social et scolaire* donne souvent des résultats opposés à ceux que l'on visait. Sans compter les institutions non étatiques, qui, *même conventionnées*, parviennent à maintenir des classes moins hétérogènes et attirent les enfants de la bourgeoisie.

A partir de la classe de seconde, par une pratique nullement officielle mais connue, se rassemble dans un lycée parisien, Louis-le-Grand, un nombre impressionnant des meilleurs élèves des lycées (ou C.e.s.) parisiens et même provinciaux. On y compte sept classes de seconde C. Pour ceux qui atteignent à la terminale, le baccalauréat ne constitue plus une épreuve. Accéder à une classe terminale de Louis-le-Grand est autrement difficile que décrocher un vénérable parchemin, à tout jamais dévalorisé.

Le deuxième cycle de Louis-le-Grand apparaît ainsi *l'antichambre des classes préparatoires* aux grandes écoles, classes elles-mêmes antichambre de *Polytechnique* (environ 30% de la liste) et de Normale supérieure. Qualité du recrutement, qualité des enseignants, esprit de compétition expliquent les résultats.

Fault-il condamner le rassemblement des *forts en thème* dès la quinzième (et parfois la quatorzième) année, le '*chauffage*' précoce de la future élite intellectuelle et parfois sociale? Le jugement ne va pas de soi: certains des bons élèves dépistés par les représentants de Louis-le-Grand réussiront mieux et plus vite qu'ils ne l'auraient fait ailleurs. Il s'agit non pas d'une sélection qui élimine, mais d'une sélection qui favorise, sinon ceux qui possèdent le quotient intellectuel le plus élevé, du moins ceux qui obtiennent les meilleures notes à l'école.

A la sortie du baccalauréat, la sélection, au sens précis auquel ce mot est pris en France, continue d'être excommuniée et exclue. Louis-le-Grand n'accepte pas n'importe quel élève en 2C, il choisit *sur dossiers*. De même les classes préparatoires aux grandes écoles choisissent sur dossiers. Les exigences des classes préparatoires varient, selon les établissements. Tout bachelier n'est pas assuré d'entrer dans une classe préparatoire aux écoles scientifiques. En revanche, tout bachelier, sur le papier, selon la loi et en fait, peut entrer dans une université.

Curieusement, la querelle sur la sélection portait exclusivement sur l'accession des bacheliers aux universités. Le baccalauréat étant un grade universitaire, seule une loi rendrait légale une sélection des bacheliers à l'entrée des universités. Tous les ministres de l'Education nationale ont jusqu'ici reculé devant *cette mesure symbolique*.

En revanche, toutes les écoles, même de réputation modeste, sélectionnent ou bien sur dossiers, ou bien, le plus souvent, par un concours. Nul ne doit donc s'étonner que les diplômes ou grades universitaires ne bénéficient pas, sur le marché du travail, du prestige souhaitable. Les quelques centaines de milliers d'étudiants en lettres trouveront de moins en moins de débouchés dans l'enseignement (le corps enseignant est très jeune et la population n'augmente pas), ils passent, parfois à tort, pour *les laissés-pour-compte* du système, ceux qui n'ont pas de plan précis de carrière et qui n'ont pas affronté un concours ou un examen après le baccalauréat.

La sélection à l'entrée des universités s'insinue par le biais de la loi d'orientation de 1968. Comment répartir les bacheliers qui, dans le district parisien, veulent continuer leurs études? Une méthode, celle dite de *la sectorisation* (en fonction du lieu de résidence), a été supprimée, elle allait en sens contraire de l'autonomie, désormais affirmée. La sectorisation éliminée, aucune méthode n'est prévue ou imposée par le ministère. Que se passe-t-il? Pour les études littéraires, Paris IV est le meilleur (ou *passe pour* le meilleur). Paris IV choisit sur dossiers. Comment faire autrement? Il y a trois ou quatre fois plus de candidats que de places. De même, pour la gestion des entreprises, Dauphine tient le premier rang; là aussi, une sélection est inévitable.

En revanche, il est inacceptable que soient reçus ceux qui déposent leur dossier les premiers (surtout si le président de l'université avait déclaré auparavant que le choix résulterait de l'étude des dossiers). Faire queue au secrétariat des universités, se présenter une nuit avant l'ouverture des guichets, comme le font des amateurs de spectacles sportifs, ne me paraît ni décent ni équitable.

Les universités, désormais autonomes, ne *doivent* pas accepter plus d'étudiants qu'elles ne *peuvent* en recevoir, mais le mode de sélection, connu de tous, ne changerait pas *au gré de l'humeur* du président.

SOURCE: R. Aron, *L'Express* (11-17 sept. 1978) p.52.

Exploitation du texte

1. Expliquez en quelques mots les phrases/termes en italique.

2. Résumez en moins de 300 mots les arguments du texte de manière à expliquer le sens du titre.

3. Dans quelle mesure l'auteur justifie-t-il sa constatation, à savoir que le système d'enseignement en France a subi une 'révolution'?

4. Expliquez les allusions des phrases suivantes:
   Les réformateurs obéissent...l'égalité des chances.
   Accéder à une classe terminale...dévalorisé.

Il s'agit non pas d'une sélection...à l'école.
La sélection à l'entrée...de 1968.

5. Quelle semble être l'opinion personnelle de l'auteur concernant le système d'enseignement en France?

6. Rédigez un paragraphe à la première personne qui aurait pu servir de conclusion à cet article et qui présente en termes directs l'opinion de l'auteur sur la question de la sélection dans l'enseignement.

Texte 4.7   L'ENA, trente ans après: démocratisation à rebours

Ils sont environ 1 800; ils ont entre 30 et 55 ans; ils sont *PDG* ou ministres, inspecteurs des Finances ou chefs de bureau, membres influents d'un cabinet ministériel ou modestes administrateurs civils. Les uns sont chez Giscard, les autres chez Mitterand. Mais tout ces 'anciens élèves de l'école nationale d'administration' de quels maux ne les accuse-t-on pas? Les voici tour à tour *'mandarins'*, *'jeunes loups'*, *'princes qui nous gouvernent'*, *'technocrates sans âme'*, *'franc-maçonnerie du régime'!* Le fait est là: aucune institution n'a provoqué, comme l'Ena, autant de réactions acerbes.

Depuis la fin de la guerre, la haute fonction publique s'est incontestablement démocratisée, et cela grâce au concours interne réservé aux fonctionnaires: sur les quelques 1 800 anciens élèves, moins de la moitié (47,5 % exactement) sont fils d'industriels, de cadres supérieurs, de médecins, de hauts fonctionnaires. . .

Toutefois, au fil des ans, cette démocratisation relative n'acessé de se détériorer: *'les catégories socio-professionnelles qui ont le plus augmenté en France ont le plus diminué à l'Ena'.*

Deux raisons expliqueraient cette démocratisation à rebours: d'abord la diminution des élèves en provenance du concours fonctionnaires; ensuite, l'effacement des classes moyennes au profit de la classe supérieure. Inquiète des bouleversements introduits par l'Ena, cette dernière *a beau en effet avoir boudé dans un premier temps le secteur public,* dès 1955 on assiste à *la montée en flèche* d'un recrutement plus bourgeois.

Une fois admis, le candidat n'est pas au bout de ses peines. Durant toute sa scolarité, une *épée de Damoclès* restera suspendue au-dessus de sa tête: le concours de sortie, le célèbre *'amphi-garnison'.* Car il ne suffit pas d'entrer à l'Ena, il faut encore en sortir. . . dans un bon rang!

O mystère des énarques! On aurait pu penser que ces jeunes gens et ces jeunes filles, avides de servir l'Etat, avaient des vocations précises. Eh bien, non! Sur tous, les *'grands corps'* ne cessent d'exercer leur extraordinaire fascination. A quelques très rares exceptions près les *'caciques'* veillent, travaillent, luttent pour sortir dans l'Inspection des Finances, le Conseil d'Etat ou la Cour des comptes. Les autres se partageront *les dépouilles des vainqueurs* selon une hiérarchie non écrite: le corps diplomatique, le corps préfectoral, le ministère des Finances. . . et les autres ministères.

Or, là encore, les statistiques montrent que la probabilité de réussite au concours de sortie n'est pas égale pour tous. Il vaut mieux être parisien que provincial, étudiant que fonctionnaire, appartenir de préférence aux classes aisées de la société et être diplômé de l'IEP de Paris.

Reste une question: les énarques sont-ils vraiment ces 'princes qui nous gouvernent'? Une mythologie, aussi tenace qu'insinuante, *véhicule* cette image dans presque tous les milieux. Le destin de la France dépendrait, selon certains, de cette école du pouvoir. Plus encore: les énarques seraient, dit-on, de plus en plus tentés par une vie politique active, à la recherche de *mandats électifs*.

Les énarques ne font pas toutefois profession des cabinets ministériels: pour la plupart, ils les quittent à 38 ans. Mais avoir vécu pendant quelques années à l'ombre d'un ministre semble accélérer le déroulement des carrières. Et surtout augmenter les possibilités de *pantouflage*. La moitié des anciens membres de cabinet quittent leurs 'corps' ou ministères *d'affectation* deux ans après leur sortie de cabinet. Et presque la moitié de ces départs ont lieu vers des entreprises, des établissements ou offices publics, des organismes internationaux. Le nombre des *mises en disponibilité* est très élevé.

En fait, les anciens élèves de l'Ena n'existent pas, ou, tout au moins, ils ne constituent pas la 'mafia' que l'opinion imagine et redoute. Au vrai, le mot énarque recouvre deux univers assez différents. D'un côté, celui des fonctionnaires *sans histoire* dont les administrateurs civils forment *les gros bataillons*. A leur tête: les chefs de bureau et les sous-directuers. De l'autre, le monde des dirigeants, des managers qui passent indifféremment du pouvoir administratif au pouvoir économique et politique. Ce sont les énarques dont on parle, beaucoup moins nombreux que les autres et dont *le vivier* est constitué en grande partie par les cabinets ministériels. Bref, il ne suffit pas d'entrer à l'Ena, il faut, aussi, 'bien' en sortir pour faire partie de la nouvelle 'aristocratie'.

SOURCE: C. Sales, *Le Point* (15 août 1977) pp.24-6 (adapté).

Exploitation du texte

1. Expliquez en quelques mots les phrases/termes en italique.

2. Expliquez le titre de l'article.

3. Donnez des exemples de postes qui seraient inclus dans la fonction publique.

4. Pour quelles raisons faut-il bien sortir de l'ENA?

5. Faites le portrait d'un énarque typique et de sa carrière, en vous servant des tournures suivantes: tour à tour, ou encore, il reste à savoir, en un mot, toutefois, au fil des années, en provenance de, au

profit de, à quelques exceptions près, tout au moins, au vrai, d'un côté...de l'autre, bref.

Texte 4.8 L'école et les cloisons

Quand bien même Bourdieu-Passeron ne nous auraient appris qu'une seule chose: l'école favorise ceux qui sont déjà favorisés, socialement favorisés; elle exclut, repousse, dévalorise les autres; c'est aux héritiers des situations privilégiées qu'échoit aussi l'héritage scolaire; les succès scolaires, la possibilité d'une scolarité prolongée, l'accès à l'Université, donc l'accès aux postes dirigeants, pour lesquels sous une forme directe ou implicite les diplômes les plus élevés sont requis, vont massivement à ceux dont la famille est déjà installée en position dominante – ils marqueraient une date définitive dans l'histoire de la pédagogie.

Quand bien même Baudelot-Establet ne nous auraient appris qu'une seule chose: 'l'école unique' n'est pas unique, ne peut pas être unique dans une société divisée en classes; la culture dispensée par l'école n'est pas une, partout d'une même coulée, avec seulement du plus ou du moins selon le nombre d'années de scolarité; les itinéraires, les points d'aboutissement sont non pas simplement différents, mais opposés, tout ce qui se passe à l'école est traversé par la division en classes antagonistes – leur apport serait d'une importance décisive.

Faut-il dire qu'ils nous l'ont appris ou qu'ils nous l'ont rappelé? Car en fait tout cela était déjà contenu dans les analyses de Marx et de Lénine; mais nous l'avions pour ainsi dire, oublié, nous l'avions laissé en marge, tant il est dur de regarder en face une réalité qui dément les idéaux que l'on proclame, bien plus: les idéaux pour lesquels on est effectivement en lutte.

Il était si important de défendre l'école laïque contre l'école inféodée à tel dogme, l'école républicaine contre l'école directement, ouvertement réactionnaire, l'école publique contre la mainmise patronale – et surtout l'école elle-même, l'instruction en face de l'ignorance et de la mise au travail des enfants de huit, dix, douze ans – que nous avions chassé du champ de la conscience claire le caractère de classe du monde scolaire. Pour les combats que nous avions à mener, était-il nécessaire de mettre, même provisoirement, de côté cette terrible dépendance de l'école?

SOURCE: G. Snyders, *Ecole, classe et lutte des classes* (Paris: PUF, 1976) pp. 17–19 (adapté).

Exploitation du texte

1. Expliquez ce que l'auteur veut dire par 'socialement favorisés' et faites un résumé des mécanismes moyennant lesquels l'école favorise ceux qui le sont déjà.

2. Expliquez en quoi '"l'école unique" n'est pas unique'.

3. Quelles sont les luttes auxquelles l'auteur fait allusion dans l'avant-dernier paragraphe?

4. Expliquez ce que l'auteur entend par 'le caractère de classe du monde scolaire' et la 'terrible dépendance de l'école'.

5. Quelle semble être l'opinion personnelle de l'auteur sur la matière qu'il commente et de quelle manière la révèle-t-il?

6. Récrivez le texte en vous servant d'un langage et de structures plus simples de manière à présenter les arguments de l'auteur à un membre du grand public.

Exercices de comparaison et d'application

1. Reprenez les rubriques suggérées dans la première question des Exercices de comparaison et d'application du Chapitre 2 pour résumer, sous forme d'un tableau, les caractéristiques de chacun de ces textes.

2. Faites une comparaison des traits que vous avez relevés dans votre tableau afin d'identifier les caractéristiques des différentes variétés de langue que les textes représentent.

3. Imaginez un débat dans lequel des enseignants dans le primaire, le secondaire et l'enseignement supérieur, un représentant du Ministère de l'Education, un parent, un élève, un étudiant et un membre du grand public discutent du thème: l'enseignement devrait être un service social.

4. Ecrivez une dissertation d'environ 1500 à 2000 mots sur un des sujets suivants:
   (i) 'Offrir à tous les individus de l'espèce humaine les moyens de pourvoir à leurs besoins, d'assurer leur bien-être, de connaître et d'exercer leurs droits, d'entendre et de remplir leurs devoirs;
   Assurer, à chacun d'eux, la facilité de perfectionner son industrie, de se rendre capable des fonctions sociales, auxquelles il a droit d'être appelé, de développer toute l'étendue de talents qu'il a reçus de la nature; et par là établir, entre les citoyens, une égalité de fait, et rendre réelle l'égalité politique reconnue par la loi.'
   Analysez ces principes proposés par Condorcet pour l'instruction publique en 1792 et comparez-les avec ceux qui sont aujourd'hui appliqués dans le système d'enseignement en France.
   (ii) D'après Frappat, 'l'école à tous les égards renvoie encore souvent son image à la société, même si les traits y sont plus accusés, comme en un miroir grossissant'. Examinez le bien-fondé de cette constatation dans le contexte de la société française contemporaine.

5

Leisure

In 1977 a committee[1] was set up to study the ways in which the government should act to encourage and channel the increasing amount of leisure in present-day French society. Their report stressed that the state should have a leisure policy, but it was cautious about the degree of control to be exercised and anxious that individual and group initiative should not be precluded. The committee therefore proposed that the state should focus its attention on improving economic efficiency, national solidarity, and individual freedom of choice in the provision of amenities and access to leisure activities, especially holidays, as befits a democratic society committed to promoting social justice.

The report raises the main issues which are generally investigated in studies of leisure in contemporary Western societes and which will be examined in this chapter with reference to the French context: leisure is presented as a new social value characteristic of the post-industrial phase of economic development and closely related to the desire for a better quality of life and greater social equality; the work ethic is questioned, and the potential of leisure to solve the problems associated with alienation in everyday life is discussed; freedom from the constraints imposed by factors limiting available time and access to resources is advocated, as reflected in the title of the report *Choisir ses loisirs;* ways are sought of ensuring a less wasteful distribution of time, by reorganising the working week, year and life, and by educating members of the public so that they are able to gain maximum benefit from leisure.

The topicality of the report and the relationship it establishes between leisure and the quality of life are important indicators of the stage of development reached by contemporary French society: as elsewhere in the post-industrial world, social or qualitative policies are increasingly given priority over economic or quantitative objectives. It is significant that governments have now begun to formulate coherent policies for leisure, an area in which their intervention would have been anathema a century ago. Leisure has entered the political arena. For example, the French Communist and Socialist Parties, in their *Programme commun de gouvernement* of 1972 and in other policy statements, while continuing to demand an increase in the amount of available free time for all workers, emphasise the positive ideology of leisure as time for cultural enrichment and self-development, and it is significant that the government formed after the election of President Mitterrand in 1981 included a Minister for Spare Time.

Although the preoccupation with leisure is common to all post-industrial societies, the problems associated with leisure time and leisure provision vary from one country to another, as do the ways in which governments and the public are reacting to them: for example, until recently workers' claims in France have centred on increasing the number of paid holidays rather than on reducing the length of the working day, with the result that the French are now amongst the nations with the longest paid annual holidays but also one of the longest working weeks. Since it has become socially abnormal not to go away on holiday, policy is focusing on how to ensure that members of all social categories can take satisfying holidays and how to minimise the threat to the economy and to the natural environment which has arisen from the excessive concentration of holidays for more and more people over a short period of time and in a limited number of areas.

Definitions, concepts and functions of leisure

Most definitions of leisure include the dimensions of both time, the temporal framework, and the activity which it allows, but a third component is nowadays generally taken into account to provide a fuller understanding of the meaning of leisure: namely, the conceptual dimension defined in terms of individual or collective attitudes and behaviour in relation to free time and to the activities which it makes possible. One of the main exponents of leisure theory and of the sociology of leisure in France, Dumazedier,[2] describes leisure as time orientated towards self-fulfilment, and research workers elsewhere also stress the positive value of leisure as an opportunity for resourcefulness and creativity.

Free time is generally defined as residual time, or that which remains once the individual has acquitted himself of his institutional or primary obligations, said to comprise professional duties (including travel to and from work and preparation for work), attention to personal or physiological needs (for example dress, health care), family obligations (covering care for children, domestic chores, time spent over meals and home maintenance), socio-spiritual and socio-political activities (for example religious worship, voting and attending political and trade union meetings). Time spent sleeping is excluded from leisure. The individual is then 'free' to use his surplus time to pursue physical, practical, artistic, intellectual or social activities which will enable him to relax, to enjoy himself or to cultivate his mind gratuitously, either through the acquisition of knowledge or through voluntary involvement in social organisations. Leisure is expected to fulfil at least one of these functions (the frequently quoted three ds of Dumazedier, *délassement, divertissement, développement*, described in Texte 5.1). The most complete leisure activity will satisfy the three functions simultaneously. Real leisure is then characterised by four important properties: it releases the individual from his obligations, whether they be concerned with work or family roles (*libératoire*), the activities pursued are without materialistic, utilitarian or ideological intent (*désintéressé*), they should procure pleasure and personal satisfaction (*hédonistique*) and answer the personal needs of the individual (*personnel*).

It is only recently that leisure has come to be investigated as a separate sphere of human activity and as a social value in its own right. In the late nineteenth and early twentieth centuries the main objective in the struggle to increase the amount of free time available for workers was to allow recovery from alienating work. Leisure was thought to fulfil a compensatory function (a theory expounded in France by Friedmann in the 1940s) and to act as an antidote for the industrial worker carrying out soul-destroying routine mechanical tasks. More recently, particularly since the Second World War, other types of relationship between work and leisure have been described and documented, indicating that leisure may reflect and extend work patterns, that it may be segmented into a separate or opposed sphere of activity, or that the relationship between the two may be neutral. Surveys in the past few years in France suggest that the majority of the population no longer accepts work as a supreme social value: more than three quarters of the sample in the Annecy study[2] cited an activity outside work as their central life interest. There is probably still an important interactive relationship between work and leisure, although its nature may be changing: the better educated and younger generations, according to some surveys, now attach more importance to the interest of their work than to the salary and expect to find in their employment the satisfaction which they derive from leisure. For those condemned to carry out monotonous and uninteresting work, employment may be no more than an unpleasant means of earning a living and enough income to be able to consume leisure goods. The shift away from the work ethic is borne out by the attention firms devote to providing opportunities for after-work activities in order to attract employees. Some authors are concerned that in a consumer dominated and state-directed society, leisure may become so institutionalised and commercialised that it takes on many of the same characteristics as work, becoming routine, standardised and outside the control of the individual. Texte 5.2 examines the way in which leisure may serve as a status symbol through conspicuous consumption and thereby act as a divisive force and encourage competitiveness.

As a proportion of the family budget in 1978, spending on leisure and related consumer goods in France had probably reached about one sixth of the total expenditure of an average family with two adolescent children, according to the *Union Nationale des Associations Familiales*. They spent approximately twice this amount on food but less on housing, clothing and sundry items. It is difficult to ascertain the exact amount spent on leisure activities since special clothing, transport and expenditure on a secondary residence is often counted under a different heading, but there are two significant features which emerge whatever accounting system is adopted: firstly that spending on leisure is increasing more rapidly than almost any other budgetary item; and secondly that the proportion of the family budget devoted to leisure rises regularly with socio-occupational status, indicating that leisure-spending increases with the marginal propensity to consume.

Leisure is then a complex and ambiguous contemporary social phenomenon, which gives rise to much debate and theorising. It has been made possible by scientific and technological progress, combined with social reforms improving living and working conditions. The general affluence characteristic of the post-1945 era, accompanying changes in the economic and social structure of France, has provided the incentive for the rapid growth of a leisure industry. But, as can be shown by a study of the different components of leisure described above, leisure is an area of social life which may be as much a source of problems and conflicts as of communal development and individual fulfilment, an aspect which is humorously portrayed in Texte 5.3.

Leisure time

The belief in leisure as time during which every member of society should be free to pursue activities of his own choice is a characteristic of Western post-industrial nations. Modern historians investigating leisure in France in the Middle Ages show that there was no clear cut distinction between work and non-work activities, and that in a rural economy leisure was generally synonymous with feast days, which served as an opportunity to express a sense of community life. At the beginning of the eighteenth century there were eighty-four feast days and probably about eighty more days in the year when work was impossible because of weather conditions, illness and other impediments. Such unoccupied time was, for the majority of the population, a substitute for work rather than a complement or compensation, and feast days came to be considered as an imposition, since they meant a loss of income. The new calendar, introduced after the Revolution of 1789, abolished religious feast days, in an attempt to undermine the influence of the Catholic church. A ten day unit was instituted with only one rest day. The industrial revolution of the nineteenth century brought about a radical deterioration in the living conditions of the working population. The working day was lengthened, leaving little time for freely chosen activities, and the idleness of the masses came to be considered as a social evil resulting in moral decadence. The demand for free time began to take the form of a political, social and humanitarian conquest by workers' movements in an ideological struggle against capitalism. In 1893 a weekly rest day was reintroduced for women and young people under the age of 18 employed in factories and mines. In spite of the campaigns waged by the church to reinstate time for religious observance, the day was not fixed until 1906 when all workers were granted a day of rest on Sundays.

Due to the pressures exerted by trade union movements and to the changing climate of opinion, the demand for a shorter working week and paid annual leave gained momentum in the first quarter of the twentieth century. In 1936 the Popular Front introduced a law guaranteeing a forty-hour week and twelve days paid leave a year. This important date in the conquest for leisure was celebrated by the creation of a Ministry for Leisure and Sports, which confirmed a new political stance: leisure meant more than simply the right to free time, it was to provide the opportunity for personal development and fulfilment, which had hitherto been the prerogative of only the privileged social classes. In 1967 however the average working week in the non-agricultural sectors was still forty-six hours. The Grenelle agreement between the unions, management and the government after the events of May 1968 gave a new impetus to the demand for a shorter working week, and during the 1981 election campaign President Mitterrand stated he would give top priority to reducing the working week to thirty-five hours.

Although there has undoubtedly been a very substantial reduction in working hours for the whole population over the past century, in spite of legislation, the amount of free time, as defined earlier, is still unevenly distributed. Men work on average more hours a day outside the home than women, and workers at both ends of the social scale spend more time working: the longer day is explained in the case of higher administrative grades, professional and independent workers by financial incentives and by their sense of responsibility and commitment, whereas for the low paid, overtime and moonlighting are necessary to improve their standard of living; for workers in agriculture, a high average figure results from the need to work exceptionally long hours at certain times of the year. As working hours have been reduced, the time spent travelling to and from work has often been lengthened, particularly in the Paris area where it is estimated that manual and lower grade non-manual workers spend on average more than an hour and twenty minutes a day travelling, a problem commented on in Texte 5.4. The trend towards shorter lunch breaks is becoming widespread, and probably about half the working population returns home at midday, but flexible working hours are operated for only a million or so workers. A more adaptable working week has proved difficult to implement. In comparison with their counterparts in Northern Europe and the United States, it would seem that the French have fewer hours of free time during the week. The English weekend is gradually being adopted, but schools still function on Saturday mornings with Wednesday as a free day, or half day in secondary schools, a practice justified by claims that a mid-week break is essential for the mental well-being of school-children. In fact it has been suggested that this distribution of the working week should be exploited elsewhere in preference to the English weekend. Many shops in France open on Sundays and close on Mondays (as well as staying open much later in the evening than do shops in Great Britain). In 1979 proposals to extend Sunday employment in the interests of trade were given a hostile reception by female employees who argued that their family life would be disrupted. Already as a result of irregular work schedules, including shift work and unsocial hours, it is not uncommon for the members of a family to be free at different times during the week. For those employed in the tourist trade or in the service industries, more leisure for the population at large has often meant extremely long working hours at weekends and during holiday periods.

Since 1968 most workers in France have one month of annual leave plus about ten days for public holidays. Almost a third already have a fifth week of leave, whereas in Great Britain not all workers as yet have four weeks. In France individual firms are responsible for negotiating agreements granting extra holidays for long service, non-absenteeism or for breaking up annual leave and taking part of it outside the summer months. The recently introduced fifth week must be taken at another time of the year. When a public holiday falls midweek, it is often permissible to bridge the gap, by adding another day of holiday, although this time may have to be made up later. For example, the Monday may be taken if the public holiday falls on a Tuesday (known as *faire le pont*, a longer bridge being referred to as a *viaduc*).

As already shown, non-work time does not necessarily imply free time, for there are other primary obligations which are big consumers of time. Several large scale surveys have been undertaken in recent years to ascertain the characteristics of time budgets, or the distribution of time usage, by the population of working age. The results confirm the trends mentioned in the second chapter: men generally devote less of their non-work time to household tasks and to their children; women who do not go out to work spend more time than working women on household chores, indicating the elasticity of domestic work; predictably women with children who go out to work full time have, on average, less free time than any other category.

As the level of unemployment and the number of the elderly in retirement increases, more people in the course of their life are exposed to longer periods of 'freed time', and for many of them this is not synonymous with leisure. Reference has already been made to the problems of the aged due to psychological, physical and financial constraints. The attitude of the unemployed to their 'freed time' is a less studied phenomenon, but it would seem that the insecurity associated with unemployment does not encourage a positive approach to ways of using the time made available. Indeed the evidence would suggest that a leisure ethic has not yet replaced the work ethic and that leisure behaviour still tends to reflect socio-occupational status rather than providing a socially acceptable alternative.

Leisure activities and behaviour

A number of important discriminating factors influence the type and variety of observable leisure behaviour: the time available which has already been shown to depend to a great extent upon socio-occupational and family obligations at different stages in the life cycle; social conditioning and economic status, which, as demonstrated in earlier chapters, correlate closely with socio-occupational membership and the level of educational attainment; public and private provision of leisure amenities, which may vary considerably from one geographical area to another and from one social environment to another.

There have been many attempts to classify the different activities engaged in during free time. Some authors base their classification on the issues involved, for example, movement or sociability; others take as their criteria types of experience; while others group leisure activities according to their functions or properties. Since the aim here is to survey the general characteristics of the leisure preferences of French people and to highlight some of the peculiarities of the French context, a few of their most typical leisure activities are briefly reviewed within the framework of three very broad categories which simplify and cut across the various classification systems adopted elsewhere: physical and practical activities, concentrating primarily on sports and other outdoor pursuits, all of which may entail group participation; cultural and social activities, covering the media, the arts and religion, as well as voluntary participation in associations and other forms of social intercourse; a separate category for holidays, which constitute such a prominent feature of social life in France today that they deserve special attention. Holidays provide an opportunity to pursue almost any type of leisure activity and are subject to many of the restraints affecting other leisure behaviour.

Studies in France reveal that in general terms there are a dozen or so dominant leisure activities, and that these are essentially home-based, requiring little effort, specialised equipment, training or knowledge. They are generally undertaken with other family members, except in the case of teenagers for whom leisure is a means of escaping from the family environment. The weekend is characterised by a wide range of activities as compared with the rest of the week, and they are less home-based but remain predominantly family centred. Holidays further extend the range of pursuits and explain the very irregular nature of some leisure behaviour.

Physical and practical activities

In general terms leisure pursuits in these categories may be expected to provide satisfaction and pleasure for the individuals undertaking them, while affording an opportunity for relaxation and personal development. Analyses of the characteristics of the groups participating in the activities falling within this broad area indicate that sports, and in particular team sports depending upon prior arrangements, specialised facilities and regular training, are confined to a small minority of the population. Surveys by the INSEE in 1967 and the Ministry of Cultural Affairs in 1973 of leisure behaviour show that only about 9 per cent of a representative cross-section of French adults (discounting students) participate regularly in a sporting activity throughout the year. The relative lack of participation – spectator sports enjoy great popularity as testified by attendance at football and rugby matches, albeit on a much smaller scale than in Great Britain, and by the interest shown in the annual cycle race (*Tour de France*) – used to be attributed to the limited availability of sports facilities, particularly in the non-urban areas. The poor performance of French athletes in international competitions has for many years been a source of great concern to policy-makers and has prompted investment in sports complexes and other amenities, with the result that the French have in some respects caught up with and passed their neighbours: there are now said to be more public swimming pools *per capita* in France than in the United States, Russia and Eastern Germany. Despite the fact that swimming is one of the most popular sports amongst adults, it is estimated that only about 1.5 million French people go swimming regularly throughout the year. This may be due to the same factors which limit participation in other sports.

The population taking part regularly in sporting activities can be characterised according to several variables. Age is an important discriminating factor: the 1967 and 1973 surveys found that participation fell steeply after the age of 20. The physical state of the individuals concerned and the family obligations associated with different stages in the life-cycle are both related to the age parameter. Marriage and the entry into professional life bring about a reduction in the level of participation. Women are less likely than men to pursue sporting activities and some sports remain a male prerogative. The conditioning received through the family and educational environment, as well as physical limitations, explains sex-based attitudes to sports, but it is also a major factor determining the rates of participation for different socio-occupational groups. Those who have had an opportunity to learn sports at school or in higher education more often continue to pursue them in later life. The higher the level of educational attainment and professional status, the more likely an individual is to pursue sporting activities. In the past the lack of provision of sports facilities in schools implied that only the wealthy had the opportunity to participate in sports through membership of private clubs. Even today the majority of sports clubs are administered by members of higher social categories. In spite of attempts to democratise sports,[3] many sporting activities remain the preserve of the wealthier social categories due to the exclusiveness of the clubs – still an integral part of their organisational framework – as for example tennis, golf, sailing, and because they require special facilities or locations, which are still dependent upon financial status, as for horse-riding or skiing.

This inequality of access to sporting activities is not offset by the training provided in schools. It is still rare for a school to be well equipped with sports facilities, and although sport is now a compulsory part of the curriculum – the Seventh Economic Plan stipulates that there should be two hours a week in the *lycées* and three in the *collèges* – the number of trained teachers is insufficient to provide physical education for all pupils. There is no traditional consensus in France, as in Great Britain, that physical education should be an essential part of character building and socialisation, training the young for a competitive society or preparing them to work as effective team members.

In mitigation it must be remembered that sport, and particularly team sports, are dependent upon regular practice outside the home, require expensive facilities and equipment and demand physical effort. They are therefore subject to constraints on time and space: as already mentioned, the French tend to work longer hours during the week than in Great Britain, they generally arrive home later in the evening and spend longer over meals. It is difficult to arrange regular training sessions at the weekends, as they compete with other family-based activities. The best facilities are in the urban areas, where people spend more time travelling to and from work, and this is the environment from which they seek to escape at the weekend.

It is significant that, after football with nearly 14,000 clubs, the most popular outdoor game which can be played within an organisational framework is *boule,* a game requiring very little prior planning, specialised equipment of facilities. In its Lyons version (*lyonnaise*) and in the southern version (*pétanque*), described in Texte 5.5, it has become a very common activity amongst all social categories and all age groups, as well as being a spectator sport when played for competition.

There is evidence to suggest that individual physical exercise, which does not require specialised equipment, may be gaining in popularity. Amongst activities such as jogging, cycling (more than a quarter of the 1973 sample were adepts of cycling), keep fit exercises, one of the most popular is probably walking. It seems however that the main enthusiasts of hiking and rambling are adults who have grown up to consider voluntary physical activity as a normal part of their daily routine and who are conscious of the advantages of being physically fit. The most typical hiker is male, either a teacher or a professional worker, aged about 32 and from the Paris area. He is seeking to improve his physical condition in the natural environment and considers hiking as an opportunity for social contact.

In a less strenuous form, walking is a physical activity which is accessible to almost everybody. It also requires no prior arrangement and can be undertaken for an unspecified length of time, thereby allowing maximum flexibility and independence. It is a common activity in the evening when it is carried out most often with family members. On weekdays it is generally confined to the immediate vicinity (the town square in the Midi or the local park on a summer's evening become a social meeting place), whereas the weekends are the time to travel away from the urban environment into the surrounding countryside. For more than one Frenchman in four, and more than one in every three town dwellers, walks in the country are the preferred activity at the weekend. Picnic spots have sprung up to cater for the demand, national parks[4] have been created, and sign-posted trails and tracks (*sentiers de grande randonnée*, known as GR) have been set up.

The most common means of transport used for reaching the country is the motor car. More than two thirds of all households now possess a car, and 10 per cent have more than one motor vehicle, but it is more frequently used for pleasure trips than for journeys to and from work. As well as providing a means of transport to a place of leisure, for many motorists, especially in the younger generation, driving is in itself a source of enjoyment.

Angling, sometimes described as the national sport, is another outdoor activity easily accessible to all age groups and all social categories. One in five of the 1973 sample had used fishing tackle in the year preceding the survey. The most enthusiastic anglers belonged to the 15-19 age group, to the categories of semi-skilled manual workers or foremen and lived in medium-sized or large towns. Shooting is also a peculiarly French sport, and the French account for approximately half of the total number recorded for the whole of Europe. More than 9 per cent of the 1973 survey sample had used a gun in the preceding year, and most regular adepts were found to belong to the 25-39 age group and to the agricultural and rural population.

Many practical activities may by definition have a utilitarian end and may be perceived as worklike and as an obligation. They are therefore better described as semi-leisure, but it is often difficult to distinguish between the various reasons for undertaking a particular activity, and the functions fulfilled may also be hard to identify. The motivation of gardeners for example can vary considerably, even for a single individual over time. Approximately two thirds of all French households have a garden, compared with about 80 per cent in Great Britain. Half of all gardens in France are attached to the main place of residence, and the trend towards terrace and roof gardens for the city dweller is fast gaining in popularity. Other gardens are on allotments or at secondary residences, of which there are over two and a half million in France, more than in any other country. 35 per cent are owned by Parisians, for in the Paris area only one fifth of households have a garden at their primary residence. As shown by Texte 5.6, the category most likely to use free time for gardening is that of workers in agriculture. Gardening is a more common activity amongst the elderly and those with a lower level of educational attainment, but the professional and higher administrative grades are often adepts. It is significant that about half of all gardens are used to grow vegetables, and it may be speculated that the utilitarian function of gardening is most prevalent amongst the low income groups.

Although do-it-yourself activities (*bricolage*) are often pursued for practical reasons, nearly three million French people are said to consider this as their favourite leisure occupation and to derive from it satisfaction, pleasure and relaxation. More than one in every two French people claims to occupy himself in this way occasionally, according to the 1973 survey, and men are predictably greater adepts than women, particularly at the age of 25–39 and in the INSEE category for middle-management and administrative staff. According to recent press reports, the do-it-yourself man is becoming more adventurous: in the past the handyman would undertake small repairs and improvements to his home, then interior decorating became more popular, and by the late seventies major works, such as the installation of insulation or of bathrooms, were considered feasible for the amateur. The market has reacted by producing adaptable tools and information banks, as well as courses in electrics, plumbing and carpentry, encouraging individual initiative and resourcefulness (*système D* for *débrouille*).

The fact that many semi-leisure activities, such as do-it-yourself and gardening, and also cooking and sewing, are so often cited as favourite pastimes indicates that activities which may be perceived as an obligation can nonetheless be a source of pleasure. The preference for practical rather than sporting activities is a sign that the traditional conception of sport as a preserve of the wealthy is still prevalent, and it is clear that the provision of more facilities – and the same argument applies for other categories of leisure activities – is not enough to change such firmly entrenched attitudes.

Cultural and social activities

The term 'cultural' is used in a very loose sense here to refer to intellectual rather than physical faculties, and it in no way implies that the activities presented necessarily contribute to the intellectual development or enrichment of the individuals or groups described. The term 'social' refers to activities involving some form of contact or interchange with other individuals, when this is perceived as one of the main functions of the activity.

Although the French generally have less time available every day for leisure than other comparable Western nations, in common with them, almost half their free time is occupied by the mass media, and in particular by television. As illustrated in Texte 5.6, almost 90 per cent of households were equipped with a television set in 1973, and on average every individual watched it for more than two hours a day. These average figures conceal a wide range of viewing habits: a study by the *Institut National de l'Audiovisuel* in 1977 found that 30 per cent of viewers aged 15 and above were responsible for 61 per cent of all viewing. Studies of younger age groups show that television viewing is the main leisure activity of 40 per cent of children aged 8–14. The youngest age group in the sample surveyed in 1973 (aged 15–19) spent the smallest amount of time viewing each week, and the elderly spent by far the largest number of hours watching television.

Viewing time is inversely proportional to the level of educational attainment, as shown in Texte 5.6. The categories with the highest socio-occupational status spent substantially less time watching television than did, for example, manual workers. There would seem to be two fairly distinct extreme patterns of viewing: those who watch every day and whose viewing habits can be described as 'passive', as judged by the fact that they continue to watch programmes they do not like rather than switching off the set, and that they feel they would be very upset if deprived of television for several weeks; viewers in the second category are distinguished by their low level of viewing and their interest in high or elite culture (*culture cultivée*), as typified in Texte 5.7, and by their careful selection of programmes. The choice of high culture programmes is found to be less bound by socio-economic variables than is attendance at live performances of, for example, concerts or theatrical productions.

Viewer ratings for 1977 showed that by far the most popular programmes were those classified as 'fiction', especially feature films (of which a large proportion are imported from abroad), with more than one a day over the three channels[5], followed by drama, serials, series and television films. Television quizzes and other games also enjoy widespread popularity, and light entertainment programmes are watched slightly more than the average for all broadcasts. Amongst the current affairs programmes, the daily news broadcasts attract a particularly wide audience. Documentaries, broadcasts about the arts and religion and children's programmes attract the least interest from viewers, and sports also come below the average.

According to an opinion survey by the SOFRES in 1973 almost half of those questioned watch television for entertainment rather than for information. The place that television occupies in the French home has changed over the years: it seems now to have been accepted as a member of the family, and viewing has become a habit rather than a freely chosen activity. Indeed the attitude of the French public to its television is ambivalent, as demonstrated by reactions in 1979, when strikes disrupted weekend broadcasting (analysed in Texte 5.8). It would seem that even if they watch it regularly, the vast majority of the French public is not satisfied with the service television provides.

Television ownership has not resulted in a dramatic decline in the interest shown in radio broadcasts, but it may have brought about a

change in their function. Almost every family owns at least one radio,
and in 1973 (see Texte 5.6) more than three quarters of the population
surveyed listened to it almost every day. Unlike television, radio attracts
the 20-40 age groups and is less popular amongst the elderly and the
least well educated groups. The indications are that those who listen
frequently tend to do so while pursuing other activities. For some
categories it obviously provides an important source of information
through news bulletins. If the elderly shun the radio, this may be due
to problems with hearing or to the fact that they can devote undivided
attention to one activity and are therefore able to watch television
instead.

As shown in Texte 5.6, the social categories who spend the smallest
amount of their time budget each week watching television are the
groups most likely to read political and social periodicals. However,
readership of daily papers increases regularly with age, after the age of
20, and is more common with men than women. Although several
socio-occupational groups show similar figures for daily readership,
their choice of newspaper may be very different. A survey in 1975 of
four national dailies showed that the Catholic paper *La Croix,* with a
circulation of 127,000, is most popular amongst the non-working
population and the middle and higher administrative grades, and it is
the only daily to attract more women than men. The elderly in retirement are more likely than any other category to read *L'Aurore,* with a
circulation of 280,000, or one of the very popular regional papers. The
higher status groups more often read *Le Monde* than do other categories.
Lower grade non-manual and manual workers are characterised by their
relatively low readership figures.

After its Golden Age between 1881 and 1914, the popularity of the
French press has declined and its function has changed. The circulation
of newspapers today is relatively low compared with that in neighbouring countries: no daily paper in France sells more than a million copies.
With the take-over by the radio and then television of the function of
providing coverage of news events as they occur, the press has had to
adapt to satisfy alternative and often complementary needs. The provincial press has been able to survive and indeed to flourish through its
ability to cover local news. As the regional radio and television net-
works extend their sphere of influence, this function may be usurped,
but it may be some time before they transmit all the minutiae, such as
obituary notices, local cinema programmes and small advertisements,
which are one of the main attractions of the provincial press.

The daily press still serves to explain events and to entertain, but
these functions are being taken over by the growing number of weekly
magazines which can aim at a very specific readership. If concentration

has been characteristic of the dailies, diversification and proliferation apply to periodicals. The most popular weeklies are those associated with television viewing (*Télé 7 jours* and *Télépoche* sold 2,334,301 and 1,491,865 copies respectively in 1975). Amongst the thirty-eight periodicals selling more than half a million copies, the largest single category is aimed at a female readership, and the feminine press accounts for more of the total sales of magazines than any other category of periodicals. About half of the most popular titles deal with issues affecting the family, a further indication of the family-centred orientation of leisure in France. Several weeklies are aimed at a well-educated middle class readership, interested in and informed about a wide range of social, economic and political issues. Although only *L'Express* sells more than half a million copies, other weeklies, such as *Le Nouvel Observateur* and *Le Point,* appeal to a large proportion of the readers who are looking for stimulating discussion of events and ideas.

Readership of daily newspapers does not necessarily coincide with readership of books, for as shown in Texte 5.6 those who read daily papers most regularly often belong to the social categories which in 1972–3 had not read a single book. More than 30 per cent of the population investigated were non-readers: the proportion increases steeply with age and is closely related to a low level of educational qualifications. It is estimated that 80 per cent of all the books published are read by only 15 per cent of the population, and there is a close correlation between ownership of books and of other leisure goods, such as stereo equipment, paintings or a musical instrument. The same categories of individuals tend to buy books and to borrow them from public and private libraries. Library provision is poor compared with Great Britain, and in 1972 only a tenth of the population was using libraries.

If 30 per cent of the population surveyed in 1973 had not read a book in the preceding year, 93 per cent had not been to a concert of classical (as opposed to popular) music given by professionals, and only 12 per cent had been to the theatre. As shown in Texte 5.7, activities associated with high culture concern only a minority of the French population. Visits to museums and historical monuments were more frequent in 1973, but still applied to little more than 30 per cent of those questioned. The general lack of interest shown by the majority of the population in the performing arts and their cultural heritage does not seem to have changed in recent years. Despite the offical claims that France is witnessing an explosion of the arts, it cannot be demonstrated that policies intended to democratise and decentralise cultural facilities have succeeded in raising the level of cultural awareness and involvement of all social categories. The multi-purpose arts centres (*maisons de la culture*), launched in 1963 by Malraux, De Gaulle's Minister of Culture, have not lived up to expectations. Encouragement of the theatre through grants and subsidies has done little to change the overall picture, and the theatre is still not economically viable. The Centre Pompidou, an enormous and costly cultural centre opened in the heart of Paris in 1977, has become a popular tourist attraction but a major financial burden for the Ministry of Culture and Communications, and its role in stimulating interest in the arts is debatable.

The decision taken in 1979 to reduce central government involvement in the arts reflects the general move in recent years away from the organised institutional framework towards what has been called 'industrialised' or 'commercial' culture: people prefer to watch television rather than go to the cinema; they would rather listen to recorded music than go to a concert. The commercialised culture has many of the same advantages as those attributed to the more popular physical and practical activities in that it is generally home-based and family centred. It requires equipment which is readily available and easy to operate, and the individual is relatively free to choose when and how he uses it.

The institutional framework is however being increasingly exploited in order to prepare children for leisure: in primary schools time is set aside for extracurricular activities (*tiers temps pédagogique*); in secondary schools provision is made for educational and cultural project work; after-school activities, ranging from handicrafts to dance and reading groups are provided in *maisons des jeunes et de la culture, centres municipaux des loisirs* and *centres aérés* under the auspices of local authorities. But here as elsewhere it can be demonstrated that it is the middle class families which are likely to make most use of these public amenities, whereas they are not the categories whose need is the greatest.

Another institution which has seen its role as a leisure provider challenged in recent decades is the church. Since it can be classified as a primary obligation, time spent in religious observance is often excluded from studies of leisure. For many people however activities associated with religion fulfil the functions attributed to leisure, providing an opportunity for self-realisation and enrichment, social contact and enjoyment. In some cases they may compete for time with other leisure pursuits, not only on Sundays, but also during the week. The state must guarantee time for schoolchildren to receive religious instruction, and this is normally scheduled on a Wednesday, on which there is no schooling at primary level. But it is very unlikely that the expansion of leisure opportunities alone explains the fall in recent years in church attendance.[6] Rather, both phenomena can be seen as the outcome of the underlying social changes in the structure of the living and working conditions described in previous chapters. Probably less than a third of the French population attends church sometimes and little more than one tenth regularly, although most French people still claim to be Catholics. It is generally thought that the elderly, and particularly elderly women, are most fervent in their religious observance, but studies of the readership of the Catholic paper *La Vie* show that an impressive number of practising Catholics do not fall into this category. Whereas young people are more and more prepared to admit that they do not believe in God, religious sects and mass demonstrations of faith, such as the oecumenical gatherings organised by the Protestant movement at Taizé, have no difficulty in attracting the young.

Observers of the changing scene in Annecy – and it is likely that similar situations prevail elsewhere – comment that the church is finding increasingly that its sphere of action is being confined to spiritual needs and that its cultural functions are being relinquished. If church premises continue to be used for activities not connected with religion, these are less frequently organised by church leaders. There were in 1978 still about twenty associations with religious affiliations catering for groups such as students, rural youth, doctors and the police. The most thriving of the youth movements, *Jeunesse Ouvrière Chrétienne*, which was founded in 1925, today fulfils many of the functions of a trade union, while also maintaining a religious and educational role.

In general membership of associations is characteristic of only a minority of the population: in 1973 fewer than 10 per cent of those aged over 15 were found to belong to a sports club, little more than 3 per cent to a cultural association and 2 per cent to a religious movement. Trade union and political movements attracted only 3.6 and 0.8 per cent of the sample respectively, and it seemed unlikely that even half of the members participated regularly. Membership of associations is more characteristic of men than women, it decreases with marriage and is more common in the better educated social categories and the higher socio-occupational groups. Studies show that positions of responsibility are in most cases held by those who exercise responsibility in their work, and that the hierarchical structure of everyday life tends to be reproduced within this leisure context.

A widely studied social activity which takes place in less formal surroundings and appeals to a broader cross-section of the population is that provided by the café. Most of those who go to a café are looking for company and social contact. The amount of time spent there and the reasons for going are related to sex and socio-occupational status. Going to a café is a predominantly male activity. For members of the working classes, particularly in rural areas and small towns, a visit to a café, generally in the company of work associates, is part of normative behaviour. It may provide an apportunity to play card games and *pétanque* or for betting and chatting. For the lower income groups and unmarried men, the café may also be a substitute for entertaining at home. The higher social categories tend to use cafés only in the more urbanised areas, where they have a wider choice, and they expect to go there for a chat or a business discussion over a meal.

It has been demonstrated that some social groups will be more likely than others to participate in particular leisure activities, and that the more privileged social categories will have access to a wider range of pursuits and be able to exercise greater choice. Where the same activities are engaged in by all social categories, as is the case for walking, watching television or going to a café, there is evidence to suggest that those who do work which is both demanding and absorbing, and who have a high income and a good education, are most likely to exploit their leisure opportunities in an active and satisfying way. The cumulative effect of these advantages in life-styles and social expectations is particularly salient in any analysis of the holiday phenomenon which serves as a microcosm of leisure behaviour.

Holidays

Whereas the English word 'holidays' has religious connotations, the French terms (*vacances* and *congés*) emphasise the interruption in routine activity and that the worker is being granted leave of absence. The break in the work schedule and the escape which it allows from the constraints of everyday life have produced a situation in which holidays have come to be perceived as a social value, a necessity and a right for every individual.

In 1976–7, however, according to the INSEE, little over half the French population went away on holiday. In comparison with 1964, this represents an increase of 9 per cent. The number of holidays taken in the winter increased over the same period by 14 per cent to reach 29 per cent. The low status social groups are slowly improving their position but, as shown in Table 5.1, the higher income groups remain more privileged in terms of the length of stay and the nature of the holiday as well as the number of departures. The low figures for the non-working population are explained by problems associated with age, such as poor health and low income. Those who do take a holiday tend more often than other categories to do so in winter, and the length of stay is greater than the average for all holiday-makers. It is important to remember that this social category groups together individuals from extremely divergent social origins, and that the in-

Table 5.1

Holidays in relation to socio-occupational categories, 1976-7 (%)

	Departure rates	Average number of days	Type of holiday			
			Hotel	Relations, friends' house	Tent, caravan	Holiday village
0*	19.3	19.2	17.6	34.7	17.3	5.2
1			1.9	53.6	29.5	3.5
2	56.6	23.9	17.4	33.0	13.0	1.6
3	90.5	40.1	18.6	37.7	7.9	3.3
4	79.9	31.0	15.1	41.9	14.3	4.4
5	65.8	26.1	16.8	37.5	15.8	5.8
6	48.8	25.3	8.8	42.3	23.6	4.0
7	50.2	28.0	10.4	48.6	15.4	7.3
8	81.5	32.3	7.4	62.2	7.4	2.6
9	38.5	32.2	19.8	49.3	5.9	2.7
Total	53.3	29.4	14.8	42.2	13.9	3.9

* INSEE socio-occupational categories.

SOURCE: *Economie et statistique*, 101 (June 1978) pp.14, 15, 24 (adapted).

equalities which exist amongst the elderly are much greater than those amongst the working population. The low departure rates for the agricultural population are explained in part by their professional obligations, and when they do go away they tend to take shorter holidays than the average.

An important feature of the French holiday scene is their concentration: half of holiday-makers are away in August, and 80 per cent take their holidays between 1 June and 1 October, although probably only about 40 per cent are obliged to do so because of school holidays. Many factories and shops close down completely in August, and the mass migration which ensues is the source of congestion, shortages of accommodation, carnage on the roads and a significant reduction in any economic activity not associated with the tourist trade. Efforts to stagger holidays by juggling with the dates of school holidays or by changing the closure dates for large firms have as yet done little to improve the situation. Alternative solutions are sought in policies to increase the amount of available accommodation and of amenities during the peak periods particularly on camping sites.

As shown in Table 5.1, the most common type of holiday is that spent at the home of friends or relations, but this is the form of holiday which tends to be the least satisfying and is rarely 'freely' chosen. Few holidays are spent in hotels, only 7 per cent of holiday-makers tour, and less than 5 per cent of all trips are package holidays, compared with 15 per cent in Great Britain. As more low income families begin to take holidays and as fewer holiday-makers stay with friends or relations, the number of campers is growing rapidly. Analysts of camping show that this type of holiday is particularly popular amongst the young and amongst manual workers from small towns and rural areas and that campers tend to congregate in the busiest coastal resorts, often it is claimed in overcrowded and unhygienic conditions, although some camping sites are luxurious by British standards.

A much studied phenomenon in the French holiday scene is the attempt by profit-motivated organisations to provide the ideal holiday. Of the main holiday clubs perhaps the best known is the *Club Méditerranée*,[7] which in the early 1950s began to popularise a special brand of open air holiday in makeshift accommodation often in exotic resorts. Their clientele is drawn almost solely from the higher and middle administrative grades with a smaller proportion of employers in industry and commerce, and very few industrial and agricultural workers. Nearly three quarters of the holiday-makers are from the Paris area, the age group 19–49 predominates, more women than men are attracted and a high proportion of unmarried persons. Over the years the villages have become increasingly sophisticated. Their advertising, as described in Texte 5.9, provides an idealised representation of the holiday ethos, which is contrasted with the negative aspects of everyday life.

Although organised touring is less popular in France than in most Anglo-Saxon countries there are some fifty non-profit-making organisations which have been established since the beginning of the century, helped by grants from public funds, which concentrate their efforts on providing cheap accommodation for people who could not otherwise aspire to a holiday. Organisations such as *Tourisme et Travail, Villages-Vacances-Familles* provide facilities for families on low incomes, by adjusting prices and opening their accommodation to pensioners at low rates outside the main holiday season. Some firms subsidise cheap holidays for their employees in their own holiday villages, and the state sponsors a scheme allowing employers to offer holiday subsidies in return for which they are exempted from social security contributions for employees earning less than three times the minimum wage. The old age pension funds and workers' organisations can also issue holiday subsidies. The state has arranged a system of relief workers to enable the agricultural community to take holidays, and public transport provides cheap travel for special categories of individuals, in addition to the standard annual leave reduction (*billet de congé payé*) for all workers.

Over the years the problems of how to occupy schoolchildren during the very long summer holidays – lasting eleven weeks in 1979 – have prompted a number of government policies. Leisure and sports centres (*centres aérés*) have been created in the towns, and holiday centres (*centres de vacances*) have burgeoned in the country and at the seaside. These state-approved centres now cater for several million children each year, and the state, together with local authorities or large organisations which provide facilities for their employees, covers most of the expenditure on capital investment and training facilities as well as running costs. Thereby it is possible, at least in theory, for some children, who might not otherwise do so, to derive benefit from their holidays.

As with other leisure activities it would seem that the functions fulfilled by holidays differ substantially from one social category to another. Ideally holidays are expected to provide an escape from daily routine, but they may simply substitute one routine for another: a holiday with relations or camping does not provide respite from menial tasks, nor does a crowded camping site offer a peaceful contrast to suburban living. The same phenomena of elitism, selectivity and cumulative advantage (described in Texte 5.7 with reference to other leisure activities) tend to determine the quality of the holiday experience.

The report, *Choisir ses loisirs,* referred to at the beginning of this chapter, undoubtedly gives an accurate assessment of the main factors inhibiting a more equitable distribution of leisure opportunities, and of access to activities which are qualitatively satisfying, when it mentions temporal, fincancial and cultural constraints. As has been demonstrated, the amount of free time available for each individual varies considerably according to factors such as age, sex, nature of employment and social status. Income levels fluctuate according to the same variables and affect the type of leisure activities to which different social groups can aspire. It is not however sufficient to provide amenities, whether they be for sports, the arts or for holidays, since the cultural constraints, which make some social categories less likely than others to exploit the available facilities, are deeply rooted in traditional attitudes and behaviour patterns. There are clearly no easy ways of achieving the objectives set out in the Blanc Report: namely to give every individual the possibility of choosing how to organise and use free time and to ensure that leisure provides an opportunity for cultural enrichment and personal development. It may be that in leisure, as in other areas of social life, if amenities are provided indiscriminately, state intervention could even contribute to greater inequality in leisure behaviour, or at the most to only a negligible reduction in the distance between social groups.

Bibliographical guidance

General works examining the growth of leisure in French society and its implications:

C. Guinchat, *Bibliographie analytique du loisir: France (1966-1974)*, (Prague: Centre Européen pour les Loisirs et l'Education, Série Bibliographique 11, 1975)

J. Blanc, *Choisir ses loisirs* (Paris: Documentation Française, 1977),

B. Cacérès, *Loisirs et travail du Moyen Age à nos jours* (Paris: Seuil, 1973)

G. Coronio, J.-P. Muret and C. Guinchat, *Loisirs: du mythe aux réalités* (Paris: Centre de Recherche d'Urbanisme, 1973)

J. Dumazedier, *Sociologie empirique du loisir: critique et contre-critique de la civilisation du loisir* (Paris: Seuil, 1974)

J. Dumazedier, *Vers une Civilisation du loisir?*, new ed. (Paris: Seuil, 1971)

J. Fourastié, *Des Loisirs pour quoi faire?* (Paris: Casterman, 1970)

G. Friedmann and P. Naville, *Traité de sociologie du travail*, 2 vols (Paris: Colin, 1970-2)

'La durée du travail', *Le Monde: dossiers et documents*, 70 (April 1980)

R. Sue, *Le Loisir* (Paris: PUF, 1980)

Studies of leisure behaviour in France:

A. Brasseur, P, Debreu and Y. Lemel, 'Typologie des loisirs', *Collections de 1 'INSEE*, M 72 (1979),

P. Debreu, 'Les comportements de loisirs de Français: enquête de 1967 (résultats détaillés)', *Collections de l'INSEE*, M 25 (1973)

J. Dumazedier and A. Ripert, *Le Loisir et la ville*, I *Loisir et culture* (Paris:Seuil, 1966)

J. Dumazedier and N. Samuel, *Le Loisir et la ville*, II *Société éducative et pouvoir culturel* (Paris: Seuil, 1976)

P. Le Roux, 'Les comportements de loisir des Français', *Collections de 1 'INSEE*, M 2 (1970)

Secrétariat d'Etat à la Culture, *Pratiques culturelles des Français*, 2 vols (Paris: Service des Etudes de la Recherche du Secrétariat à la Culture, 1974)

Y. Lemel, 'Les budgets-temps des citadins', *Collections de 1 'INSEE* M 33 (1974)

Studies of leisure activities:

'Le Sport', *Après-demain*, 191 (Feb 1977)

J.-M. Brohm, *Sociologie politique du sport* (Paris: Jean-Pierre Delarge, 1976)

'La télévision', *Après-demain*, 208 (Nov 1978)

G. R. Hughes, *Les Mass Media en France* (Edinburgh: Oliver & Boyd, 1973)

M. Souchon, *La Télévision et son public (1974–1977)*, (Paris: Documentation Française, 1978)

C. Bellanger (ed.), *L'Histoire de la presse française*, V *De 1958 à nos jours* (Paris: PUF, 1976)

E. Derieux and J.-C. Texier, *La Presse quotidienne française* (Paris: Colin, 1974)

'L'expression culturelle', *Après-demain*, 210 (Jan 1979)

J.-C. Bécane, 'L'expérience des maisons de la culture', *Notes et études documentaires*, 4052 (1974)

A. Laurent, *Libérer les vacances?* (Paris: Seuil, 1973).

E. Mossé and J.-L. Lesage, *Changer les vacances: rapport sur l'aménagement des temps de loisirs*, 2 vols (Paris: Documentation Française, 1978)

Reviews:

There are no specifically French leisure studies publications, but analyses of current trends are made in *Données sociales* and *Economie et statistique*.

Illustrative texts and linguistic exercises

Texte 5.1   Les trois fonctions du loisir

Le *délassement* délivre de la fatigue. En ce sens, le loisir est réparateur des détériorations physiques ou nerveuses provoquées par les tensions qui résultent des obligations quotidiennes et particulièrement du travail. Malgré *l'allègement* des tâches physiques, il est sûr que le rythme de la productivité, la complexité des relations industrielles, la longueur des trajets du lieu de travail au lieu de résidence, dans les grandes villes, accroissent le besoin de repos, de silence, de *farniente*, de petites occupations sans but.

   La seconde fonction est celle du *divertissement*. Si la fonction précédente délivre surtout de la fatigue, celle-ci délivre surtout de l'ennui.

   Vient enfin la fonction de *développement* de la personnalité. Elle délivre des *automatismes de la pensée* et de l'action quotidienne. Elle permet une participation sociale plus large, plus libre et *une culture désintéressée du corps*, de la sensibilité, de la raison, au-delà de la

formation pratique et technique. Elle offre de nouvelles possibilités d'intégration volontaire à la vie des groupements récréatifs, culturels, sociaux. Elle permet de développer librement les aptitudes acquises à l'école, mais sans cesse dépassées par l'évolution continue et complexe de la société. Elle incite à adopter des attitudes actives dans l'emploi des différentes sources d'information traditionnelles ou modernes (presse, film, radio, télévision).
Ces trois fonctions sont solidaires. Elles sont étroitement unies l'une à l'autre, même lorsqu'elles s'opposent entre elles. En effet, ces fonctions existent à des degrés variables dans toutes les situations, pour tous les êtres. Elles peuvent se succéder ou coexister. Elles se manifestent tour à tour ou simultanément dans une même situation de loisir; elles sont souvent *imbriquées l'une dans l'autre* au point qu'il est difficile de les distinguer. En réalité, chacune n'est le plus souvent *qu'une dominante*.
Le loisir est un ensemble d'occupations auxquelles l'individu peut s'adonner de plein gré, soit pour se reposer, soit pour se divertir, soit pour développer son information ou sa formation désintéressée, sa participation sociale volontaire ou sa libre capacité créatrice *après s'être dégagé de ses obligations professionnelles, familiales et sociales.*

SOURCE: J. Dumazedier, *Vers une Civilisation du loisir?* (Paris: Seuil, 1962) pp. 26–8 (adapté).

Exploitation du texte
1. Formulez une défininition des termes 'délassement, divertissment, développement' à partir des données du texte.

2. Donnez en exemple une activité de loisir qui pourrait remplir chacune des trois fonctions en précisant les conditions dans lesquelles elle devrait être exercée.

3. Expliquez comment ces trois fonctions du loisir sont 'solidaires'.

4. Expliquez en quelques mots le sens des autres phrases/termes en italique.

5. Récrivez les deuxième et troisième paragraphes en utilisant d'autres structures afin d'éviter la répétition des pronoms 'elle/s'.

6. Relevez tous les vocables à sens évaluatif et groupez-les en fonction de leur portée positive ou négative et de leur catégorie grammaticale, par exemple substantifs positifs: délassement, allègement, repos, etc.

Texte 5.2   Le loisir signe

Cette approche reprend la notion de besoin par un autre angle. Qu'est-ce qu'un besoin sinon ce que je déclare tel? Ce que je déclare tel, est-ce la conséquence d'un *'besoin humain fondamental'* ou le résultat d'une opération dont je connais mal des règles, où se conjuguent mes pulsions et ma détermination par le contexte, et en particulier par mon milieu socio-économique et par les *'créateurs de besoins'* que sont les media? Le seul besoin fondamental qu'identifient les partisans du loisir-signe et les manipulateurs du loisir comme signe, c'est le besoin de se signifier à travers des pratiques de loisir devenant – dans *une société de forte division du travail* et consécutivement d'indétermination potentielle des activités de temps libres – l'empire privilégié du signe. Le loisir, lieu de l'ostentation, devient alors l'endroit où opère par excellence *la dialectique de la différence* et dont s'empare la sphère de la marchandise. En vacances, il s'agit dès lors moins de rompre avec la vie quotidienne que de manifester cette rupture (non plus Palavas-les-Flots mais Bali) et de la manifester différemment, donc peut-être même l'inverser en continuité (ne pas quitter Paris au mois d'août).

Le loisir, comme *'utopie concrète'*, c'est un système d'images-signes consommées comme telles plus que comme *porteuses d'un contenu;* le loisir devient alors le lieu par excellence d'une aliénation, puisque 'l'homme de loisir' est transformé en un consommateur de signes, en un usager toujours en quête de nouveaux symboles de son identité, définie uniquement comme sa différence.

Dans cette perspective, *l'enjeu du loisir* échappe au politique. En effet, l'inégalité est indestructible, puisqu'elle n'est en fait qu'une différence perpétuellement régénérée dans un processus dialectique.

SOURCE: J. Blanc, *Choisir ses loisirs* (Paris: Documentation Française, 1977) pp. 220–1.

Exploitation du texte

1. Formulez une définition des termes en italique et proposez des exemples pour les illustrer.

2. Faites une paraphrase du texte entier.

3. Présentez en vos propres mots les arguments du texte de manière à faire ressortir les différentes étapes et à démontrer ce que l'auteur entend par le 'loisir signe' et 'se signifier à travers des pratiques de loisir'.

Texte 5.3   C'est papa qui décide

Tous les ans, c'est-à-dire le dernier et l'autre, parce qu'avant c'est trop vieux et je ne me rappelle pas, Papa et Maman se disputent beaucoup pour savoir où aller en vacances, et puis Maman se met à pleurer et elle dit qu'elle va aller chez sa maman, et moi je pleure aussi parce que j'aime bien Mémé, mais chez elle il n'y a pas de plage, et à la fin on va où veut Maman et ce n'est pas chez Mémé.

Hier, après le dîner, Papa nous a regardés, l'air fâché et il a dit – Ecoutez-moi bien! Cette année, je ne veux pas de discussions, c'est moi qui décide! Nous irons dans le Midi. J'ai l'adresse d'une villa à louer à Plage-les-Pins. Trois pièces, eau courante, électricité. Je ne veux rien savoir pour aller à l'hôtel et manger de la nourriture minable.

— Eh bien, mon chéri, a dit Maman, ça me paraît une très bonne idée.

Papa, il a ouvert des grands yeux, comme il fait quand il est étonné, et il a dit: 'Ah? bon.'

— Il faudra faire la liste des choses à emporter, a dit Maman.

— Ah! non! a crié Papa. Cette année, nous n'allons pas partir déguisés en camion de déménagement. Des slips de bain, des shorts, des vêtements simples, quelques lainages...

— Et puis des casseroles, la cafetière électrique, la couverture rouge et un peu de vaisselle, a dit Maman.

— Et la plage, c'est des galets? a demandé Maman.

— Non, madame! Pas du tout! a crié Papa tout content. C'est une plage de sable! De sable très fin! On ne trouve pas un seul galet sur cette plage!

— Tant mieux, a dit Maman; comme ça Nicolas ne passera pas son temps à faire ricocher des galets sur l'eau. Depuis qui tu lui as appris à faire ça c'est une véritable passion chez lui.

Et moi j'ai recommencé à pleurer, parce que c'est vrai que c'est chouette de faire ricocher des galets sur l'eau; j'arrive à les faire sauter jusqu'à quatre fois.

Maman m'a pris de nouveau dans ses bras et elle m'a dit de ne pas pleurer, que Papa était celui qui avait le plus besoin de vacances dans la famille et que même si c'était moche là où il voulait aller, il fallait y aller en faisant semblant d'être contents.

— Moi je veux faire des ricochets! j'ai crié.

— Tu en feras peut-être l'année prochaine, m'a dit Maman, si Papa décide de nous emmener à Bains-les-Mers.

— Où ça? a demandé Papa, qui est resté avec la bouche ouverte.

— A Bains-les-Mers, a dit Maman, en Bretagne, là où il y a l'Atlantique, beaucoup de poissons et un gentil petit hôtel qui donne sur une plage de sable et de galets.

Papa s'est passé la main sur la figure, il a poussé un gros soupir et il a dit:

— Bon, ça va! j'ai compris. Il s'appelle comment ton hôtel?

— Beau-Rivage, mon chéri, a dit Maman.

Papa a dit que bon, qu'il allait écrire pour voir s'il restait encore des chambres.

— Ce n'est pas la peine, mon chéri, a dit Maman, c'est déjà fait. Nous avons la chambre 29, face à la mer, avec salle de bains.

SOURCE: J.-J. Sempé and R. Goscinny, *Les Vacances du petit Nicolas* (Paris: Denoël, 1962) pp. 9–15 (adapté).

Exploitation du texte

1. Relevez les traits linguistiques qui indiquent que c'est un enfant qui parle, et les vocables et structures caractéristiques du langage parlé.

2. L'histoire est racontée à travers les yeux d'un petit enfant, décrivez les mêmes événements vus par l'un des parents.

3. Comment est-ce que les auteurs du texte représentent les rôles familiaux?

Texte 5.4   Travail: guerre à l'horloge

Comment, dans la pratique, l'homme de la civilisation industrielle, esclave de *l'horloge pointeuse, des cadences de production,* des vacances à dates fixes et du renouvellement accéléré des modes, soumis jusque dans ses loisirs à *la grille des programmes* de télévision, peut-il encore faire sa part au hasard, à l'imprévu, choisir sa vie?

Malades du temps, les ouvriers qui se relaient par équipes autour de machines tournant vingt-quatre heures sur vingt-quatre – les 3 x 8 comme on dit – le sont. Physiquement. L'organisme humain n'est pas une machine, il a ses rythmes propres et *on ne les bouscule pas impunément.*

Mais qui n'est pas malade du temps, de nos jours, au moins moralement? A commencer par tous les salariés obligés de vendre leur temps à un patron, de perdre leur vie à la gagner. Métro, boulot, dodo, jusqu'à la retraite. Et, ce jour-là, il ne reste plus qu'à crever, parce qu'on a tellement perdu l'habitude d'avoir du temps à soi qu'on ne sait plus quoi en faire. On jure de se rattraper pendant les week-ends, pendant les vacances.

Mais, dès qu'on a un moment de libre, on a si peur de s'ennuyer, de 'perdre son temps', qu'il faut à tout prix trouver des distractions et qu'on finit par faire appel à des techniciens de l'animation ou à de gentils organisateurs.

Même les privilégiés de ce monde, ceux qui volent en 'Concorde' pour 'gagner du temps', se plaignent tous de ne jamais avoir une minute à eux. Et c'est vrai qu'ils sont débordés, harassés, qu'ils peuvent se payer n'importe quel caprice, mais qu'ils ont de moins en moins la possibilité de se consacrer à ces activités qui ne coûtent rien, qui ne demandent qu'un peu de temps libre: profiter de l'instant, d'un bon livre, de la conversation d'un ami, vivre en famille. Ou même simplement avoir une vraie nuit de sommeil, sans recourir aux somnifères.

On croyait, au XIXe siècle, que les machines, en libérant l'homme des tâches serviles, lui permettraient de consacrer plus de temps aux activités nobles, à l'art, à la pensée, à l'action politique. Les machines ont en effet permis d'accroître la production des biens matériels dans des proportions qui dépassent tout ce qu'on pouvait espérer. Mais *jamais l'homme n'a été moins disponible,* jamais la place de l'art, de la pensée, de l'action politique désintéressée n'a été aussi chichement mesurée. Parce qu'on avait oublié que consommer prend autant de temps, sinon plus, que produire. Et plus on produit, plus il faut consommer, c'est un cercle vicieux.

On a inventé un tas d'instruments pour alléger *les corvées ménagères,* mais les enquêtes américaines démontrent que les femmes consacrent autant de temps à manipuler ces instruments qu'à la cuisine et au ménage traditionnels. L'automobile devait accélérer les déplacements. Mais, pour permettre à toutes les automobiles de circuler, il a fallu augmenter sans cesse la distance entre la maison et le lieu de travail. Aujourd'hui, compte tenu des temps de déplacement et des heures de travail correspondant à l'achat et à l'entretien de la voiture, on a calculé que l'automobile dévore, en moyenne, cinq heures par jour de la vie des Français. Ils ne vivent plus que des journées de dix-neuf heures. Comment rendre aux gens un peu d'autonomie, les faire profiter des promesses du temps? On parle *d'étaler les vacances,* d'assouplir les horaires de travail. Mais on veut aussi que ces mesures améliorent le fonctionnement de la gigantesque machine collective qu'est devenue la société industrielle et qui est l'exacte transposition, dans les rapports humains, du déterminisme scientifique. De sorte qu'elles risquent de se retourner contre ceux qui en bénéficient et de transformer encore un peu plus l'individu en *rouage anonyme.*

SOURCE: G. Bonnot, *Le Nouvel Observateur* (9 oct. 1978) pp.66–8 (adapté).

Exploitation du texte

1. Expliquez en quelques mots le sens des phrases/termes en italique.

2. Faites un résumé en moins de 300 mots des arguments présentés par l'auteur.

3. Quelle est l'attitude de l'auteur envers son sujet et envers ses lecteurs? Comment le sait-on?

4. Relevez les termes et les mécanismes linguistiques exploités par l'auteur pour retenir l'attention du lecteur et pour souligner son point de vue.

5. Les expressions suivantes sont du ressort du langage familier. Remplacez-les par des expressions plus recherchées: métro, boulot, dodo, il ne reste plus qu'à crever, de gentils organisateurs, débordés, chichement mesurée.

6. Rédigez une réponse à cet article critiquant le point de vue de l'auteur et défendant une opinion opposée.

Texte 5.5   Règle du jeu de pétanque

La partie se joue entre deux équipes composées chacune de 2 ou 3 joueurs ayant chacun deux boules. On peut également jouer à 2 personnes, qui prendront alors 3 ou 4 boules chacune.

On tire au sort l'équipe qui lancera *le cochonnet* la première. Un joueur de cette équipe choisit l'emplacement de départ en traçant un cercle suffisamment grand pour que les pieds puissent y tenir et envoie le cochonnet dans le *'port'* réglementaire qui se situe entre 6 et 10 mètres.

Le principe du jeu est le suivant: la boule la plus près du cochonnet donne le point à son équipe.

Un joueur quelconque de l'équipe désignée par le sort lancera sa première boule, en prenant bien soin de garder ses pieds à l'intérieur du rond jusqu'à ce que la boule ait touché le sol.

La boule une fois immobilisée, un joueur de l'autre équipe entrera à son tour dans le rond pour lancer sa première boule et chercher à s'approcher encore plus près du cochonnet en *'pointant'* comme le premier joueur.

Il pourra aussi, si le premier jet de son adversaire était très bon, et s'il juge qu'il ne peut faire mieux, *'tirer'* sur la boule en jeu.

Si le tir est réussi, c'est-à-dire si sa boule reste plus près du cochonnet, c'est à un joueur de la première équipe à rejouer une autre boule, soit le même que pour le premier jet, avec sa seconde boule, soit un quelconque des autres joueurs composant l'équipe.

Si le tir est manqué, et cela arrive souvent, le joueur qui vient de pointer ou tirer, joue à nouveau avec sa deuxième boule, ou bien un autre de son équipe.

Aussi longtemps qu'une boule d'une équipe est gagnante, c'est aux joueurs de l'autre équipe à jouer, soit en pointant, soit en tirant, pour réaliser *un point meilleur*.

Quand toutes les boules ont été jouées, l'équipe qui a la boule la plus près du cochonnet marque un point pour chaque boule plus près que la meilleure boule de l'équipe adverse.

On commence alors une deuxième *'mène'*. N'importe quel joueur de l'équipe qui a gagné la *'mène'* précédente trace un nouveau rond, lance le cochonnet et joue dans les mêmes conditions que pour la première *'mène'*.

Et ainsi de suite, jusqu'à ce qu'une équipe ait gagné la partie qui se joue en 13 points.

SOURCE: Jeu de pétanque fabriqué par La Méridionale (adapté).

Exploitation du texte

1. Expliquez en quelques mots le sens des termes en italique.

2. Cherchez l'origine du mot 'pétanque', et montrez comment le jeu de pétanque se distingue de celui de la boule lyonnaise.

3. Décrivez le terrain, l'équipement et l'ordre des joueurs pour une partie de pétanque.

4. Prenez le rôle d'un adulte expliquant le jeu de pétanque à un enfant au cours d'une démonstration pratique.

5. Rédigez une description d'un jeu de *bowls* destinée à un Français en vous servant du jeu de pétanque comme point repère.

6. Expliquez pourquoi le jeu de pétanque est si populaire en France.

Texte 5.6 Fréquence de quelques activités de loisirs

Activité	Ensemble	Hommes	Femmes	Mariés	Célibataires	15 à 19 ans	20 à 24 ans	25 à 39 ans	40 à 59 ans	60 ans et plus	Agriculteur exploitant	Patron de l'industrie et du commerce	Cadre supérieur et profession libérale	Cadre moyen	Employé	Ouvrier qualifié, contremaître	OS, manœuvre et personnel de service	Femme inactive de moins de 60 ans	Inactif de 60 ans et plus	Pas de diplôme	Certificat d'études	Brevet ou CAP	Baccalauréat et études supérieures
Lecture d'un quotidien [1]	55,1	60,3	50,2	58,6	43,4	37,1	35,2	47,9	64,1	67,6	61,2	60,2	61,1	57,9	60,4	54,3	50,0	41,5	66,3	47,5	58,4	54,4	59,1
Lecture d'une revue d'actualité politique ou sociale [5]	16,6	21,3	12,3	16,4	17,2	9,2	16,4	18,8	18,6	10,7	21,1	17,2	57,2	34,6	20,8	10,7	12,2	13,1	14,1	9,1	13,2	21,9	40,1
Lecture d'un magazine [5,11]	42,8	37,9	47,4	43,5	41,5	45,3	48,0	48,0	44,9	30,9	30,9	34,2	48,1	62,0	51,8	27,3	31,3	45,8	40,0	28,1	43,4	49,0	61,8
Lecture de plus de 20 livres [3]	28,4	30,9	26,1	27,3	31,5	10,8	20,5	34,2	34,1	20,5	8,7	20,8	65,3	48,9	36,3	23,3	26,3	33,3	19,9	14,8	25,4	41,5	52,3
Pas de lecture de livre [3]	30,3	28,3	32,1	32,1	25,6	11,3	13,7	22,4	39,2	43,0	66,3	28,9	8,7	4,0	12,7	23,3	34,1	34,1	43,0	43,3	31,2	20,8	3,6
Écoute de la télévision [2]	74,4	72,3	76,4	78,7	62,9	77,6	53,6	73,7	78,5	82,0	78,9	76,7	52,3	67,0	72,4	78,7	81,7	73,4	82,0	78,8	78,9	73,4	60,6
Durée moyenne d'écoute de la télévision (en heures) [3,12]	15,7	14,1	17,1	16,3	12,4	16,3	12,4	13,5	15,5	19,6	15,7	12,6	7,9	13,4	13,4	15,9	17,1	17,1	19,6	18,1	16,2	13,4	11,2
Écoute de la radio [3]	76,9	75,9	77,8	76,6	80,2	82,2	85,1	80,2	76,4	66,6	78,9	79,0	88,2	86,2	83,2	79,3	81,7	73,7	78,7	69,2	79,2	79,3	78,9
Écoutent la radio seulement pour les informations	35,2	42,5	28,5	39,1	24,6	14,2	31,9	40,5	40,5	39,1	42,2	36,9	48,0	36,0	35,0	38,3	35,5	24,5	24,6	28,3	36,7	36,1	42,4
Utilisation d'un instrument de musique [4,8]	11,3	13,4	9,4	9,0	21,7	25,3	17,1	14,5	9,0	2,8	2,0	8,1	25,3	18,9	12,4	7,1	10,8	14,0	1,8	7,1	8,1	14,5	21,7
Utilisation d'un appareil photographique [4,8]	45,5	49,4	41,9	47,3	41,9	33,3	44,3	54,2	47,3	17,0	33,3	54,2	71,6	64,5	67,4	45,9	48,6	46,8	14,6	26,9	45,9	64,1	67,4
Utilisation d'un électrophone [4,8]	44,8	46,1	43,6	40,9	69,9	75,9	64,6	64,6	41,5	15,0	28,0	47,2	75,9	69,9	61,8	49,4	53,6	48,6	14,6	31,8	39,6	62,4	69,0
Utilisation d'un magnétophone [4,8]	17,3	20,7	14,2	13,5	34,5	35,7	35,4	20,5	15,0	2,7	4,0	32,9	35,0	34,5	22,4	22,0	20,5	16,5	3,4	8,3	14,3	28,1	37,5
Monument historique [3,7]	31,8	33,3	30,4	30,8	35,4	20,7	29,1	39,1	37,5	18,7	18,0	31,0	58,0	43,9	40,1	23,3	24,8	29,0	19,8	18,0	31,0	38,1	54,9
Fréquentation d'un musée [3,7]	27,4	29,4	25,6	25,5	35,7	29,1	29,1	32,5	24,8	16,4	14,7	29,1	53,2	46,9	31,0	24,8	29,0	24,8	16,4	12,8	25,4	44,0	51,8
Sortie le soir [9]	47,1	53,6	40,8	43,0	77,4	76,7	76,7	61,1	38,9	20,4	43,6	52,0	65,0	61,1	50,5	49,1	52,0	40,3	20,4	26,6	44,0	53,6	77,2
Concert [10,7,8]	6,9	8,4	5,4	6,3	8,0	4,1	7,2	7,1	6,7	4,9	6,3	5,2	21,5	14,6	8,0	4,9	9,6	9,6	4,9	3,8	4,8	8,4	19,8
Fréquentation d'un théâtre [6,7]	12,1	12,2	12,1	10,1	16,7	12,0	14,6	14,6	13,7	6,0	1,5	9,4	35,8	22,9	12,0	7,4	6,0	10,1	6,0	6,3	7,1	18,5	36,7
Non fréquentation du cinéma [6]	48,3	44,4	51,9	56,3	17,0	1,5	13,7	33,5	68,7	80,3	68,7	53,6	25,5	16,1	36,9	47,1	46,3	49,9	80,3	65,8	53,6	24,4	17,0
Cinéma [6,8]	21,8	26,9	17,1	11,1	54,3	55,8	50,1	25,0	9,2	4,3	9,9	22,9	55,8	50,1	33,3	26,1	27,6	21,4	4,3	11,9	17,2	33,1	47,7
Assistance à un match ou spectacle sportif [6,7]	24,3	34,0	15,0	22,9	28,0	31,5	27,1	28,6	27,5	8,9	22,9	27,1	27,5	28,6	25,0	33,3	27,6	21,4	8,9	22,9	25,5	24,4	26,2
Fréquentation d'une fête foraine [6,7]	47,2	46,5	47,9	46,5	51,9	63,1	62,9	56,5	43,4	20,4	35,9	42,3	34,8	39,5	56,9	54,7	56,5	49,8	21,7	43,8	49,8	51,9	43,0
Fréquentation d'un bal public [6,7]	25,4	29,8	21,4	21,9	43,2	62,3	43,2	33,2	13,5	0,8	35,9	33,2	10,6	21,4	24,2	34,7	34,7	22,6	0,8	21,0	24,3	29,8	21,4
Jardinage [4,6]	28,4	31,7	25,3	35,3	11,5	5,0	10,6	22,6	34,7	34,7	63,1	35,9	25,0	27,1	22,0	28,6	18,1	22,6	37,5	31,6	33,0	17,2	19,0

Sexe ; *Situation de famille* ; *Age* ; *Catégorie socio-professionnelle individuelle* ; *Niveau d'études*

1. Tous les jours. 2. Un jour sur deux au moins. 3. Hebdomadaire. 4. Souvent ou de temps en temps. 5. Régulièrement. 6. Plus de dix fois. 7. Au moins une fois. 8. Au cours des douze derniers mois. 9. Au moins une ou deux fois par mois. 10. Concert de grande musique « joué par des professionnels. 11. Revue d'actualité politique et sociale, magazine féminin et familial, revue littéraire, artistique, scientifique, d'histoire, etc. 12. Sur cent personnes disposant d'un téléviseur.

SOURCE: *Données sociales* (1978) p.310, à partir des chiffres du Secrétariat d'Etat à la Culture, *Pratiques culturelles des Français*, I *Données quantitatives* (Paris: Service des Etudes et de la Recherche du Secrétariat d'Etat à la Culture, 1974) pp. 127-32.

Exploitation du texte

1. Décrivez les caractéristiques des activités de loisirs d'une femme par rapport à un homme à partir des données du tableau, et indiquez les changements qui pourraient intervenir dans son comportement lors du mariage.

2. Présentez les grandes lignes de l'évolution dans les activités de loisirs couvertes par le tableau au cours de la vie d'un individu appartenant à la catégorie socio-professionnelle de votre choix.

3. Expliquez les écarts, quant à l'utilisation des médias, d'une catégorie sociale à une autre, en faisant intervenir les variables âge et niveau d'études.

4. Comment peut-on expliquer les différences de comportement quant à l'âge et à la catégorie socio-professionnelle en ce qui concerne le jardinage.

5. Quels sont les facteurs qui, d'après ce tableau, semblent être les plus déterminants dans le comportement de loisirs pour les activités présentées?

Texte 5.7   Pratiques culturelles des Français

1. On peut désormais évaluer le poids réel (et il est faible) des pratiquants culturels dans la population française. Si on se limite à *une définition non extensive de la culture* (définition administrative dans une certaine mesure puisqu'il s'agit en grande partie des secteurs *sous tutelle* du Secrétariat d'Etat à la Culture), on s'aperçoit que le public réel, permanent, de la culture, ne représente que 20% des Français, qui cumulent la majorité des activités et des fréquentations (et donc indirectement le bénéfice d'une grande partie des subventions culturelles de l'Etat).

2. Par ailleurs, cette typologie éclaire bien la leçon que l'on pouvait tirer déjà des *croisements socio-démographiques,* à savoir que la culture (prise au sens restreint, mais d'usage le plus courant, de culture cultivée: spectacles, lecture, visites diverses, presse, pratique amateur, etc..) reste globalement:

● *élitaire* (parce qu'elle ne touche qu'une faible partie de la population);

● *sélective* (parce qu'elle atteint de manière inégale les diverses couches sociales: on voit bien dans les trois premiers types la place prépondérante occupée par les classes privilégiées);

● *et cumulative* (dans les deux sens du terme, c'est-à-dire à la fois que la culture va aux gens cultivés – un peu comme on dit que 'l'argent va aux riches' – et que la pratique entraîne la pratique).

3. Il faut substituer à la vision monolithique d'un 'privilégié culturel' une représentation plus nuancée: il existe 3 modalités distinctes

d'appartenance à cette catégorie socio-culturelle. Cette description empiriste de la réalité ne remet cependant pas en cause la notion très réelle et globale de privilège culturel, dont la nature sociale, c'est-à-dire de classe, apparaît très clairement dans cette enquête.

4. Par contre, il serait très hasardeux d'épiloguer sur la répartition en trois types des plus défavorisés du point de vue de la pratique culturelle, dans la mesure où ce qui les différencie réellement les uns des autres n'appartient justement pas en grande partie au domaine des *pratiques culturelles 'reconnues'* et recensées ici, et est donc mal saisi par la présente enquête (cela nécessiterait une approche théorique complémentaire à l'enquête quantitative sur des *pratiques comptabilisables*). De plus, on court le risque de voir interpréter l'analyse de ces trois types en termes d'absence totale de pratiques 'culturelles', alors qu'on est sans doute en présence de pratiques culturelles autres, de l'ordre de la quotidienneté et des relations sociales, qu'on ne saisit ici ni au niveau de leur existence, ni au niveau de leur contenu.

SOURCE: Secrétariat d'Etat à la Culture, *Pratiques culturelles des Français*, I. *Données quantitatives* (Paris: Service des Etudes et de la Recherche du Secrétariat d'Etat à la Culture, 1974) pp. 142–3 (adapté).

Exploitation du texte
1. Expliquez en quelques mots le sens des phrases/termes en italique.

2. Faites un résumé en quatre phrases des conclusions que les auteurs ont tirées de leur étude de différents types de Français du point de vue de leurs pratiques culturelles.

3. Reformulez la dernière phrase du troisième paragraphe de manière à expliquer ce que les auteurs entendent par la nature sociale du privilège culturel.

4. Exprimez la dernière phrase du texte en vos propres mots, et donnez des exemples de ces 'pratiques culturelles autres' que l'enquête n'a pas su saisir. Cherchez à expliquer cette lacune.

5. Rédigez un article de presse exprimant votre opinion sur les conclusions présentées dans ce texte.

Texte 5.8   Le prix de la création

Les Français n'ont jamais vraiment accepté leur télévision. Ils entretiennent avec elle d'étranges relations, faites de fascination et de haine, qui les conduisent à réagir avec passion à tout mouvement de grève. Depuis près de trois semaines, deux attitudes apparemment contradictoires s'affirment ainsi au fil des jours. D'une part, on s'indigne d'être privé des programmes habituels ou tout au moins, les soirées n'étant que peu touchées, de ceux de l'après-midi et du week-end. Pensez aux personnes âgées, aux malades, aux familles, gronde *la rumeur publique*, relayée par quelques journaux prompts à saisir l'occasion de manifester leur colère.

D'autre part, comme par l'effet d'*un dépit amoureux,* on se dit satisfait d'échapper pendant quelque temps au *bombardement de l'image électronique* et l'on découvre avec émerveillement les plaisirs de la conversation, le bonheur de la lecture, les joies du cinéma ou de la promenade. Voyez comme les enfants sont sages, font bien leurs devoirs et se couchent de bonne heure quand ils sont arrachés à la contemplation du petit écran, susurre la *vox populi,* qui, faisant écho à la méfiance ancienne des intellectuels, communie dans le mythe du paradis perdu de la *'galaxie Gutenberg'.*

Ces deux thèmes – la tristesse de la frustration et le contentement de la liberté retrouvée – ne sont pas aussi opposés qu'ils en ont l'air. Ils ont en commun de refléter la faible estime dans laquelle sont tenus les gens de télévision.

Même quand elles attirent une vaste audience, les émissions semblent frappées d'une sorte de suspicion aux yeux des téléspectateurs, qui prétendent les regarder *faute de mieux* et qui, lorsqu'ils en sont privés, feignent d'être soulagés, tout en reprochant aux réalisateurs et aux techniciens de se moquer du *contribuable.*

Certaines réactions se comprennent. Il est normal que ceux qui, pour une raison ou une autre, sont immobilisés se plaignent de la grève et il est possible que l'arrêt des émissions ait eu, sur les enfants notamment, une influence bénéfique. Ce qui est remarquable en tout cas, c'est la façon dont ces faits assez banaux sont utilisés pour *dénigrer les grévistes.*

Boudée par les représentants de la culture classique, qui, pour l'avoir ignorée ou méprisée à ses débuts, n'ont pas su ensuite s'y faire une place, la télévision suscite encore, dans toutes les couches de la population, une certaine mauvaise conscience, qui se traduit par un sentiment d'hostilité diffuse. Des responsables des chaînes vont même jusqu'à supposer que le gouvernement trouve son avantage à cette situation, qui encourage, à intervalles réguliers, de vigoureuses interventions au Parlement et qui permet de contrôler un instrument, tenté, par sa nature même, d'abuser de sa puissance.

Toujours est-il que de nombreux téléspectateurs se délectent à la lecture d'articles ou de rapports vengeurs sur *la gabegie régnante* et, en période de grève, ne manifestent pas la moindre compréhension. Il serait pourtant souhaitable que cessent *les condamnations sommaires et les affirmations péremptoires.*

SOURCE: T. Ferenczi, *Le Monde* (27 fév. 1979) pp.1, 16 (adapté).

Exploitation du texte

1. Expliquez en vos propres mots le sens des phrases/termes en italique.

2. Résumez en environ 100 mots ce que l'auteur veut dire lorsqu'il constate que les Français entretiennent avec leur télévision 'd'étranges relations'.

3. Relevez tous les antonymes employés dans le texte pour présenter les attitudes contradictoires des Français envers la télévision.

4. Commentez les remarques faites par l'auteur sur l'attitude des représentants de la culture classique.

5. Préparez une lettre à la presse en réaction à cet article, présentant soit le point de vue d'un parent content d'échapper aux contraintes de la télévision, soit celui d'une personne âgée privée de son occupation préférée.

Texte 5.9   L'idéologie hédoniste-consommatrice du Club

La thématique du discours publicitaire représente les vacances-club comme *l'image inversée* de la société urbaine-industrielle et de sa vie quotidienne; elle s'articule selon *une succession d'antithèses mani-chéennes* opposant quotidienneté et vie de vacances comme s'opposent le clos, le cloisonné et le fermé à l'ouvert, la rationalité à l'irrationnel de l'affectivité, le compliqué et le sophistiqué à la simplicité et la pureté de l'originel et d'une manière plus large la médiocrité au bonheur:

1. alors que la vie quotidienne se déroule dans un milieu urbain grisâtre et bétonné, loin de l'eau et de la lumière, dans *un espace sur-chargé et quadrillé* et *un temps fonctionnalisé,* le plus souvent dans la fadeur sinon la laideur, la vie de vacances, elle, s'épanouit au sein d'un environnement ensoleillé et lumineux, près de l'eau et de la nature vivifiante, c'est-à-dire dans un cadre où l'espace est illimité et le temps fluide et où règne la beauté;

2. alors que la vie quotidienne nous plonge dans la foule solitaire et nous abandonne à la froide indifférence des contacts anonymes, la vie de vacances nous fait connaître la chaleur de l'existence villageoise où l'on trouve le sentiment communautaire et surtout la communication directe et sympathique avec les autres;

3. alors que la vie quotidienne *subit le joug de la rentabilité* et nous accable de tensions et soucis de toutes sortes, la vie de vacances nous immerge dans le monde de la détente, c'est-à-dire de la spontanéité, de la fantaisie et de l'insouciance;

4. alors que la vie quotidienne est menée sous le signe de la limite et du rationnement, la vie de vacances offre la plénitude, l'abondance et le libre jeu de toutes nos possibilités;

5. alors que la vie quotidienne nous enserre continuellement dans un réseau d'obligations, de restrictions et de contraintes les plus diverses (hiérarchies, horaires, interdits....), la vie de vacances est le passage au règne de la liberté;

6. enfin, alors que la vie quotidienne nous impose l'ennui du travail (bureaucratisé et parcellisé) propre au monde industriel et par suite nous atrophie, nous sépare de nous-mêmes et finalement nous mène à l'alié-nation, la vie de vacances – dans les villages du Club, bien sûr – nous fait accéder au bonheur dans le jeu et la fête retrouvés, ce qui nous permet

d'être nous-mêmes et de jouir joyeusement de notre personnalité. Le Club n'a d'ailleurs pas besoin de longuement décrire *l'enfer-repoussoir* de la quotidienneté: il lui suffit d'insister sur les 'biens' qu'elle met à notre disposition pour que du même coup nous ressentions par contraste à quel point nous végétons dans la triste vie ordinaire, pour que nous éprouvions un violent désir de rupture et d'évasion et pour que nous sentions encore davantage le caractère éminemment *attrayant-attractif* des vacances au Club.

SOURCE: A. Laurent, *Libérer les vacances* (Paris: Seuil, 1973) pp. 116–18.

Exploitation du texte

1. Expliquez en quelques mots le sens des phrases/termes en italique.

2. Commentez l'emploi de 'nous' dans le texte.

3. A partir des données du texte, dessinez un tableau représentant d'un côté les aspects caractéristiques de la vie quotidienne et de l'autre les traits attribués aux vacances.

4. Relevez les qualités des vacances-club qui répondent aux différentes fonctions du loisir proposées par Dumazedier (Texte 5.1).

5. L'auteur semble reprendre lui-même le ton du discours publicitaire dans ce texte. Relevez et analysez les termes et les expressions, ainsi que les autres mécanismes qui donnent cette impression. Ensuite montrez comment il obtient un effet ironique.

6. Préparez un document publicitaire pour le Club Méditerranée visant les cadres moyens.

7. Ecrivez une lettre au directeur du Club exprimant votre déception lors d'un séjour dans un village du Club à Cefalu.

Exercices de comparaison et d'application

1. Reprenez les rubriques suggérées dans la première question des Exercices de comparaison et d'application du Chapitre 2 pour résumer, sous forme d'un tableau, les caractéristiques de chacun de ces textes.

2. Utilisez les résumés que vous avez préparés pour les textes de tous les chapitres afin de dresser un bilan des traits particuliers aux différentes variétés de langue que vous avez examinées au cours de cette étude.

3. Imaginez un débat sur le thème suivant: 'Le travail n'est plus qu'un moyen plutôt désagréable de gagner sa vie et de se procurer le plus de loisirs possible. C'est seulement pendant le temps de loisir que l'homme pourra essayer de se réaliser.' (Cacérès).

4. Ecrivez une dissertation d'environ 1500 à 2000 mots sur un des sujets suivants:

(i) En 1965, il semblait que le loisir allait cesser d'être un sous-produit de la civilisation pour devenir un produit base. Examinez le bien-fondé de cette proposition dans le contexte de la société française contemporaine.

(ii) D'après Dumazedier, le loisir constitue une nouvelle valeur sociale de la personne qui se traduit par un nouveau droit social. Analysez les conséquences politiques et pratiques d'une telle conception du loisir dans le contexte français.

Conclusion

In the course of this study of contemporary French society reference has frequently been made to other Western post-industrial nations, particularly Great Britain and the German Federal Republic, in order to highlight the similarities and differences in the ways in which they are developing. There is much evidence to suggest that countries in the Western world are adopting more and more the same models of behaviour and attitudes. Similar changes are occurring in population structure: due to greater life expectancy and fluctuations in the birthrates and deathrates, the proportion of young and elderly people in relation to the population of working age has altered dramatically, creating problems associated with the dependency ratio; the acceleration of urbanisation and industrialisation in the post-war period has encouraged migratory movements and brought about major shifts in the socio-occupational structure of the population. Family patterns and the relationships between the generations are changing; the new models are being reinforced by the norms presented in the media, and they are sanctioned by legislation. The demand as of right for a higher standard of social welfare provision, including facilities for education and leisure, is common to all post-industrial societies, as emphasis shifts from quantitative to qualitative concerns.

Within each of these areas there remain important differences from one country to another, whether it be in the organisational structure of the existing systems and the process involved, or in the nature and intensity of the current demands. It has been demonstrated that many features of the post-war growth and change in the distribution and composition of the population are peculiarly French: the imbalance in the structure by age and sex is more acute than in most other Northern European nations; France is characterised by a particularly high concentration of population and resources in the capital and by a relatively late changeover from a mainly rural and small craft economy to one dominated first by the industrial and then by the service sector, a structure considered typical of the phase of mature industrialisation. Al-

192

though the French seem to be adopting the same model of family size as their neighbours, this pattern is by no means universal, and the role expectations of members of the family have not changed to the same extent as in some Northern European countries. The French social security system has been shown to differ markedly from that introduced in Great Britain, in the underlying principles on which it is based, in the way it is financed, the part played by the private sector and the degree of protection it affords. The educational system in France shares the same general objectives as those upheld elsewhere in Europe, but it is distinguished from them by the problems it has inherited from a rigid centrally-controlled bipartite structure dating from the nineteenth century, by the way in which the process of reform operates and by the firmly entrenched attitudes of the pressure groups concerned. More free time and a greater variety of leisure activities are common to all post-industrial societies, but the French still tend to have less free time during the working week and to prefer longer holidays. The range of leisure pursuits to which different social groups have access continues to be determined to a greater extent than in most other countries in Northern Europe by cultural factors dependent on traditional attitudes and patterns of behaviour and the ways in which leisure socialisation takes place.

An attempt has been made in this study to produce a snapshot of contemporary French society. The information used has often been the most recent available, and it must be remembered that it may be several years before the analyses of data collected in a national census or a major survey are published. Some trends and changes have been recorded and interpreted almost as they are taking place, and therefore without the 'distance' of the historian. The 1981 victory of the Socialists after twenty-three years in opposition is expected to bring substantial shifts in policy, such as cannot be predicted at the time of writing. The advantage of this approach is that it stresses the dynamic dimension of the subject matter, but it also places the onus on the reader to pursue constantly the course of events through the contemporary press and the periodical literature. Equipped with the necessary analytical apparatus the observer of social change should be able to compare trends from one survey to the next and evaluate the hypotheses formulated.

A number of interrelated themes have recurred regularly throughout this study: the cumulative effects of different variables influencing the life chances of individuals and resulting in different forms of social inequality; a concern for improving the quality of life for every member of society; increasing state intervention in social life, ostensibly to bring about greater social justice and to satisfy qualitative demands. These themes reflect the main preoccupations of the French in the 1970s and are fundamental to an understanding of the present stage of the country's development.

In the description and analysis of the major social sub-systems reference has been made continually to the variables of sex, age, ethnic and geographical origins, socio-economic and cultural factors, which determine an individual's social status, his normative behaviour and the way he interacts with other members of society and social institutions. This process can be observed throughout the life cycle of any member of society. It affects his chances of being born into a particular type of family, which in turn influences language acquisition, cultural development and physical well-being. Progress through the educational system, access to information and the ability to understand it compound situations of privilege or of disadvantage and exclusion, both in terms of the rewards received and the risks incurred. The evidence suggests that longer schooling and more higher education have not reduced inequalities of opportunity. Rather it would seem that the educational system has been exploited by the privileged social groups to legitimatise their position, enabling them to continue to dictate cultural and ideological values to the rest of society. Once established, and in the absence of compensatory mechanisms, these inequalities of condition and opportunity remain throughout the working life. They are mirrored in non-work activities and become even more acute in old age. Life expectancy and the causes of death are affected by the same variables, completing the cumulative process. It would seem that the welfare services are virtually ineffective in eliminating such deep-seated social differences, and it has been argued that the extension of welfare provision may accentuate inequalities and thereby ensure the reproduction of the social hierarchy.

Since this situation of cumulative privilege or disadvantage is perpetuated from one generation to another through the medium of the family, opportunities for mobility are limited. Studies of the process of social mobility in the post-war period show that individuals tend to move only short distances to neighbouring categories. Structural mobility, caused by changes in the distribution of the working population according to economic sectors, conforms to the same pattern, bringing about movements such as that of agricultural labourers to manual work of a similar status in the industrial sector. The attitude of the public at large towards inequalities of condition fluctuates according to their perception of the opportunities for promotion, but it is also influenced by the state of the nation's economy, and in a period of recession the level of tolerance is lower, The most strongly resented inequalities in the late 1970s, according to surveys, were the differences in working conditions between manual and non-manual categories, those between wage earners and the self-employed in respect of income tax and social security contributions and those between men and women in access to employment and in salary levels. Wage differentials within the working population, which are probably greater in France than in many neighbouring countries, are generally underestimated, as are differences in access to goods and services. Most people agree that there should be inequalities: the concept of an egalitarian society and of hereditary privilege is rejected in favour of equality of opportunity and achieved privilege, since importance is attached to avoiding a situation of uniformity and to preserving incentives. There is much evidence to suggest that, although the general feeling is that existing inequalities are excessive and should be reduced, a principle stressed in left-wing propaganda, it is doubtful whether anyone is prepared to forgo his own advantages or to see his own standard of living deteriorate.

Most observers of the present—day scene in France agree that the overall rise in living standards in the post-war period, the extension of the social services and in particular the introduction of basic minima, whether it be a statutory minimum wage, a family supplement or old age pension, have brought about a substantial reduction in the number of people living in absolute poverty. The causes of hardship have not however been eliminated, nor has relative poverty disappeared. As demonstrated throughout this study the distance between the two extremes of the social scale had not been significantly reduced by the end of the 1970s. The assumption implicit in the concept of equality of opportunity, and the much used formula of greater social justice, which most people advocate instead of social equality, has been that needs should not be satisfied directly. Rather individuals should be rewarded for their labours and must therefore be made capable of working and of earning the means with which to satisfy their needs in the market situation. This is borne out by the trend in the 1970s towards rehabilitation and reintegration of social misfits on the assumption that they should be expected to adopt the dominant norms of society. The exploitation of the concept of equality of opportunity and social justice by Barre's government has been much criticised, particularly by left-wing intellectuals, for the stress it laid on market mechanisms and consequently on the ability to work. It could be seen, they claimed, as a pretext for not interfering with the underlying social structure and consequently with basic social inequalities.

The search for greater social justice is frequently referred to in conjunction with that for a better quality of life, evoking not only the reduction of hardship and suffering, but a concerted effort to improve living and working conditions. Increasingly concern is expressed about the organisation of working hours, the work ethic is questioned, and job enrichment has become a keyword. Publicity is given to the problems of pollution and industrial accidents, to the need for preventive medicine, protection of the environment, avoidance of waste, improved standards of housing and community life, better facilities for children outside school hours and easier access to welfare services. Leisure is by definition the area of social life which is perhaps most closely concerned with qualitative objectives. Recent studies indicate that public opinion, particularly amongst the more privileged social groups, is giving less weight to opulence, status and the need for achievement in social life and attaching more importance to self-fulfilment, enjoyment, comfort and happiness, qualities which correspond closely to the functions often attributed to leisure.

Perhaps the most frequently recurring theme in the present study has been that concerning the interventionist role of the centralised, bureaucratic and technocratic machinery of the state. It has been argued that the welfare state has not become so pervasive in France as in Great Britain: the French social security system emphasises individual responsibility and the insurance principle; incentives to work hard have been maintained through relatively low income tax and concessions for high wage earners on social insurance contributions; and the provision of health care, education and subsidised holidays depends to a large extent on a strong private sector under contract to the state. The anonymous hand of the state is however felt in all areas of social life and throughout the life-cycle. In spite of policies for regionalisation and devolution, the tradition of strong centralised control remains intact, whether it be in determining the conditions for divorce and abortion, appointing teachers, building cultural centres or setting up national parks.

In the 1970s the emphasis of state intervention shifted from quantitative to qualitative objectives. It was suggested in a report by the government commission set up to investigate social inequalities during the preparatory phase of the Seventh Economic Plan that in the future the planning procedure should be reversed: social objectives should be established and their economic consequences studied rather than designing social policies in response to economic trends. In any event it was stressed that social objectives should not be sacrificed to economic ones and that quality and quantity should be seen as complementary aims.

It has been shown that the role of the state is ambivalent: in a democracy, governments must respond to the demands of their voters and react to individual and group pressures, while at the same time serving as a collective conscience and instigating policies designed to protect the interests, well-being and security of the nation, which may not always be compatible with those of its individual members or with personal freedom of choice. In France this conflict of interests has resulted in widespread opposition to a system based on the notion of national solidarity, reminiscent of the traditional individualistic values considered characteristic of the French. The implication behind the social policies pursued since 1945 has been that the state should enable individuals to take better advantage of the economic system, and that absolute poverty and relative inequality would progressively disappear as a consequence of this action. As already demonstrated, these objectives had not been achieved by the end of the 1970s. It is still doubtful whether more state control of social life would be acceptable to the public at large. Awareness of this attitude was reflected in the cautious approach adopted during Giscard d' Estaing's presidency in policy documents on leisure, an area of social life in which state interference had remained relatively limited. It is significant that the proposals made emphasised individual freedom of choice and collective responsibility at the community level, rather than a major increase in state control.

It could be argued that because of the evolutionary nature of society, many of the questions debated here may become less topical during the 1980s. The gradual shift in individual and group values — from materialistic and economic objectives to a search for greater equality of opportunity and social justice, a better quality of life, more individual freedom of choice and more satisfying human relationships, ideals generally considered characteristic of the post-industrial phase of development — would seem to correspond closely to the social policy objectives of the Socialist government. Whether or not they are embraced by the whole of French society will depend upon economic and political events over the next few years. It remains to be seen whether the many fundamental changes advocated by the Left can be carried through, and if so how such changes will affect the social systems and social structures of the country. Whatever the outcome, it is likely that the issues examined here will remain central to any discussion about developments in contemporary French society over the next decade.

A General Bibliography

General works analysing social systems and processes in post-war France and depicting present-day social life:

J. Arbois and J. Schidlow, *La Vraie Vie des Français* (Paris: Seuil, 1978)

J. Ardagh, *The New France: a Society in Transition 1945–1977*, 3rd ed. (Harmondsworth: Penguin, 1977),

J. Blondel, *Contemporary France: Politics, Society and Institutions*, (London: Methuen, 1974)

D. G. Charlton, *France: a Companion to French Studies* (London: Methuen, 1972)

A. Codevilla, *Modern France* (LaSalle: Open Court Publishing Company, 1974)

G. Dupeux, *La France de 1945 à 1969*, 3rd ed. (Paris: Colin, 1972)

J. E. Flower (ed.), *France Today: Introductory Studies*, 4th ed. (London: Methuen, 1980),

V. Giscard d'Estaing, *Démocratie française* (Paris: Fayard, 1976)

P. George, *La France* (Paris: PUF, 1972)

S. Hoffman, *Essai sur la France: déclin ou renouveau?* (Paris: Seuil, 1974)

E. H. Lacombe, *Les Changements de la société française* (Paris: Editions Ouvrières, 1971)

P. Longone, *53 Millions de Français* (Paris: Centurion, 1977)

P. Miler, P. Mahé and R. Cannavo, *Les Français tels qu'ils sont* (Paris: Fayard, 1975)

P. Miquel, *Economie et société dans la France d'aujourd'hui* (Paris: F. Nathan, 1971)

M. Parodi, *L'Economie et la société française de 1945 à 1970* (Paris Colin, 1971)

A. Peyrefitte, *Le Mal français*, 2 vols (Paris: Plon, 1971)

P. Sorlin, *La Société française*, II 1914–1968 (Paris: Artaud, 1971)

E. Stillman (ed.), *L'Envol de la France: portrait de la France dans les années 80* (Paris: Hachette, 1973)

Y. Trotignon, *La France au XXe siècle*, 2 vols (Paris: Bordas-Mouton, 1968, 1972)

G. Vincent, *Les Français de 1945 à 1975* (Paris: Masson, 1977)

Annotated bibliographies of works about social and cultural life and education in contemporary France:

R. Lasserre (ed.), *La France contemporaine: guide bibliographique et thématique* (Tübingen: Niemeyer, 1978)

Reviews:

Actualités service, Après-demain, Autrement, Cahiers français, Collections de l'INSEE, Données sociales, Droit social, Economie et statistique, Esprit, Faits et chiffres, Intérêts privés, Liaisons sociales, Le Monde: dossiers et documents, Le Nouvel Observateur, Notes et études documentaires, Le Point, Population, Population et sociétés, Problèmes politiques et sociaux, Revue française de sociologie, Revue française des affaires sociales.

Notes to Chapters

1. Demographic features

1. An urban area, as defined in 1962, is based on a group of units of more than fifty inhabitants, formed by dwellings of less than 200 metres apart and together making up a community of more than 2000 inhabitants.

2. Defined by official sources as independent and salaried workers, family members carrying out paid work, the product of which is included in the figures for national income, and also those seeking paid employment. Hence the unpaid family workers in small shops and firms and on farms are part of the working population, whereas housewives are not.

3. Although many objections can be raised about this system of classification: for example, large and small farmers are grouped together, as are large and small employers in commerce and industry, although a separate sub-category is created for those with a very small number of employees. It is argued by the INSEE that criteria such as the surface area cultivated by farmers would not be a good indicator of social status, and that income level would not afford an accurate means of assessment. The grouping of foremen with industrial workers is also criticised, but the INSEE maintains that they should be grouped with workers rather than management and administrative staff, since they often rise through the ranks. The grouping of family helpers with the person for whom they are working can also be misleading.

4. In its *Classification of Occupations*, the Office of Population Censuses and Surveys regroups the categories to form five 'Social Classes' and seventeen 'Socio-economic Groups'. The groupings for social classes are based on the general standing in the community of the occupations concerned, and this is taken to correlate closely with, and depend upon, factors such as education and economic environment, but it is not considered to be directly related to average income levels for different occupations. The Socio-economic Groups contain individuals whose social, cultural and recreational standards and behaviour are similar, as determined from consideration of their employment status and

occupation. From a cross-classification of the Social Classes and Socio-economic Groups, the Office of Population Censuses and Surveys has produced a new classification referred to as 'Socio-economic Class'.

2. The Family

1. As described by E.Burgess, H. Locke and M. Thomas in *The Family: from Traditional to Companionship*, 4th ed. (New York: Van Nostrand Reinhold Co., 1963).

2. Until 1970 Article 213 of the *Code civil*, read out in the wedding ceremony, stated: *'Le mari est chef de la famille'* and *'la femme concourt avec le mari à assumer la direction morale et matérielle de la famille'*. It now reads: *'Les époux assurent ensemble la direction morale et matérielle de la famille. Ils pourvoient à l'éducation des enfants et préparent leur avenir'*

3. 39 per cent of households are made up of couples living with their children and a further 9 per cent include one other person in addition; in 21 per cent couples are living without their children, 20 per cent are made up of one person living alone, and 11 per cent are single-parent families.

3. Social Welfare

1. The term social security was first used in the American *Social Security Act* in 1935. In 1948 the United Nation's *Universal Declaration on Human Rights* recognised that every individual, as a member of society, should have the right to social security. The term has come to mean the efforts made in this direction as well as the organisations intended to carry them out.

2. The *Commission des Finances* estimated in 1973/4 that on a monthly salary of 1000 to 1500 francs, 3.5 per cent of income is paid in contributions, for 2040 to 3000 francs, 2.7 per cent, and for 10000 francs, only 1.51 per cent. The employers' contributions decrease in the same way.

3. Recent housing policy has adopted three main objectives: improvement of aid to low income families through the *aide personnalisée au logement*; grants for builders and home buyers for housing which conforms to certain conditions through the *aide à la pierre*; lifting the freeze on rents for property built before 1949, approximately 60 per cent of all housing, in order to encourage modernisation.

4. Education

1. Traditionally the Right has supported the view that the roles of the

family and school in the socialisation process are complementary. At the Centre of the political spectrum, similar precepts have been stressed, and both the Right and Centre have advocated a high degree of individual choice and freedom from political involvement. The Left has argued that the school system is simply a reflection of society and that there can be no changes in the latter without radical changes in the former. It emphasises that a left-wing government would ensure that the educational system serves the population and not the state, and it suggests a more unified rather than uniform system in order to provide better educational opportunities for all members of society.

2. 10 per cent of the school timetable in secondary schools is set aside for activities which are not part of the syllabus, providing opportunities for innovation and experimental teaching and for pupil initiative. The intention was to make corresponding reductions in the syllabus and to allow a free choice of activities. In 1979 the '10 per cent' was replaced by a system of educational and cultural projects, intended to complement academic studies.

5. Leisure

1. Jacques Blanc, the Member of Parliament for Lozère was appointed as its chairman. The committee's report, made to the President in August 1977, is generally referred to as the Blanc Report.

2. In 1945 he founded the movement *Peuple et Culture* in order to expand and develop opportunities for popular education and cultural activities, and he has led the leisure research team of the *Centre National de la Recherche Scientifique*, which was set up in 1953 and has achieved an international reputation. Many of the findings presented by Dumazedier are the result of observations of the various dimensions of leisure behaviour in Annecy since the early 1950s and are based on surveys and interviews as well as an analysis of the town's ecology and leisure amenities.

3. Under the banner of 'sport for all', in 1978 the Ministry of Youth and Sport introduced two national certificates to encourage interest in sport: the *brevet sportif populaire* and the *décathlon olympique moderne*. Subsidised school trips to the mountains, seaside or countryside (*classes de neige, classes bleues, classes vertes*) have opened up opportunities for a wider cross-section of the public.

4. In 1979 there were twenty-one regional and twenty-five national parks, covering 5 per cent of the total surface area of France, set up by the state in order to protect the environment, to allow scientific observation and to educate the public. Attention was focused on ecological problems in April 1977 when the National Day of the Tree was established.

5. In 1975 the French television service was reorganised into three state-controlled national broadcasting companies (*Sociétés Nationales de Programmes*): *TF 1*, covering the largest number of hours of broadcasting over the year, followed by *Antenne 2* and then *FR 3*, which broadcasts for less than half the time of the other two channels. A fourth company was put in charge of radio. Each company has a director appointed by the French President for a period of three years, a system much criticised both for the limited length of the term of office and for the method of appointment.

6. As explained in *Sondages*, 3-4 (1977), surveys of religious practice are notorious for their divergent results, due either to the abuse of statistics or to the type of population sample involved and the untruthfulness of some replies.

7. By 1972 the *Club Méditerranée* was employing some 9000 people. It organised sixteen holiday villages in the mountains for winter sports and forty villages in the sun in twenty-three different countries, including Tahiti, Mexico and the Ivory Coast.

Index

References to texts, for convenience, are printed in **bold** type.

FOR READER'S NOTES

FOR READER'S NOTES

FOR READER'S NOTES

FOR READER'S NOTES